Fighting planning appeals

Lewis Keeble

Illustrations drawn by Betty Trevena

CONSTRUCTION PRESS
London and New York

Construction Press
an imprint of:
Longman Group Limited
Longman House, Burnt Mill, Harlow
Essex CM20 2JE, England
Associated companies throughout the world

*Published in the United States of America
by Longman Inc., New York*

First published 1985

British Library Cataloguing in Publication Data
Keeble, Lewis
  Fighting planning appeals.
  1. City planning and development law —
  England 2. Regional planning — Law and
  legislation — England
  I. Title
  711'.1   KD1125.Z9
ISBN 0-86095-732-2

Set in 10/12 pt. Linotron 202 Baskerville
Printed at The Bath Press, Avon

Contents _____

List of illustrations _____

Throughout, unless the context dictates otherwise, the following common notation is used. Additional items are shown on the drawings where necessary.

Appeal site

Industry

Town centre or sub-centre

Shopping or centre that is predominantly shopping

Offices and other business

General urban area

Open space

Green belt

Introduction _____

There are many good publications which describe the law and procedures which affect planning appeals, predominant among them Sweet and Maxwell's *Encyclopedia of Planning and Property Law and Practice*, to which numerous references will be made herein. But all deal almost exclusively with law and procedures not with merit, evidence, the preparation and presentation of a case, and how to meet and counter opposition; in short how to win if you are a disputant in a planning appeal, or on what principles and in what form to adjudicate if you are an adjudicator. It is with these latter matters that this book is concerned, though naturally the framework of law and of statutory and customary procedures forms a necessary background.

That so little should have been written about these aspects of planning appeals, which affect most of the people involved in them most of the time, is strange. In this country, on a rough calculation, at any given time, up to a quarter of a million people are working on planning appeals in a fashion which necessitates or ought to necessitate knowing something about the merits of the issues involved and the criteria for their sound resolution, not merely being able to type or file relevant material. Of that notional quarter of a million, how many, I wonder, know enough about the subject to perform as well as they are able? There can be no authoritative answer to that, but I should be surprised if more than 20 per cent do. On that assumption, therefore, at any given time there are about 200 000 people who, to do their current work better, need a book something like this. To these must be added an indefinite number of student town planners, architects, surveyors, engineers, solicitors, geographers, barristers, sociologists, economists and others.

I therefore thought that a book written frankly as a 'How to do it' book would be useful, and this is it. It is addressed to all the kinds of people referred to in the previous paragraph as well as to those lay people who are aware that town planning appeals are quite important things which affect the personal welfare of individuals and the safety, pleasantness and convenience of the physical environment quite substantially, have little idea how these appeals are managed, yet feel they ought to know, or would like to know, something about it.

That being said, let us at once make clear exactly what the subject matter of the book is, in the very simplest terms. In this country, if you want to build anything sizeable or to make a substantial change to the existing use of land (whether this involves building or not) you have to apply to the local council for permission, known as 'planning permission'. The council may give you unconditional permission, give you permission with conditions attached to it, refuse permission or, regrettably, fail to make a decision within the period (usually two months) within which they are allowed to make up their minds. Unless you get an unconditional permission you have a right of appeal to the Secretary of State for the Environment (hereinafter SoS) who, after investigation, can dismiss or uphold your appeal, or uphold it in part and reject it in part. The investigation takes the form either of a public inquiry or hearing, or if all parties – applicant, council and Department of the Environment (hereinafter DoE) – prefer it, an exchange of written representations in which the council state why they took the decision they did and the applicant, who by now has become technically an appellant, states why he thinks it was the wrong decision. The parties may argue back and forth with each other in several repudiatory replies and counter attacks. In either procedure third parties may join in the argument on either side. Nowadays most appeals are determined by an inspector employed by the DoE and appointed by the SoS to carry out the investigation, but a small proportion are still determined (formally) by the SoS himself. Except in a tiny number of cases, where some particular legal point arises and can be taken to the High Court by one or other of the parties, that is the end of the matter: everyone is bound by the decision.

I have been personally involved in many hundreds of appeals over nearly forty years in England, Wales, Northern Ireland and Australia, and I have played nearly every role there is to play in an appeal: I have been a one-man tribunal, a member of a three-person tribunal, an advocate for appellants, councils and third parties, and a witness on behalf of all of these. I therefore know a good deal about appeals, but far from everything, and, as will become very clear in later pages, opinion is about 90 per cent of the game and facts only about 10 per cent, so a great deal of what I have to say is only informed opinion, about which it is perfectly possible for there to be informed disagreement.

I say 'a game', and that is what it is, and a fascinating one. To say so is not to regard appeals frivolously, far otherwise; given competence and sincerity, fighting appeals successfully is to make the world, to some tiny extent, a better place to live in each time you win. This imposes a responsibility on planning officers representing councils, consultants representing appellants and third parties, and inspectors. An inspector is not there to pronounce the cleverer team of performers the winner but to decide which way the decision should go. Often none of the mass of spoken or written words and pictures thrown at him will have any considerable effect on his decision, though he may be enlightened, confused or even convinced against his previously formed opinion by some of it. By contrast, lawyers and technical people who are not planners do not have the same kind of moral responsibility as planners; they are quite legitimately concerned simply to win without considering whether to win will make the world a better or worse place.

To take the 'game' analogy further, the parts of a planning appeal dealt with by means of inquiry which consist of cross-examination are very much like a game of cricket in which the cross-examining advocate is the bowler and the witness the batsman. However, it is rather nicer than cricket, since practically no one ever actually gets out; the worst that happens is that the witness (batsman) may fail to score, or the bowler (advocate) may have a lot of runs knocked off him. However, there are limits to the game concept; as a professional person you are not fighting an appeal for yourself but for another or others, who are paying for your services and who will be directly affected by the result as you will not be. So the game has to be played with seriousness and sobriety, and big risks should not be taken without the knowledge and consent of the client, whether the client be a developer, a local authority or an objector.

Though I have referred to this as a 'How to do it' book, it should be noted that I have not dealt with the minutiae of procedures, the finer points of filling in the forms involved when making an appeal, the time limits which have to be observed, and so forth. These are omitted partly because some of them change from time to time, but also because the DoE already does an excellent job in this regard in the booklet *Planning Appeals: a guide* (HMSO 1983).

It should be added that I have not tried to be exhaustive. Some appeals, notably those concerned with mineral workings and outdoor advertising, are so specialised in character that much of their subject-matter falls outside the range of the general town planning practitioner. They, and others, are very briefly discussed in Chapter 19.

To set the whole book in perspective, it may be useful to say that though the numbers vary appreciably from year to year, in a fairly lively year, something like half a million applications for planning permission are made in England. Of these, some 60 000 (12 per cent) are likely to be refused; a third of these refusals will probably be taken to appeal (4 per cent of all applications) and about a third of those appeals (a little more than one per cent of all applications) are likely to succeed. Prima facie, therefore, councils err on the side of severity in only about one in a hundred of the cases they consider. How often they err on the side of leniency is anybody's guess.

Part I

Framework

1

How appeals come about

Appeals may come about in many ways, but let us start with the simplest and probably by far the most common. Someone has bought or secured an option to buy a piece of land and wants to build a house on it. He has plans and elevations of the proposed house prepared, fills in an application form for planning permission and sends it to the appropriate district council with the drawings. In due course he receives back from the council a document known as a 'Refusal of Planning Permission' which gives the reasons why the council think he ought not to receive permission as well as stating that permission has been refused. Thereupon he writes to the Department of the Environment (DoE)asking for the appropriate form on which to make an appeal. This form will require him to give his reasons for disagreeing with the council's decision.

If this admirable simplicity of procedure continues, he will next be invited to, and will, agree to his appeal being dealt with by means of written representations, and so will the council. The council will then send him, via the DoE, a statement in amplification of their reasons for refusal, and he, by the same route, will write a rebuttal. An inspector will visit the appeal site. If the site can readily be seen and appreciated without his going on to private property, i.e. from the road, the inspector need not even be accompanied. Otherwise an appointment is made for the inspector and representatives of the appellant and the council to meet him at the site and inspect it.

Eventually, this being a case in which the power to make a decision has been transferred by the Secretary of State (SoS) to the inspector, the inspector sends to the appellant and the council a letter, probably no more than one-and-a-half pages long, stating whether he allows or dismisses the appeal and why, and that is that: clean, clear, neat.

The justice of the decision depends upon the inspector having been given sufficient and accurate information, having enough technical knowledge to evaluate that information, and making an unbiased judgement in the light of it.

Would it were ever thus. The complications and consequent delays which may beset this simple process are so numerous that they need to be tabulated (see Fig. 1.1). Even this is probably not exhaustive.

Apart from actual variations of the route which an appeal may follow, the following complications are quite likely to creep in at one or more points:

1. Discussions with officers/members of the council before an application is submitted, which may give rise to much misunderstanding and subsequent confusion about what has been agreed, undertaken or suggested.
2. Doubts about exactly what has been applied for. Withdrawals, resubmissions, amendments, alternative applications may all appear on the scene and may play havoc if allowed to get out of control.
3. Doubts about the identity of the land in respect of which permission is being sought and even about which of several alternative and overlapping sites relates to alternative layout or building plans.
4. Doubts about which among different decisions relates to which among several alternative applications or plans.

Some comments are needed to clarify Fig. 1.1. Disputes arise very frequently, much more frequently than they ought to, about whether planning permission is needed for a particular operation or activity on a particular site. The interests of councils and of applicants or potential applicants diverge here somewhat.

Developers, (to use a generic term to include developers and potential developers and people who are not developers but seek to do something which needs or may need planning permission) are naturally concerned to do as much as they can without going to the trouble and expense of seeking council approval. Since 1 April 1981 the mere act of applying for planning permission costs money. On the other hand, councils, more perhaps the officers than the elected members, are interested in keeping things neat, tidy and under control. (There may often also be an element of ingrained authoritarianism present.) Moreover, and here the elected members' views may predominate, questions about the need for planning permission often arise from the complaints of neighbours. Neighbours see something going on which they think harms, or may harm, the quiet enjoyment of their homes, and protest to their councillor, usually, understandably enough, wholly ignorant of whether or not what is going on is something the council has power to control or not. The councillor, often little better instructed than the complaining neighbour, wants something to be done, both because of a wholly laudable belief that he must safeguard his electors' interests, and often, less laudably, from a touch of officiousness. The council take the easy way out and tell the developer that he needs planning permission for what he is doing. The developer can then choose between three courses of action: write back and say 'Oh no I don't'; apply for planning permission; or put in a section 53 application, seeking determination of whether planning permission is needed. He may, but need not, link this with an application for planning permission, which is ignored if the council decide permission is not needed, determined if they think it is.

The third course is seldom to be recommended unless there is real doubt

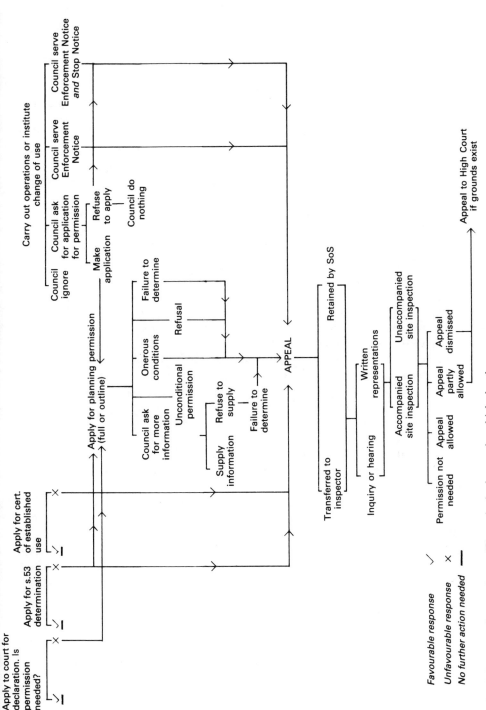

Fig. 1.1 Appeal procedures. The principal ways in which development or an intention to develop proceeds to determination via an appeal

5

about whether planning permission is needed and unless what is being under-taken is fairly costly, since the very making of such an application implies that planning permission *might* be necessary. Nevertheless, it is a route to lodging an appeal against an unfavourable reply, which appeal will result in a deter-mination not merely of whether planning permission is needed, but whether it should be given; this may save time. However, it is to be emphasised that it is a procedure to be used with caution, since, as will be explained in Chapter 11, inspectors do not seem very keen to say flatly 'No, planning permission is not needed for this', which is the answer the applicant wants.

The first course may be the best to follow from the point of view of a devel-oper if, in the event of ultimate failure, the cost of undoing what he has done would not be too great to bear. All the hard work, initially at least, is cast upon the council, and he does not have to pay a fee. If the council want to pursue the matter, they have to go to all the trouble of serving an Enforcement Notice, with all the rather horrible administrative and legal work which has to be done, and then fight an appeal. This is unlikely to be an attractive prospect for them, especially in view of the somewhat discouraging terms of Circular 22 of 1980 and the distinct possibility in some cases of their not only having to fight an appeal on its merits but also having to contest a claim for the issue of a Certificate of Established Use.

At this point readers may well ask why there should ever be any doubt whether planning permission is needed: surely the law should be definite enough to make plain what does and what does not need permission? The answer to this is that however carefully definitions are drawn up there is always bound to be doubt at the fringes about what constitutes 'operations' and 'material change of use', just as there must always be doubt about what, for example, constitutes 'mental cruelty' and what constitutes 'incompatibility'. In the case of our uniquely flexible planning system, this 'grey area' is inevitably larger than it is in a more formalised or 'legalistic' system, but the increase in doubt is more than made up for by the increase in the sensitivity with which the system can respond to particular needs and problems.

Our definitions, contained principally in the current General Development Order of 1977 (plus amendments in 1980 and 1981), the Use Classes Order of 1972, and also, a little confusingly, in the current principal legislation, the Town and Country Planning Act of 1971 do their best to narrow the grey area as much as is compatible with flexibility but it can never be eliminated, as will become clear on reading Chapter 2.

The second course, namely applying for planning permission even if you are not sure whether you need it, is in one sense an easy way out. If you are reasonably sure that permission will be given, all you lose by applying for plan-ning permission is the fee charged for making it and the loss of the moral and tactical advantage (even more so in this case than in the case of a section 53 application) of being able to declare that it is impossible for a reasonable person to think that planning permission could possibly be needed. By making an application for planning permission you have conceded that a sensible person might think it necessary and implied, almost, that *you* think it is necessary.

It should be noted that planning permission is quite independent of consent under building regulations; there is little or no leakage between the two. Sometimes both are necessary for a particular operation, sometimes one, sometimes the other. Building regulation consent relates to specific requirements about the stability, safety, drainage, incombustibility, etc., of a building and the means of access to it and, usually in a much less stringent way than planning control requires, the space about buildings. The giving or refusal of planning permission or building regulation consent cannot properly or lawfully influence the grant or withholding of the other.

To conclude this chapter, it will be useful to summarise the main kinds of reasons which lead councils to refuse applications for planning permission or to impose onerous conditions:

- Incompatible use (e.g. factory in a housing area);
- Intensity of development: excessive or, more rarely, inappropriately low (e.g. development proposed at twenty houses to the acre, council think fourteen should be the limit);
- Effect on neighbours (e.g. development likely to be unreasonably annoying to neighbours because proposed buildings are too close to them or because of noise, smell or general disturbance likely to be caused by the proposed use);
- Safety and convenience (e.g. bad access on to road, development likely to cause traffic increase incompatible with capacity of road, inconvenient proposed road layout with insufficient provision for pedestrians);
- Appearance of proposed development unsatisfactory (e.g. poor design of building or buildings, bad grouping of buildings, insufficient provision for planting, removal of beautiful trees involved).

2

Relevant law

Indispensible information is contained in *the Encyclopedia of Planning Law and Practice*, especially in Part VI, 'Planning Law and Practice from the Decisions', a lengthy commentary, whose author Harold J. J. Brown enlivens its pages with much quiet wit. Even here there is, rightly, no discussion at all of planning merits, no more than the very occasional exclamation of anguish or astonishment at a perverse decision. A point made over and over again in this commentary is that the law and the courts are concerned, as regards planning, solely with the law itself and its interpretation, while it is for planning authorities and the SoS to decide how the *facts* of a case fit the law.

It is therefore impossible to avoid a good deal of discussion of the points at which law and facts meet. No one can effectively advise a client unless he is prepared to consider and give an opinion on, for example, whether a particular activity does or does not require planning permission, and part of this advice may often be to make sure one way or another that steps are taken to keep the activity definitely one side or the other of what is always a somewhat hazy borderline.

To be fully conversant with planning law one would need to be familiar with hundreds and hundreds of pages of legislation and commentary, yet, and this is an interesting paradox, few practitioners are likely to need from one year's end to another, close knowledge of more than the definition of development contained in sections 22 and 23 of the Town and Country Planning Act 1971, the current General Development Order, the current Use Classes Order, the special restrictions which apply in conservation areas, and the law governing building preservation orders and tree preservation orders, Enforcement Notices and Stop Notices. Nevertheless, a practitioner who was not aware of the mass of other legal material looming over him which might occasionally affect his activities, and sufficiently aware to know how to look it up, would be at peril. It also goes without saying that it is perilous for any non-lawyer to try to argue with lawyers about what the law *means*. Fortunately, interesting though they are, the number of appeals at which the law and its meaning come into the picture at all is very small; even rarer are those where a legal issue is the predominant one. What happens much more often is the question of whether a particular set of facts and circumstances constitutes a situation which brings the matter within the ambit of planning law. Here, unless it somehow gets dragged before the courts, the matter is for planners, not lawyers, to decide. In a notable judgment by Donaldson, L J and Kilner Brown, J, the latter said: 'I would hope that henceforth inspectors and planning officers would be able to approach the growing problem using their common sense, assessing each situation upon the facts as they appear to be.' Earlier he had said: 'But in the end it is always a matter of common sense'. (Queen's Bench Divisional Court, 15 December 1980.)

The current principal legislation governing development control is the Town and Country Planning Act 1971. Section 22 of this Act defines development as 'the carrying out of building, engineering, mining or other operations, in, on, over or under land, or the making of any material change in the use of any buildings or other land'. It is important to note the two limbs of this definition: 'operations', and 'material change in the use of any buildings or other land'.

Section 22 then exempts certain operations and uses from the definition of development, namely works for maintenance, improvement or other alteration of a building which affect only the interior, or which do not materially affect the external appearance; work by the local highway authority for the maintenance or improvement of a road, inspecting or repairing or renewing sewers, etc.; use of any buildings or land within the curtilage of a dwelling-house for any purpose incidental to the enjoyment of the dwelling-house as such; use of land for agriculture or forestry and use for those purposes of any building occupied together with land so used; and use of buildings or land for any purpose within a class specified in an order (the Use Classes Order).

Conversely, 'for the avoidance of doubt', the use as two or more separate dwelling-houses of any building previously used as a single dwelling-house (i.e. conversion of a house into flats) and the deposit of refuse or waste materials are declared to involve a material change of use.

Section 23 provides that planning permission is required for carrying out any development of land, subject to various exceptions with which we need not here be concerned.

Section 24 deals with Development Orders, and provides that the SoS shall by order provide *inter alia*, but especially for the grant of planning permission, for development specified in the order. Development Orders may be either general, that is applicable to all land, or special, applicable only to such land as may be specified.

General Development Orders are important pieces of delegated legislation, and whether or not a particular operation falls within one of the exemptions from the obligation to obtain planning permission set out in the order is quite often an issue at an appeal, though fortunately the current order is well drafted and does not leave a very great deal of room for doubt and argument. Difficulty usually arises only when someone tries to twist its meaning, not when a genuine attempt is made to understand it.

The current General Development Order is the Town and Country General Development Order of 1977 (SI No. 289, as amended by No. 1946 of 1980 and No. 245 of 1981). The most important part for appeal purposes is the 23 classes in it which are specified as exempted from the obligation to obtain planning permission. These include minor development within the curtilage of a dwelling-house, including house extensions, garages, greenhouses, etc., up to certain specified maxima, and subject to certain limiting conditions as to position; minor operations such as the erection of gates, fences, walls or other means of enclosure, again subject to certain maxima; a very odd switch-over from the Use Classes Order, placed here instead of there for some legal reason, which enables a general industrial building's use to be changed to that of a light industrial building and the use of a special or 'nasty' shop deemed likely to be objection-able in some way to be changed to use as an ordinary shop; the erection of agricultural buildings, again subject to certain maxima as to position, and a number of other items which it is very unlikely that any ordinary planning authority or planning practitioner will be concerned with more than once in a lifetime.

The current Use Classes Order is that of 1972 (SI 1972 No. 1385). As already mentioned, Use Classes Orders stem from section 22 of the Town and Country Planning Act 1971, sub-section 2(f). Disputes about whether a particular change of use falls within the exemptions, similar in intention to the exemptions of the General Development Order, provided by the Use Classes Order, are likely to be rather more frequent than those arising from the General Development Order. The first thing to bear in mind about the Use Classes Order, and it is surprising how many people fail to bear this in mind, is that in no sense does it try to set out a full list of the possible uses of land. It does nothing of the kind; for example, it does not even mention houses. All it does is to list certain groups of uses sufficiently similar in character and in their implications for effects upon surrounding property, for it to have been felt safe not to require the trouble and nuisance of an application for planning permis-sion to be undergone before changing from one of them to another. Such changes may well, in terms of the definition of development given in the Act, be material changes of use, but the Order says that they can be carried out without planning permission being sought and obtained.

Seventeen Use Classes are set out in the schedule to the Order. Class 1, for example, provides that a shop can be used for any shop purposes, e.g. you do not have to seek planning permission to change from a grocer to a stationer though permission is needed for change to a 'nasty' shop (one for the sale of hot food, tripe, pet animals or birds, catsmeat or motor vehicles). Similarly, one office use can be changed to another office use without getting permission; so can a light industrial building use to another light industrial purpose and a general industrial building use to another general industrial purpose. These are kinds of use which tend to feature fairly often in planning appeals and in which disputes over the meaning of the Use Classes Order or the actual facts of the change contemplated (or more often the change already made)are likely to arise. It is not only the Use Classes themselves which may cause problems, but the definitions of various uses in the body of the Order, such as 'shop', 'office', 'light industrial building', and so on; the last named, particularly, constitutes a minefield of doubt.

In any particular case, care needs to be taken to make sure that the provisions of the General Development Order and the Use Classes Order, themselves complex, have not been overridden or modified by the imposition of a Special Development order in the area concerned, or by what is known as an Article 4 direction. A Special Development Order, not very widely used, usually imposes extra obligations, i.e. withdraws from permitted development one or more kinds of development in a particular area because of the particular problems, needs or attractions of that area. Somewhat similarly, an Article 4 direction, which can be made with rather less formality, is made under Article 4 of the General Development Order and in effect reimposes control over one or more kinds of development exempted by the General Development Order.

Moreover, the conditions attached to permissions previously given may legitimately remove from a particular site the advantages given by either the General Development Order or the Use Classes Order. For example, as regards the former, a condition attached to a permission may provide that the erection of fences which would otherwise be permitted development shall not be carried out without planning permission therefor being obtained. Quite commonly, a permission for the use of a building as a light industrial building may be accompanied by a condition which says that, e.g., 'the premises to which this permission relates shall be used for croggle perging and for no other purpose within Class III of the Use Classes Order'. Class III of the Use Classes Order relates to light industrial buildings.

Conservation areas: here the demolition of all buildings except very small ones is brought under development control. Conservation areas are 'areas of special architectural or historic interest, the character or appearance of which it is desirable to preserve or enhance'. Whether or not permission is ever required to demolish a building outside conservation areas, and where the building is not listed as one of special architectural or historic interest, is an open point. The weight of opinion suggests that it would not be reasonable to regard it as development which requires permission. Conservation areas are, as it were, especially prone to Article 4 directions since some encouragement is given to councils to make them in Circular No. 23 of 1977.

Powers to control development would be useless if they were not accompanied by powers to enforce them. Although section 23(1) of the Town and Country Planning Act 1971 states that planning permission is required for the carrying out of development of land, it is not illegal (though it may be unlawful) to carry out development without first seeking planning permission. The distinction here is perhaps a fine one, but not without importance, since councils, sometimes quite unfairly try to suggest at appeals that it is somehow wicked to have carried out development without first having obtained permission. It is not wicked at all: it may be financially very imprudent. The position is that where development has been carried out without planning permission having been obtained, the council may serve an Enforcement Notice. This requires the people on whom it is served to cease the use or remove the development complained of and restore the land to its original condition within a stated period. An appeal can be made against an Enforcement Notice and will be dealt with much like any other planning appeal. It will often be divided into two parts, namely argument about whether what is complained of by the council needs planning permission, and argument about whether, even if it did need planning permission, it ought to be allowed. Only after an appeal, if lodged, has failed, does continuation of the offending activities or continued existence of complained-of buildings become a legal offence, and even then only after a specified period has run out.

In rather exceptional circumstances, councils may deem it necessary to reinforce their enforcement powers by issuing what is known as a Stop Notice. It can only be served after an Enforcement Notice has been served and must refer to that Enforcement Notice. It was introduced to deal with appellants who tried to delay by various tactics the determination of an appeal against an Enforcement Notice. A Stop Notice prohibits any person on whom it is served from continuing any activity specified, but it cannot prohibit the continued use of a building as a dwelling-house or of land as the site of a caravan occupied by anyone as his only or main residence. Generally speaking too, a Stop Notice cannot be served in respect of an *activity* begun more than twelve months previously, but this does not apply to building, engineering or mining operations or to the deposit of refuse. A Stop Notice ceases to have effect, of course, if the Enforcement Notice to which it relates is successfully appealed against. It is unlikely that Stop Notices will ever become very popular devices among councils since their unsuccessful use attracts what may be very formidable compensation.

This is the bare bones of the legal background to planning appeals. To go any further would necessitate going very much further and it is not one of the purposes of this book to do so. Once more I reiterate that in the vast majority of planning appeals no point of law of any kind arises: they are simple contests about whether what the appellant proposes is compatible with the sound development of the area of which the appeal site forms part. For all that it is of course very desirable, preferably before the application which gives rise to an appeal has been made, to find out the precise circumstances of the application site as regards planning law. Is it in a conservation area? Is it subject to a Special Development Order or to an Article 4 direction? Are there any conditions attached to a previous permission relating to the site which necessitate making an application for permission which would not otherwise be needed? Any council ought to be able to answer such questions very quickly.

In the foregoing I have excluded the subject of outdoor advertisements. The erection of an outdoor advertisement usually involves development under planning law but the whole business is dealt with in rather different ways and under different constraints from those applying to ordinary planning appeals. Someone might find it worth while to write a short book on the subject.

The remainder of this chapter is devoted to discussion of the very awkward and often all-important matter of whether a particular operation or activity on a particular site does or does not constitute development as defined in the Planning Act of 1971 and/or whether it really falls within the exemptions given by the General Development Order and the Use Classes Order. It lies awkwardly astride the fields of law and town planning technique and so will initially be dealt with here though it will crop up again a number of times in subsequent chapters.

From a council's point of view, it is obviously undesirable and confusing for a lot of operations and activities to be carried on without planning permission if, in law, they need planning permission, even if such permission would readily be given for many of them. Questions of established use may subsequently arise and be incapable of accurate resolution. A council which lets the situation get out of hand in this regard sows the wind and may later reap the whirlwind. People may get to know of things which have been done without planning permission and, innocently or otherwise, conclude that they can do similar but more ambitious things without seeking permission. If there is a build-up of such activities, the council may find itself faced with the need for a mass of difficult, time-consuming and enmity-producing Enforcement Notices and proceedings to be undertaken. On the other hand, no council ought to want to receive applications for permission in respect of matters which do not need permission. If, as some do, they assume that if an application is made for permission, that is sufficient evidence of the need for permission, they get themselves into a hopeless tangle. Eventually there is fairly certain to be an embarrassing confrontation: 'Look what X has done. Did she get planning permission?' 'No, she didn't need it.' 'But I did the same at my house, and I applied for planning permission', (or, worse, 'I wanted to do the same as Mrs X has done and you refused me planning permission; I've only just found out what she's done!').

Such occurrences must lead to a loss of confidence in the council, and it is surprising how careless councils can be in such matters. For example, a friend of mine asked an officer of her local council whether she needed planning permission for a proposed operation and was told without delay or hesitation that she did. She then asked my opinion and I told her that planning permission was quite certainly not needed. She went back to the council, quoted my opinion, and the officer she spoke to readily agreed with it!

From the point of view of a developer (i.e., once more, anyone who wants to do or has done something which might need planning permission) the situation, always unsatisfactory, has been made worse since 1 April 1981, since when a fee has had to be paid for making an application for planning permission. These fees are not negligible. They were first imposed by regulations made under section 87 of the Local Government, Planning and Land Act 1980. These regulations have already been altered twice. The latest are The Fees for Applications and Deemed Applications Regulations 1983 (SI 1983 No. 1674). Because of the strong possibility of early further changes only a few examples will be given.

Outline applications (we shall see later what these are) are charged at the rate of £47 for each 0.1 ha, up to a maximum of £1,175. Full applications for the erection of dwelling-houses are charged at £47 for each dwelling-house, again to a maximum of £1,175. Full applications for most other buildings are charged on a sliding scale, ranging from £24 where the floor space to be created is less than 40 m^2, to a maximum of £2,350. Applications for most changes of the use of land attract a charge of £47, as do applications for continuance of a use or retention of buildings or works without compliance with a condition subject to which a previous planning permission has been granted.

There are some concessions and exemptions. For example, no fee is charged for extensions and alterations to a disabled person's house; for applications needed because of an Article 4 direction; for applications needed because of the removal of permitted development rights by a condition attached to a planning permission; for renewal of temporary permissions and revised applications for development of the same character or description within twelve months of refusal or withdrawal of an earlier application. A duplicate application made by the same applicant within twenty-eight days attracts a full fee for the first application, but only one quarter of the full fee for the second one.

How very irritating to pay such a fee and then discover afterwards that there was no need to apply for planning permission! Conversely, how very much more annoying to do something which you believe does not need planning permission, but then to be served with an Enforcement Notice and be forced to go to the trouble and expense of appealing against it. Circular 22 of 1980, issued by the DoE, recognised the latter problem and suggests to councils that since the power to issue an Enforcement Notice alleging that there has been a breach of planning control is entirely discretionary and is only to be used if the authority consider it expedient to do so, having regard to the provisions of the development plan and to any other material considerations, the power should be used only where planning reasons clearly warrant it and there is no alternative to enforcement proceedings. But this disregards the possible complications mentioned a little earlier.

As already noted, an application may be made under section 53 of the Town and Country Planning Act 1971 to determine whether planning permission is required, and this does not attract a fee, but the disadvantages of this procedure have already been noted (see page 4). If what is proposed to be done involves little expenditure and is believed not to need planning permission, the best thing to do is to go ahead and let the council do as it thinks fit. In the rather unlikely event of the council serving an Enforcement Notice and winning an appeal against it, the only direct financial loss involved will be in undoing anything that has been done. Where substantial expenditure is involved, and it is therefore thought prudent to obtain the local authority's opinion, it may be well, in making both a section 53 application and an application for planning permission, to attach to them a statement in some terms such as: 'We do not believe that planning permission is needed in respect of this application. If you agree, please so inform us in writing and refund the fee which has been enclosed.' A good council ought to cooperate in doing this.

The substantial difficulty about knowing whether planning permission is needed is that in the last resort it is opinion, not law, which is the determining factor. This must be pursued with some thoroughness, even at the risk of repetition. The definitions of development in the Act and the categories of development exempted from need to obtain permission in the General Development Order and Use Classes Order are not precise or comprehensive. No definition in a field as wide and varied as this can prescribe exact limits as to what is *de minimis*, so trifling as not to fall reasonably within the definitions. '*De minimis non curat lex*', 'the law is not concerned with trifles', is an ancient and respected maxim. But one still has to make up one's mind whether a particular thing is a trifle or not, and there are many activities connected with land and buildings which fall near the *de minimis* line. Unfortunately but inevitably, this line is apt to be drawn differently by different people and even, one suspects, in different places by the same person on different days.

Changes of use, i.e. activities, are even trickier than operations in this respect. It must be repeated that the Use Classes Order does no more than list and define a number of groups of uses within each of which changes from one use to another can be made without planning permission being sought. These groups or classes are no more than skeletons, selections of uses, exchanges between which have been deemed to be harmless for planning purposes. It is therefore no use grumbling about not being able to find a particular use in the Use Classes Order; if it cannot be found there it has not been thought to be a member of a group worth defining for the sake of freedom of change within it. Moreover, as regards some of the use classes which *are* included, although a good and conscientious job has been done in drawing up the definitions, much room for doubt inevitably remains about whether a particular activity on a particular site falls within a particular defined use class.

If both operations and activities or changes of use are involved at the same time and on the same site then whether either, separately or both together, constitute development at all or are permitted development under the General Development Order or are permitted by the Use Classes Order, may be very difficult indeed to decide.

The courts have always been anxious to make it clear that they are judges of law, not of facts or of planning merit. The observations of Kilner Brown, J quoted earlier, related to a case in which one of the points at issue was whether land could be said to be used for grazing. Donaldson, L J, in his observations, neatly said:

If horses are simply turned out on to the land with a view to feeding them from the land, clearly the land is being used for grazing. But if horses are being kept on the land and are being fed wholly or primarily by other means, so that such grazing as they do is completely incidental *and perhaps achieved merely because there are no convenient ways of stopping them doing it,* [my emphasis] then plainly the land is not being used for grazing but merely being used for keeping the animals. On the other hand, of course, if the animals are put onto a field with a view to their grazing and are kept there for twenty-four hours a day, seven days a week, over a period, it would not, I would have thought, be possible to say that as they were being kept there, they were not being grazed.

15

Both learned judges stressed the relative importance of common sense rather than legal precedent in such matters.

Even the highest judicial decision about whether or not, in a particular case, development is involved, only relates with precision to a particular operation or use on a particular site. It may be that such judgements will be highly persuasive to everyone as regards very similar cases on very similar sites, but whether the similarity is great enough to justify a similar conclusion is necessarily a matter of fact and of opinion rather than of law.

One may add without disrespect that a judgement made by an experienced town planner about the probable physical effects of an operation or activity on a particular site is likely to be at least as good as that of the most eminent lawyer. Therefore, when the question 'Is it development?' has to be answered, there may be different answers of prima facie equal weight. If the answers conflict, the final and decisive answer will usually be that of the inspector deciding the consequent appeal, since only a tiny proportion of such issues ever get to the courts and only a small proportion of appeals are now decided by the SoS. Apart from the inspector's, there may also be involved the lay opinions of council members and developers (the first of which may nevertheless be the effective cause of a refusal of planning permission or unfavourable answer to a section 53 application), the opinion of the developer's professional adviser (let us hope a chartered town planner) and of the council's planning officer. An application for a judicial declaration may in some cases be made as an alternative to a section 53 application, but it is unlikely that the courts would permit this procedure to be used frequently or in ordinary cases.

An inspector, in my view, should, in the light of the evidence presented to him and his own knowledge and experience, feel entirely free to decide one way or the other whether development is involved, but perusal of relevant appeal decision letters reveals a curious reluctance on the part of inspectors to do any such thing if they can possibly avoid doing so. One has often seen decision letters which express doubt whether the activity at issue requires planning permission, assume, however, that it does and then give a decision in favour of allowing it. But what would an inspector do if, being inclined to think that permission was not needed, he nevertheless believed that if it was needed, permission ought to be refused? Unless he was then prepared to stick his neck out and say that in his opinion permission was not needed so the appeal need not be determined, he would have to find some other face-saving formula. I have not personally found an example of this: perhaps face-saving formulae have been so well devised as to be undetectable!

We must here note an interesting conflict of opinion about what constitutes a *material* change of use. Some have expressed the view that it means 'substantial' in terms of amount, without regard to its probable effect. Others have taken almost the opposite view, and consider that it is the probable 'planning effect on the surroundings' which should decide whether it is 'material'. I do not myself see why it should be necessary for one or the other view to prevail to the exclusion of the other. They are, after all, likely to run together rather than in opposition to each other. Something that looks large and/or involves movements of many people or vehicles is far more likely to have an impact on the surroundings than something which is small and/or involves few people or vehicles. By way of illustration, if you saw a handwritten notice on a front gate of a house, which had not been there the week before, stating 'a few young rabbits for sale', it is hardly likely that you would consider a material change of use had taken place even if you could see a 2 ft by 6 ft rabbit hutch in the garden and even if it looked like a new hutch. By contrast, if you saw a notice saying 'Tappitout Secretarial Agency', then even though the notice in itself might not be of a kind which required permission as an outdoor advertisement, if you also saw strip-lighting in all the rooms visible from the road, the front garden marked out with parking spaces and a dozen typists visible at their work, that would be a very different matter, likely to lead you to a quite different conclusion. That, of couse, is not to say that permission for such an activity should necessarily be refused. (There is a curious tendency when considering the General Development Order and the Use Classes Order, somehow to assume that what is excluded from the exemptions will be refused!) Not at all; it is simply necessary to satisfy oneself that they *are* excluded before their planning merits can usefully be considered at all. Once that point is reached, they need to be considered entirely on their merits.

There are obviously many places in which that sort of secretarial agency would be entirely unacceptable, in the midst of an otherwise uninterrupted area of housing for example, because of the disturbance caused by a great increase of activity, but in other places, for example within or immediately adjacent to a central area, it might be entirely acceptable.

Here is a borderline example from real life. A house was occupied by a man who earned his living by selling pottery at outdoor markets (see Fig. 2.1). At

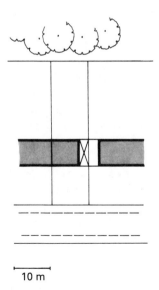

10 m

Fig. 2.1 Pottery at the side of a house

the side of the house was a covered access way leading to the back garden, hidden by a gate at the front and a 6 ft high fence at the side. Here he stored his stock of pottery: a few dozen pots at any particular time. They were invisible from anywhere except within his property, except when he was actually loading them into or out of his car. He was induced by his council to apply for planning permission for change of use for the storage of pottery in the access way. He did so and was refused planning permission; he then appealed. His appeal succeeded, the inspector concluding that development had taken place but that the activity was unobjectionable. However, he thought it desirable to impose conditions that no goods other than pottery should be stored, that the permission given should be only for the benefit of the appellant and not for the benefit of the land. A fair enough conclusion perhaps, but can it really be considered that development had taken place? The volume of goods stored was no greater than you or I might store in our garage. And since the goods were not sold at the premises the fact that they were to be sold elsewhere in the future did not really affect the matter. After all, you and I may occasionally sell or try to sell the junk stored in our garage in order to get rid of it. My own opinion is that no material change of use had taken place, that public and private time and money would have been saved if the council had taken no action. They could have taken action later if the activities in question had intensified so as definitely to constitute a change of use. As it is, with permission granted, they might find difficulty in doing anything about any abuse of it.

Another example provides a cautionary tale. Here, although there could not, I think, in anyone's reasonable view, have been any question of a material change of use having taken place, it appears that the responsible Minister at the time thought it had, or else dodged the issue. He allowed the appeal in question. This appeal is reported in the then Ministry of Housing and Local Government's *Bulletin of Selected Appeal Decisions*, No. XIII/26. A publisher had somehow been induced to apply for planning permission to use a bedroom in his house as a study in which to correct proofs and keep accounts of his business. He did not intend to put up a business sign or other advertisement, to receive business callers, or to conduct trading at his house. He had been refused permission because the council thought the proposal would harm the amenities of the attractive suburb in which the house stood. That such advice should have been given by the council, i.e. to apply for planning permission, is in itself, I think, disgraceful; that the Minister, on receiving the appeal, did not simply say that permission was not needed, therefore it could not be refused, therefore no appeal was necessary, was deplorably weak-kneed. There is no record that costs were charged against the council; they should have been. The attempted exercise of petty tyranny in local government is probably nothing like as great as is often made out, but when it does happen, as it clearly did in this case, it should be ruthlessly stamped on.

Whether a particular object (i.e. building, structure, erection, etc.) constitutes, if already in place, or would constitute development, and if it does, whether it is or would be permitted development under the General Development Order does not so frequently present problems as the question of whether a material change of use is involved, because objects are more readily susceptible to definition than are activities. Nevertheless, when a problem does arise it may be just as difficult to resolve. Once again, the reader is reminded that at that stage, merit is not in question, only whether the object falls within the scope of development control. When the 'object' is an access the difficulties may be immense.

Boats and other movable structures or objects present special difficulties as we shall find in Chapter 13, and certainly the movability of an object must have some effect on whether it can be regarded as having been the result of a planning operation. In *James* v *Brecon County Council* (1963) Lord Parker said: – 'No doubt in cases where the structure is affixed to the land it will in general be part of the land and constitute development. Equally, if the structure in question is intended to move about, and can be wheeled on and off the land, in general its installation will not constitute development, but in between one can imagine many situations in which the question may be finely balanced, and it may be difficult to decide on which side the scales come down.' This dictum was amusingly reinforced, yet modified, by Bridge, J, who in what is known as the 'Barvis case', thought that the tests proposed by Lord Parker might be necessary in a borderline case, but in that particular case it was not really necessary to apply them. It was impossible, he thought, to say that 'the enormous crane under consideration was not a structure or erection and there was nothing to take it out of the meaning of those words in the definition of building.' (*Encyclopedia of Planning Law*, p. 6055.)

Certainly permanence has something to do with the matter. One has sometimes been tempted in representing an appellant at an appeal to suggest that the object complained of should be removed while the site inspection took place. It would be rather difficult for an inspector to dismiss an appeal relating to the stationing of an object which came and went to such an extent that he never saw it.

There are a good many objects about which the reply to an assertion that controllable development had occurred, might well be, 'That's not development, that's gardening.' Let us examine a perhaps slightly improbable but by no means inconceivable series of events. Mr Aukwarde owns and occupies a house and garden. He erects some wooden trellising in a shape similar to that of an ordinary domestic garage and grows rambler roses all over it. An inexperienced and assertive enforcement officer employed by his council comes along to him and says, 'That's building or engineering work'. 'Don't be silly,' says Mr A. 'That's gardening. If you follow that line of thought through, every time I stick a spade in the ground and toss a spadeful of earth aside, it's an engineering operation, on, over and under land. Don't waste my time; go away.' Mr A. then starts parking his car under the delightful arbour or bower that he has created. The enforcement officer comes along again. 'You've built a garage,' he says. 'You've already exhausted the amount of permitted development you're entitled to under Class 1 of the First Schedule of the General Development Order. You

19

need planning permission'.'Nonsense, it's no business of yours where I put my car on my site; and, by the way, there is an existing vehicular access, so don't bring that up; go away.'

Unfortunately Mr A.'s delightful arbour then gets muddy underfoot; he has difficulty getting his car in and out, so he puts down some concrete blocks. Along comes the enforcement officer again. 'Well, anyhow, you've made a garage now.' 'Nonsense, you can't tell me how to arrange my garden. If I want to put paving down all over it, I will. Mind your own business.'

But the rains come and the rambler roses, dense though they are, don't keep out the rain, so Mr A. fastens plastic sheeting along three sides of the bower and over the top of it, though behind and under the rambler roses. 'Got you now; that *is* a structure or erection,' cries the enforcement officer. 'Nonsense, this is a new and better way of growing roses. You telling me how to garden? You'll be trying to get me to move my cloches next, and they're all over the place and essential to my personal horticulture. Political meetings in them? Of course, activity incidental to the enjoyment of a dwelling-house as such.'

Unhappily some local National Front lads come along quietly late at night, rough up Mr A.'s car, slash the tyres and paint obscene declarations on its panels. He therefore fills in the fourth side of his bower with doors, and while he is about it makes a decent job of it and replaces the plastic 'walls' with breeze blocks (I withhold his subsequent acrimonious conversation with the enforcement officer).

By now few could deny that a garage has been erected and that, permitted development under the General Development Order having previously been exhausted, planning permission is needed and it may be wholly appropriate for that permission to be given; it depends on the nature of the site and the position of the structure. The question is, *at what point* during this saga did controllable development take place? There are no prizes for the right answer; equally well informed and sensible people might well give different answers.

There is a moral in this. For developers it might be stated as 'Don't stretch your luck too far. You might eventually have to appeal against an Enforcement Notice if you do, and you might strike an inspector who doesn't agree with your line of reasoning.' The moral for councils is: 'Don't interfere with domestic activities unless you are quite sure they are controllable, and, before you press things too far, that they are sufficiently objectionable to give you a fair chance of winning an appeal against an Enforcement Notice.'

To conclude this chapter, a few miscellaneous points which are worth bearing in mind. Applications for planning permission have to be definite enough for councils to know what it is that they are approving or refusing. If application for a change of use clearly involves building operations, it is not valid; it has to be an application to carry out building operations. Refusals of planning permission have to be accompanied by reasons, otherwise presumably there has been a failure to determine. This is perhaps little more than a technical point, but an appeal against a failure to determine an application puts the council initially in a poorer moral position than an appeal against a refusal. More importantly, conditions also have to be accompanied by reasons for their imposition; if they are not so accompanied, presumably a condition is not valid and can safely be ignored. There is no doubt that conditions must relate to planning matters and must relate only to the application site or other land under the control of the applicant. To take an extreme, a condition that 'the appellant's wife shall sleep with the Chairman of the council whenever so required', would be quite invalid. A condition must not require payment of money.

There is a considerable danger of confusion in the case of outline applications between 'illustrative' material and something which is actually part of the application. The value of a clear and specific covering letter with an application to avoid such confusion can hardly be overstressed.

Outline applications are in a special category provided for in Article 5 of the General Development Order. They may be made only in respect of operations, not changes of use. The council, in giving permission, reserve certain matters for later approval in detail. These may relate to any or all of the following: the siting, design, external appearance, means of access or landscaping of the site. Permission on an outline application does not necessarily have to be followed by an application that covers all the reserved matters. Time and effort may be saved in the case of substantial and complex development by making a series of applications in successively greater detail. For example, with a proposed housing estate, the initial outline application might do no more than indicate the extent of the land and its position and state that the application was development for housing purposes. The next application might simply show a road layout and proposed positions of houses and curtilage boundaries, followed by a third, when the second one had received approval, to show plans and elevations of houses in detail and proposed planting and other landscape in detail. A great deal of fuss may be saved by adopting this extended procedure where the principle of development is not in doubt but there may be considerable controversy over the detailed design for it.

Two other special kinds of appeal need to be mentioned.

Appeals against Enforcement Notices have to be made on one or more of eight grounds specified in section 88 of the Town and Country Planning Act of 1971. The first three of these are the most important for practical purposes. They are, respectively, that planning permission ought to be given for the activity complained of or that a condition alleged not to have been complied with be discharged; that what is complained of is not a breach of planning control; and that what is alleged to have occurred has not in fact occurred. The other five grounds relate to whether times and procedures required by the Enforcement Notice have been complied with. (See Chapter 13 for an example of the use of the first three grounds.)

Appeals against refusal to issue a Certificate of Established Use arise under the provisions of Sections 94 and 95 of the Town and Country Planning Act of 1971. What is special about these is that the onus is on the appellant to show that he should be given a certificate; whether he should be given one depends upon facts. If the use in question was begun before 1964 he is entitled to a certificate, otherwise not.

3

Tribunals

It is important for the purposes of this book to make clear exactly what the role of an English planning inspector is; to do this, some comparison needs to be made with other kinds of tribunal which have been, are, or might be used, both to demonstrate the large advantages and small disadvantages of our current system and for the benefit of those who deal with, or may have to deal with, other kinds of tribunal. Further, I shall suggest that good though our current system is, it might be made even better.

A 'tribunal' in the sense in which the word is used here, means one or more persons charged with the task of resolving a dispute or, at least, of investigating it and recommending how it should be resolved. There are several ways in which planning tribunals differ from most others. First, although there is a framework of law within which they have to operate, this framework, as explained in Chapter 2, is very broad and flexible and is seldom an important factor in most English planning appeals, though when it is it may be rather spectacular and attract much attention.

Second, technical opinion looms very large in planning disputes: opinion rather than indisputable facts. There is, more often than not, no dispute about the facts in an appeal; even when there is it can usually be removed by means of an adjournment and brief discussion between representatives of the parties. If one side says a field has an area of 2.35 ha and the other that it has an area of 2.95 ha, it should not take long to discover which, if either, is right. But when it comes to opinion, there is often no sure way of demonstrating which opinion is sounder than others, because there are few aspects of planning in which there is an orthodoxy sufficiently accepted and respected to constitute an authoritative basis in favour of which there must be a presumption in the absence of specific rebutting evidence. Because of the long time and large costs involved, planning theory does not readily lead itself to experimental testing.

Third, as already emphasised, the data and the considerations are so varied that it is seldom that the circumstances in one case are so closely comparable with those in another that one could confidently and correctly say that the decision in one has constituted a reliable precedent for a decision in the other. Yet another distinguishing feature, though less definite, is that in planning appeals no one's life or liberty are at stake. No one is going to be imprisoned or fined if he loses (though this might happen if a decision is defied). At worst, someone may be denied the opportunity to do, or continue doing, something that he wants to do, whether by way of carrying out construction or carrying on a use.

Certainly, though, large amounts of money may hang on an appeal decision. The difference between an appeal decision that 5 ha of land should be permitted to be intensively developed for housing and a decision that it should remain as agricultural land may represent many thousands of pounds.

Types of tribunal

The distinguishable kinds of tribunal are: a judge, a magistrate, a Minister of the Crown, a lay civil servant, an 'independent' person, a lay private person and an inspector. As regards the last he is to be distinguished from an independent person as being a person with relevant technical knowledge and qualifications who is employed rather than merely retained by the authority responsible for determining appeals.

Any of the above might be multi-person rather than single-person tribunals and almost any two kinds might be combined into a multi-person tribunal.

Judges

The trouble with judges as planning appeal tribunals is that the necessarily formal procedures in courts of law, strict rules about admissibility of evidence, the need to 'prove' everything, the necessary but tiresome doctrine of judicial ignorance, all tend towards very lengthy and costly proceedings, because, apart from the reasons already given, in everything about planning except the law, the judge is a layman, so that quite elementary points of planning principle and technique have to be explained to him in the course of evidence. If they are not so explained, he may well get it wrong. In Queensland, for example, the planning tribunal is a judge; I still fear that in one of my few appearances there as a planning witness, I failed to get the judge to understand that, provided a road is wide enough to carry safely the traffic it has to bear, without congestion, the narrower it is the better

Judges are both learned and often quite wise people, used to listening to and weighing evidence, and therefore prima facie likely to give better decisions on planning appeals than most other laymen. But it is very doubtful indeed whether this advantage is so great as to justify their use in planning appeals, having regard to the immensely weightier and, for the people involved, immensely more serious, issues which judges more usually deal with. Certainly, I think, it is unwise to entrust planning appeal decisions to judges unless they are assisted by technical assessors, i.e. in this country chartered town planners. The chances of them not fully understanding or failing to weigh accurately the evidence presented are very great. Moreover, and this applies to all tribunals, unless they are at least constrained by an obligation to make decisions which do not conflict with established planning policies much harm may result.

What the expression 'established planning policies' means, or ought to mean, will be pursued in some detail in Chapter 10. In Queensland, where almost everything connected with the law is rather more confused than in most other places, it seemed as if the judges were not, in law, obliged to have regard to anything except the specific and fairly rigid provisions of the planning scheme relating to the area in which an appeal site lay. There was some pleased fluttering in planning dovecots when it became known that they had decided that they would take account of 'policy'. I never succeeded in discovering just what this meant, but I think it can only have meant that they would also take account of a local authority's policy in relation to permitting or refusing various kinds of applications which fell within the authority's so-called 'discretionary' powers. These related to things like shops in housing areas. If for 'policy' one substitutes 'merit' it is hard to see how a tribunal could make a sensible decision without taking it into account. Of course in this country where no planning proposals, however precisely expressed they may be on maps, are in law more than 'policy', it would be virtually impossible to arrive at a decision on an appeal without taking 'policy' into account. A further disadvantage in using judges as planning appeal tribunals is that, within the constraints of the law, they are very properly used to forming an opinion and making a judgement entirely on the weight of the evidence put before them. But planning appeals are not really quite like that; the professional opinions of the various witnesses may well be incapable of being assessed accurately except by someone who himself has professional qualifications and experience.

Magistrates

The use of magistrates as planning tribunals can be dealt with quite briefly. Here 'magistrate' means, in English terms, a JP; (for the purposes of this discussion, a stipendiary magistrate is just a special kind of junior judge). Justices of the Peace are simply lay people who have the advantage of receiving legal advice from their clerks. Until 1960 they were the tribunal for determining appeals against enforcement notices, after which, to the general relief, their powers in this regard were taken over by the planning Minister.

Ministers

The clear advantage of providing for the planning Minister of the day to be the appeal tribunal is that in this country he is the person ultimately responsible for the well-being of the planning process; his desk is the place at which the buck finally stops. Therefore, he is likely to take very serious and responsible decisions. What is more, he has a wealth of technical advice at his disposal. Unfortunately it would be physically impossible for one person (with innumerable other and even, perhaps, more important duties) actually to consider and decide the many thousands of appeals which come up annually in this country for determination. Delegation must, whether acknowledged or not, take place, and if final responsibility still rests with the Minister, although his ultimate responsibility may be a sound and sobering influence, for everyday practical purposes it does not amount to much and the question of who is actually in practical terms to make the decisions, has still to be answered.

In this country, until 1968, all except a tiny minority of appeal decisions were clearly made by administrative civil servants who had the advantage of reading the report and recommendations of the inspector who had dealt with the appeal. Up to 1958, when the recommendations of the Franks Committee were brought into operation, it is not possible to say to what extent decisions followed the inspectors' advice, because inspectors' reports and recommendations were not made known. Since then they have been available, and the inspectors' recommendations have been wholly or substantially followed in 90 per cent or more of all cases. From my personal experience I am not at all sure that administrative civil servants have often improved on inspectors' recommendations. I have seen a few cases where the inspector has patently and blatantly made a gross error of judgement, but many more in which his recommended decision was better and bolder than that of the actual decision of the civil servant. Since 1968, when statutory powers were first given for inspectors themselves to make decisions on appeals in selected classes of cases, an increasing number of appeals has been so determined, until currently the proportion stands at about 85 per cent. There has certainly been no observable deterioration in the quality of the decisions made.

How well equipped to do so are the people who still occasionally override inspectors' recommendations? The answer must surely be 'not very well'. Certainly they understand the processes of government and are thus better equipped than most lay people to understand the implications of planning decisions; they are not lawyers and so do not have particular experience or expertise in weighing evidence, they are not town planners and thus have no knowledge of town planning techniques and criteria. They are 'Sir Humphreys': the most senior are formulators, under the general instructions of the Government of the day, of policies; they and more junior officers implement those policies. They are interested in consistency, propriety and a quiet life, not in bringing about good town planning, nor, one is inclined to fear, very much in justice. Among the amusing exaggerations of *Yes, Minister* are many sad truths.

Independent persons

The notion of an independent person hardly ever causes a frown. It is indeed a popular notion that if you are going to be subject to someone's decision you are likely to fare better if that person is 'independent'. Some people, especially in Australia, would like all town planning, not just the resolution of planning disputes, to be carried out by 'independent' bodies. Independent of what? Presumably of government, local government and pressure groups. For determining planning appeals of some minor kinds the idea may have some merit, so long as the person chosen is knowledgeable as well as genuinely independent, not just a lawyer or a local worthy.

In Northern Ireland in the 1960s a good deal of use was made by Catholic organisations of a provision in the Northern Ireland Planning Act which enabled applicants who had been refused planning permission to have their appeals determined by an independent person rather than via the inspectorial machinery similar to that used in England. Among a number of other people I was invited to act as an independent person from time to time. Far from being a Catholic I rather strongly dislike Catholicism, so, although, like any decent person, I was determined to act entirely without bias, I heard and determined these appeals without any predisposition whatever to find in favour of the Catholic organisations. For all that, in seven out of eight cases I discovered that there was no discernable reason for the application to have been refused, and in an eighth case, although perhaps it was a fairly close thing, the weight of advantage clearly lay in favour of the appellants.

The inquiries were conducted in the stately surroundings of Stormont. Council and appellants had the services of distinguished advocates, (Catholic for the appellants, Protestant for the council, with Catholic witnesses for the appellants and Protestant witnesses for the council.) All behaved with impeccable rectitude and courtesy. The inquiries were shadow shows. Evidence was virtually confined to descriptions of the site and the history of the application. The reasons for refusal given were derisory. In one case I said 'I have now listened carefully for two hours and nobody has given any reason at all why this appeal should be dismissed. Before I close the inquiry, has anyone anything to say to that effect?' Nobody had anything to say.

These were minor, *ad hoc* matters; the way in which they were determined was going to affect slightly the welfare of only a few people living in quite a small area; it was not going to have an effect on whether the town concerned would become a well planned town or not. More important appeal cases often have a substantial effect on the planning and therefore the welfare of the area in which they lie, so if their determination is left to people who do not understand town planning the consequences may be disastrous. They may also be disastrous if the appeal tribunal is not to some extent committed to making decisions within the framework of planning policies and proposals applying to the area. It should not, I think, usually be open to a tribunal to say that a particular policy or planning proposal is wrong and to base a decision on that opinion. In the English planning system, that is for the SoS to decide when making up his mind whether to approve a plan.

Unfortunately, in England, we have got ourselves into an awkward situation (fully discussed in my *Town Planning Made Plain*, Ch. 5, pp. 86–91). This is not the place to repeat that discussion, but the essence of the matter is that structure plans are mostly motherhood statements capable of many and varied detailed interpretations, backed by vague and inadequate diagrams, plus local plans of varying detail and worth. These latter have not usually been approved by the SoS, only by the council.

Since any appeal eventually boils down to resolving a dispute between a developer and a council about whether the former's or the latter's idea of how the relevant area should be planned is the sounder, this is an awkward situation. The council is the planning authority, so it would be tragic if a well considered and able plan were to be wrecked by the decision of a tribunal which simply didn't agree with the plan; yet it would be wholly unjust if the tribunal were bound or even felt bound to uphold a plan if in its opinion it was a bad plan, especially if it had been adopted despite weighty objections made at the public inquiry into it (the only formal chance anyone has of getting it altered except by appealing against a refusal of planning permission). An obligation by a tribunal to uphold the plan would therefore be tantamount to doing away with the right of appeal. I hope we never get to that situation, but I sometimes hear things that suggest we may be in danger of approaching it.

Lay tribunals

The defects of lay tribunals have, I hope, been sufficiently demonstrated in my remarks above about JPs and administrative civil servants. There can, I think, really be nothing to be said in favour of a purely lay tribunal, but in the case of multi-person tribunals, one lay member may be very valuable in introducing the 'common-sense' approach which may sometimes offset unduly rigid technical ideas. The inclusion of such a person may also encourage confidence among appellants about the down-to-earth ability and impartiality of the tribunal.

There are inherent disadvantages in using multi-person tribunals. If they are paid fees the cost is clearly increased. The delay in hearing appeals is also likely to be increased because of the need to find a date on which all members of the tribunal are available: they would seldom be engaged on the work full-time. They may also perhaps have difficulty in agreeing on a decision, although my own personal experience of a multi-person tribunal, which I shall recount in the next chapter, did not contain that disadvantage. On the other hand, in special cases, to have a legal, engineering, geological or other expert assessor to sit with the tribunal and give it advice may be very helpful.

Inspectors

In the course of this book I shall have occasion to make a good many criticisms of English planning inspectors and of the framework within which they work. Let me therefore say at once that I have, nevertheless, a warm admiration for both and should be interested and surprised to know if there is anywhere else a better system or a better operated system. Except for the possibility that under sections 47–49 of the Town and Country Planning Act of 1971 a special planning inquiry commission might be appointed to determine an appeal and except for those fairly rare occasions when an assessor may also sit, inspectors deal with all planning appeals in England. There will be much to say about their functions and characteristics in later chapters. For the moment it will be enough to say that they are constrained, of course, by planning law, by national planning policy, by the relevant approved structure plan covering the area in which an appeal site lies and by any local plan, and they have to have general regard to relevant planning policies for the area. They are employed by the DoE, but have a substantial degree of independence. This will be discussed in some detail in Chapter 10. For the 85 per cent or so of appeals which they determine themselves they have the last word, subject to the rare occasions on which their decisions may be capable of being challenged in the courts. In the remainder they are recommenders or rapporteurs, the decision being made in the name of the SoS. They therefore have very important functions. As mentioned on p. viii, some 12 per cent of the half million or so planning applications made in a fairly lively year are refused and about a third of these are taken to appeal, of which, in turn, some third succeed.

Comparatively few applications which are given permission by a council, and so do not need to be taken to appeal, are very contentious, and there cannot be very many of those which are refused which are not taken to appeal if there is any appreciable chance of success. So it is fair to say that inspectors are crucially important in holding the balance between the permissible and the impermissible. They are clearly to be regarded as expert tribunals; most of them have some professional qualification in a field which has some relationship to town planning and a good many are chartered town planners. One's main worry is whether they are expert enough: there is certainly a strong argument to be put (and I shall put it in Chapter 10) that all inspectors ought to be chartered town planners. There are also the contradictory worries about whether they are independent enough or, conversely, whether they are too independent for their decisions to have, over the whole country, an acceptably high degree of consistency. These points too will be discussed in Chapter 10.

Ideally, inspectors, as I have said, ought all to be qualified and experienced town planners, ought to have sufficient intercommunication to ensure a high level of consistency in their decisions, ought to have available to them a sufficiently sound and detailed set of planning proposals everywhere to ensure that the decisions they make are truly compatible with the good planning of the area around, and ought to be able to do their work more quickly. That would indeed be perfection. At present we fall a good deal short of that perfection, but I think the level of success is still creditably high and I should be reluctant to see the system changed in any radical way.

I do not think that deciding planning appeals sensibly is an inordinately difficult business. Given knowledge, experience, an impartial approach and all relevant information, plus reasonable time in which to consider the matter, the right decision usually presents itself. In the 250 or so appeals in which I have been the single-person tribunal or a member of a multi-person tribunal, I do not think on reflection that there were more than a dozen where there can have been reasonable doubt that the decision arrived at was sound. All those dozen or so doubtful decisions were decisions which could easily have gone either way.

On first consideration the balance of advantage may have seemed exactly even. Since to call a draw is not a feasible decision in a planning appeal, one had somehow to make up one's mind on which side lay the 51 per cent of advantage and on which the 49 per cent. It is a reasonable consolation that in such cases the consequences of getting the balance wrong on some divinely infallible criterion cannot be very bad.

4

Methods of investigating appeals

This matter can best be examined by considering it separately from three aspects: the type of proceedings, whether adversarial or inquisitorial in nature; the relative amounts of verbal and of spoken exchanges; the degree of formality with which proceedings are conducted.

Adversary and inquisitorial methods

English court proceedings are conducted entirely in accordance with the adversary system. The advocate on each side argues the merits of his case, backs it up with the evidence of witnesses and at various times tries to destroy the credibility of opposing evidence by means of cross-examination. The role of the judge is comparatively passive, any questions he puts being directed towards clarifying evidence rather than probing statements or bringing out further information, though of course there are exceptions to this. In a jury case he bases his summing up on explanation of the relevant law, on the evidence presented and an analysis of it and on nothing else. And so, when a jury is not involved, does he base his verdict. Of course he keeps the parties within the framework of the relevant law, decides on the admissibility of evidence and so forth, and may from time to time take a very prominent part in the proceedings, so that to describe his role as passive may seem odd. Nevertheless, essentially it is so; he does not choose the evidence to be presented, he does not deal with merits, he decides or helps a jury to decide which side has presented the more convincing case about the truth of the matters at issue.

The inquisitorial method (one should not be put off by the hideous associations of the word) is quite different. Essentially it consists of the tribunal taking the initiative in finding out what it thinks it needs to know to arrive at a proper verdict. There are numerous possible variants.

At one extreme the tribunal, having acquired by one means or another all relevant information about the nature of the case and the undisputed facts about it, would simply ask the available witnesses such questions as it felt necessary to establish the truth about disputed facts. Advocates would have no part to play. But this is very much an extreme, casting an enormous burden upon the wisdom and assiduity of the tribunal. There is a continuum between the pure adversarial and the pure inquisitorial procedures the optimal point on which varies greatly according to the kind of issues being dealt with. In the case of planning appeals where, as has already been pointed out, so much of the dispute relates to the value of opinions rather than what the facts are, it is unlikely that the best results would be secured if advocates were not permitted to play some part in the proceedings. At this point I simply comment that I believe English planning appeals would go better if they were moved quite a long way towards the inquisitorial end of the continuum from their present position, which is very close indeed to the pure adversarial end.

Written and spoken exchanges

It would be very difficult indeed to deal with planning appeals if they had no written element in them at all, and none are so dealt with. Some appeals are in fact dealt with without any spoken element at all: appeals dealt with by means of written representations in those cases where the inspectors' site inspection is unaccompanied.

In English practice there has been an evolutionary process in the course of which the written element has gradually grown greater and greater compared with the spoken element. Before the Franks recommendations were implemented in 1958 there might be no more than a bare statement of grounds for refusal by the council and a brief statement of grounds of appeal by the appellant before spoken battle was joined. Since then, councils have been obliged to supply, twenty-eight days before an inquiry, a full statement of their case. The SoS can oblige the appellant to respond similarly before the inquiry but in practice this is seldom done, though as will appear later I believe that it should be. Even during an inquiry written material plays its part, evidence customarily being written down and handed to the other parties before being read out by the witness.

The public inquiry method

This tends very much towards formal courtroom proceedings. There are no wigs and gowns and, except in appeals against Enforcement Notices, no oaths; but otherwise many public inquiries into appeals are only otherwise distinguishable from trials by a slackening in the observance of the rules of evidence, hearsay evidence being admitted fairly freely if not too strenuously objected to by the other side, and a little gentle leading of lay witnesses frequently being tolerated. It is very much an adversarial affair; an inspector often does no more than announce the nature of the proceedings, blow the whistle for start and finish and cue the opposing advocates to make their speeches and to question witnesses. An inquiry takes up much less time than comparable court proceedings, but may still drag on for hours longer than is necessary for the inspector to be fully informed. Usually, one believes, he ends up by being fully informed, but it is my strong belief that he would usually become informed much more quickly, and quite often more fully, if he played far more of an inquisitorial role.

Appeals dealt with by written representations

These are rough justice, greater speed of determination being purchased at the cost of less thorough exploration. Here the role of the inspector is almost totally passive. The opposing parties shoot arguments back and forth at each other in writing via the DoE until both have said all they want to say. These and all other documents in the case are sent to the inspector, who then arranges to visit the appeal site with or without the parties, after which he makes up his mind and writes his decision. If the visit is unaccompanied he never sees, let alone speaks to, the parties or their representatives. If it is accompanied he is rigidly (and under present arrangements rightly) precluded from discussing the merits of the case at all. All he can do is to ask questions directed to identifying physical features on or related to the site and to clearing up any minor doubts or ambiguities in the documents he has been given, e.g. misprints and arithmetical errors.

This cannot be the best possible procedure. As an inspector dealing with written representation appeals I quite often ached to ask four or five questions which would have made foggy issues perfectly clear. I think that inspectors ought to be able to hold 'mini-inquiries' in inquisitorial fashion at the site or under cover near it. The parties, I am sure, would welcome this; they often also visibly ache to communicate further. Conversely, if, in the case of inquiries, both parties had to state their cases completely beforehand, in all except the most important and complicated cases the need for a prolonged formal adversarial inquiry would disappear; it could be replaced by a brief inquisitorial inquiry. The two methods would merge, with better decisions, less time expended and more satisfaction all round. The 'informal hearing' procedure exists, but is little used. It provides the opportunity for just such an investigation. The DoE seem nervous of it.

Degree of formality

The degree of formality necessary or appropriate to inquiries varies very much according to the subject-matter and complexity of the issues. No one, I think, would suggest that trials for murder or armed robbery should be conducted in a friendly, chatty fashion, with lots of jokes rippling around the room. Indeed at any inquiry some degree of formality is necessary to ensure that what needs to be brought out is brought out clearly and expeditiously. Planning appeals are fairly serious affairs; no one's liberty depends on their outcome, but the happiness of a number of people may well be affected and (which also no doubt affects happiness) the value of land and buildings may be considerably altered by the outcome. But they have nothing like the seriousness of murder or robbery trials, so a less strained and anxious formality is appropriate.

In talking about degrees of formality I am not talking about, e.g. 'Oyez, oyez, all ye draw nigh who . . .' 'All Stand . . . .', wigs, robes and so forth. 'In this matter, m'lud I appear for the plaintiff with me learned friend Mr Snarler; me learned frined Sir Drabface Chillihand is appearing for the defendant. May it please you m'lud.' 'I swear by Almighty God . . . '. All this I think is useless stuff, belonging more to the posturings of a Masonic Lodge than to the decent sobrieties of real life. It is likely to conduce neither to clarity of outcome nor, as is sometimes foolishly alleged, to respect for the law: conducive rather to fear in the layman lest he be put in prison by the judge for contempt committed in ignorance and, worse, calculated to suggest that not only the judge but all the lawyers concerned are super beings owed fear and respect instead of quite ordinary people doing an ordinary job more or less competently. I am talking about degrees of formality not of pomp and pomposity.

I cannot resist a short digression about oaths. Taking an oath essentially means invoking divine sanction for the punishment of anyone who under oath does not tell the truth. Divine sanction is of course backed up by humanly imposed penalties for those who commit perjury. There can be little doubt that it is the latter that exert the greater influence. People who do not care to take the oath are fully entitled to make a solemn declaration instead in any form which is binding on their conscience and no one who disbelieves in the probable reality of divine retribution should be deterred from insisting upon making a solemn declaration instead of taking the oath merely because it is a little unconventional to do so and the clerk administering the oath has some difficulty in finding the card which bears the appropriate wording.

At ordinary planning appeal inquiries there is really very little opportunity of telling lies, so oaths are seldom or never administered, but they are administered at appeals against Enforcement Notices because here there may be real dispute about the facts, especially, for example, about when a particular use was begun. But it would be much better at such occasions (and indeed in any court proceedings) for the person in charge simply to warn each witness in words such as 'Do you understand that if you tell lies or speak with reckless disregard for the truth you may be prosecuted and punished?'

Formality is, literally, about the form which proceedings take, who speaks when, in what order, and at what length; it extends inevitably to modes of address, reciprocal behaviour and even body language. There are a number of obvious points to be made.

1. Someone has to be in charge (in English appeals, the inspector) to decide when proceedings begin, when they adjourn, when they finish, who speaks when, to rule when irrelevance has set in; in short, to exercise the functions of a Chairman as well as of an adjudicator.
2. It is intolerable for more than one person to speak at the same time: valuable information may simply never get across, threads of thought may be lost and tempers frayed if they do.

3. In extension of (2), interruptions are intolerable: questions must be able to be put fully and questions answered fully without being cut off.
4. There must be no intimidation of any kind, including bullying of witnesses by advocates (and vice versa).
5. There must be enough quietness and stillness for concentration to be possible and speech to be heard easily.
6. There must be enough space and comfort for all participants to deploy their documents properly and to feel physically at ease.
7. Everyone must be able to see everything, such as plans, that is being talked about.

Let us imagine two extremes.

A. People are sitting about unbuttoned all over the room; there is no particular arrangement of seats; members of the public surround the inspector, and he can hardly see or hear advocates or witnesses, partly because of the thick haze of smoke; bottles and glasses clink; liquid glugs, there is a yammer of chat and the clump of shoes as people move restlessly about the room; several people have their feet up on desks and there is a good deal of cuddling and giggling. 'Wait till I get you outside' yells a witness at an advocate. The inspector is frequently addressed as 'mate'.

B. All persons are dressed in suits and ties, the main participants in black; the inspector sits in remote isolation on a dais. A dropped pin could be heard. Indeed the scrape of a match rasps like the rending of a forest giant. 'Remove that man instantly!' raps the inspector. 'You may now speak briefly and to the point', says the inspector to the appellant's advocate. 'Rise when I speak to you!' he adds sharply. 'May it please you, Sir . . .' says the advocate. 'Usher, hand Exhibit A. to the learned inspector. With your indulgence Sir, I shall, if you permit, be calling three witnesses . . . stop that whispering at the back! Now, I shall humbly seek to prove that in or about the year 1979, the respondent authority, in their wisdom, sought to ameliorate an acknowledged shortcoming in the provision of residential accommodation . . . '

No one, presumably, would regard either A or B as ideal. What point on the continuum between them should we aim for? I say 'we' because everyone who frequently takes part in appeals can influence the way in which they are conducted, though, naturally, the inspector, and those at the DoE who prescribe or suggest procedures to inspectors have the greatest influence.

Personally, I am for the least degree of formality which will enable requirements (1) to (7) above to be met, because no one's behaviour ought to be constrained more than is absolutely necessary and the more relaxed people are, the better their chances of giving their best. Clearly, the number of people present is an important factor. Procedure which is perfectly satisfactory when only four or five people are participating will not do when there are several dozen participants and an audience of scores.

I think everyone should feel free to dress exactly as he or she pleases. I prefer

'Mr Smith', 'Mr Jones', 'Ms Lovelace' to 'Sir', 'Madam', and 'Me Learned Friend' because we are growing out of the deferential society, and I prefer that people should 'ask questions' rather than 'cross-examine'.

Anti-tobacco hysteria has now reached such proportions that a disallowance of smoking is now regarded more as a matter of health than of formality. It used to be very much a matter of formality and the only discernible difference between an inquiry and a 'hearing' was that smoking was allowed at the latter.

In summary, to get the best results, I think there needs to be an atmosphere more like that in a good committee meeting than in a court: closer to A than to B but still a long way from A.

5

Procedures

In the last chapter desiderata for examining planning appeals were suggested. I now set out for the benefit of readers who are not familiar with them the procedures customarily followed at the present time in dealing with planning appeals. First, those dealt with by means of a public inquiry and after that those dealt with by means of written representations. I shall not attempt to deal with more than a few of the quirks and oddities which most frequently arise.

Public inquiries

The inquiry will have been preceded by the following events. An application will have been made and refused or permitted subject to onerous conditions or the council may have failed to determine it. Except in the last of these three cases reasons will have been given for the refusal (from now on I lump refusal with imposition of onerous conditions) often in very skeletal form such as: 'The proposed development does not accord with the provisions of the structure plan and is in any event premature.' The applicant will have written to the DoE for an appeal form (why are they not available in post offices?) and will have sent it back, giving grounds for appeal, usually in equally skeletal form, such as: 'The council's decision is wholly unreasonable. The proposed development is fully in accord with the provisions of the development plan and is not premature; it is indeed overdue.' The DoE will have considered whether the appeal is one which might be dealt with by means of written representations, but either it or one of the parties has decided that it should not be. The council will have produced a statement, usually quite lengthy though not necessarily very inform- ative. It has to be lengthy because in subsequently presenting its case, the council may not go outside it, though in practice it is often able to do so because the appellant's evidence itself goes wider and can legitimately be dealt with by the council.

The appellant may or may not have made a response to the council's statement. In my view he always should do so, making sure that both the council
and the DoE get a copy. If he has a good case, the sooner and more fully it is
stated and the more it is impressed upon the mind of the inspector the better
for him. Professional advocates often do not like doing this. They like to keep
things up their sleeves, but I regard this as one of the occupational defects of
professional advocates. An appeal inquiry is not a kind of game in which
surprise tactics may be useful. To the extent that surprise tactics succeed, the
less is the likelihood of a just determination being arrived at. In fact it would
be a poor inspector who allowed them to succeed.

The DoE fix a date, time and place for the inquiry, usually but not always
at the offices of the council concerned. The DoE take care to ensure that the
date and time are acceptable to the parties. A notice will have been affixed to
the site some time previously, announcing the inquiry and the date, time and
place fixed for it. The council may also have given a certain amount of local
publicity to it to enable local residents to come and take part if they wish.

The parties and the inspector arrive. The inspector rises and says: 'This is
an inquiry into the decision of the Blackmire District Council to refuse planning
permission for residential development at Bog Farm, Little Misery by Shod-
dihomes Ltd. Who appears for the appellants?' The appellants' advocate
announces his identity and calling and usually at that point provides the
inspector with the names of his witness or witnesses. The inspector then similarly enquires about the council's representation and then asks 'Are there any
other persons present who wish to be heard?' If there are he similarly takes
particulars from them.

Next, in complex cases there is usually an interim during which the inspector
makes sure that all concerned have copies of all documents so far issued in
connection with the appeal. He then invites the appellants' advocate to present
his case.

The appellant's advocate usually begins by making a statement, frequently
at wearisome and unnecessary length. Then he calls his first witness. There may
be a variety of witnesses to give evidence about all kinds of things such as the
demand for housing in the appeal locality, the frequency of bus services and so
on and so forth, but usually the main witness and quite often the only witness
for the appellant is a planning witness who, let us hope, will be a chartered town
planner. If his evidence has not already been distributed in written form it will
then be distributed and he will read it (see Ch. 7 for how he ought to do this).
Then he will be cross-examined by the council's representative and by any
hostile third parties. Sometimes sympathetic third parties may seek to cross-
examine him, but inspectors reasonably tend to discourage this since it is likely
to serve only to lengthen proceedings without enlightening them. If the appellant's advocate thinks that the witness has given away damaging things which
might nevertheless be repaired by means of further questioning he may then
conduct a re-examination. The inspector may then ask questions of the witness
though in my view he does not do so nearly often enough. If he does, he usually
feels it necessary to go through the wearisome process of asking all the advocates

concerned whether as a result of his questioning and the answers given they feel it necessary to ask further questions. Fortunately they usually do not.

After all the appellant's witnesses have finished the councils representative presents his case. By what is now a fairly well established custom, he does not make an opening statement, but calls his witness or witnesses straight away, and exactly the same procedure is gone through in respect of them as for the appellant's witnesses. It should be mentioned at this point that inspectors are, in law, entitled to conduct inquiries in any way they think fit, subject to observance of fairness, but they seldom depart appreciably from what is being described here. I suspect that they have pretty firm direction from the DoE not to do so. In my view it would often be very much better if proceedings started with the council presenting its case since bad written statements are not uncommon and a really bad one will have left the appellants with little real idea of what they have to meet. They therefore, naturally enough, fill the air with lead by dealing with all possible objections to the development whether the council entertains all of them or not. This prolongs proceedings, sometimes inordinately.

When the council witnesses have been dealt with it is the turn of the third parties, and it is at this point that matters may start to get out of hand. Third parties who object to the development and appear on their own behalf are liable to make long and impassioned speeches which incorporate disquisitions on justice, mercy, papal infallibility and the regrettable social habits of the appellant's wife. One suspects that inspectors are under instruction to give such people far freer rein than most of us would think desirable. On the other hand it is not altogether uncommon for third parties to be represented by a QC and for him to call expert witnesses. This often produces a terrible situation. A Queen's Counsel has all the time in the world and makes full use of it. Often all that emerges is a repetition of the council's case. Yet one must not be too critical; I recall at least two occasions when, acting as an advocate on behalf of third parties who objected to the application, the council had conducted its case so ineptly that I felt bound to argue and give evidence at length, having previously cross-examined the appellant's witness, and even, though in neither case did the inspector much like it, the council's witnesses, in order to bring out fully and clearly evidence which had been deplorably muffled and confused. It worked too; we won each time.

In practice, very often, third parties who oppose an application are roped in by the council to give evidence as part of the council's case and conversely those who favour the application are roped in by the appellant. Would it were ever so. It greatly shortens and simplifies proceedings.

The council's advocate then makes a closing speech in summary of his case and in rebuttal of the arguments raised against it.

Finally, the appellant's advocate makes a closing speech, which, if he is wise, will be very short. Many of mine have simply consisted of: 'I do not think I need to make any closing statement, Sir. I am sure that you have heard and understood all the factors relevant to this appeal, and if I have not convinced you of the rightness of my client's case it is unlikely that a further speech will convince you.' Inspectors clearly like this, judging from their facial expressions. Just occasionally a lengthier closing speech may be useful when there remain some matters which are still confused. Of course it must not include any new material.

Then the inspector closes the inquiry and makes arrangements to carry out a site inspection, accompanied by representatives of the council and the appellant and of any third parties who wish to attend. He is always very careful not to travel in any car except his own unless representatives of both council and appellant also travel in it.

The site inspection itself is confined to the inspector looking at what he wants to see and what anyone else wants to point out to him. Very often he has had a look before the inquiry started, and this is certainly a good idea. No argument is permitted, no discussion of merits is permitted. Those present can draw the attention of the inspector to any physical objects or features to which they want him to pay special attention and the inspector himself may well ask whether that grey building there is Misery Farm.

The inspector then goes away. If he feels able to and thinks fit, he may send the parties what is known as an Advance Notice of Decision, in which he simply says that he is going to allow the appeal, dismiss it or allow it subject to substantial conditions. Whether he does that or not he later sends a detailed decision letter. If the case is one of those few reserved by the SoS for his decision, no advance notice of decision is of course given, and the decision letter will be cast in somewhat different terms.

Proceedings are somewhat changed and simplified when professional advocates are not used by one or either side and the roles of advocate and expert witness are merged. This will be discussed further in Chapter 7.

Appeals dealt with by means of written representations

These follow the same general outline as those dealt with by means of an inquiry. After the preliminaries the council produces a statement much the same as that produced for an inquiry. The appellant replies with a rebuttal and opportunities are given, with gradually stiffening deadlines, for the council to rebut the rebuttal or the appellant to rebut the rebutted rebuttal until both sides have sunk into exhaustion and intimated that they have no more to say. In due course the inspector arranges the site inspection, either accompanied or unaccompanied; it is unaccompanied only if the DoE have decided that the inspector can see all he needs to see without going on private property. No advance notice of decision is given in written representation cases, but a decision letter, usually somewhat briefer than that which follows an inquiry, is issued in due course. Nearly all written representation appeals are those in which the power to determine has been transferred to the inspector.

Snags and breakdowns may occur in the procedure both for inquiries and written representations. Parties may simply not turn up. Required statements may simply not have been produced. Witnesses may not be available on the due date. Inspectors may die between an inquiry and writing a decision. All I can say is that, almost miraculously, such things hardly ever happen, and when they do happen are dealt with pretty adroitly by the DoE. This is a tribute to them. I only once remember an inspector turning up late for an inquiry; he was ten minutes late. The fog lay thick for miles around and I was fifteen minutes late. As an inspector I was once very late for a site inspection because the map I was using to find my way was hopelessly out of date. On one other occasion I was two minutes late. The DoE have built up a tradition of punctuality for which they deserve very great credit. Few organisations can have equalled, let alone bettered it.

Another procedure

This is the place to descibe the operations of the Siting and Design Review Committee in Canberra. This is a three-person tribunal set up to review and adjudicate upon development proposed to be carried out in Canberra by private persons of which the National Capital Development Commission (NCDC), which is in charge of Canberra, disapproves. I had the honour of being a member of it for some years. It has the admitted disadvantages of any multi-person tribunal, as described in Chapter 3, but they did not loom large in this case. It has as Chairman a local layman of distinction and the other two members are respectively a local architect and a member of the advisory National Capital Planning Committee (that was me). It has to be said that the matters with which it dealt were very minor; many of them would have been exempt from control in England under the Permitted Classes of the General Development Order. However, these were not really appeals against ordinary refusals of planning permission but against conditions somewhat like restrictive covenants in this country, imposed by the NCDC as landlord. Since the way in which the Review Committee operated had been firmly established long before I came on the scene I can say without conceit that the procedure was admirable. There was a constraint of the kind which I suggested in Chapter 3 should apply to most tribunals, namely that we were not entitled in our decisions to say that a NCDC policy which it was allegedly sought to breach, was wrong or misguided, but only whether the proposal did breach it or breached it only so trivially that its general effect would not be harmed, that in fact it was *de minimis*.

What we had to deal with were mostly house extensions which were deemed by the NCDC not to fall within tolerances permitted by them. Very often the development complained of had already been carried out; always a help, since one can then see for oneself the effect thereof instead of having to imagine it. Often it was in the nature of a basement. The reason given by the appellant was usually 'De bulladozer she slip', or 'Well, Momma she lika to store a leettle wine'. What the NCDC in fact were worried about in such cases was that a slip of the bulldozer or the provision of space for Momma's wine really resulted in the provision of extra living accommodation for an extended family. Why worry? Because, although the NCDC did not usually, I think, state this with quite the clarity they might have, the increased population, if such activities became general, would cast undue strain on the adjoining road system, commercial facilities and social facilities such as schools. The solution we generally adopted was to require alterations to the development so as to lower the roof height to an extent making it unsuitable for human habitation.

The way we tackled these matters was as follows. An admirable administrative assistant would wait until three or four cases had arisen, would then ring round and find a date suitable for each of the three of us, would pick us up in a car on the morning of that date and, having also made previous arrangements with the appellants, would take us to each of the sites concerned, which we would view in the light of plans and other papers he had supplied to us. After a fairly hectic journey, often totalling thirty or forty miles, we would get back to central Canberra in time for a coffee, would hear two cases before lunch and the other one or two after lunch. We would then sit down, agree on our decisions, compose the decision letters, relax for half an hour while they were typed and then sign them. After that there was always, although sometimes with a bit of hurry, time for me to catch the evening plane back to Brisbane. Although the decision letters did not go out until the next day, this splendid administrative assistant would, as soon as we had signed the letters, ring up each of the appellants and tell them what the decision was going to be. I don't see how anything could be more expeditious, and the costs were negligible; the fees paid to us were nominal and the only substantial cost was my air fare between Canberra and Brisbane and my hotel bed for the night.

The hearings themselves were very much towards the informal end of the scale, a little too far, I think. Some of the requirements for an inquiry set out in Chapter 4 were fairly often violated. Two people would quite often speak at the same time, and the crying infants of appellants often broke concentration. (In fact I remember making paper aeroplanes for one during the hearing in order to pacify him.) The NCDC were not legally represented, but relied upon their planning officers to present their case. The appellants often presented their own cases, but sometimes were represented professionally or semi-professionally. The qualifications and experience of some of those who represented appellants were, to say the least, scanty, and I think appellants may consequently have suffered in the pocket, though I think it unlikely that a decision ever went against an appellant because of the inadequacy of his representation. Like all sensible tribunals, we were always concerned to look behind the incompetence of the presentation of a case to the relevant facts. Where we fell down was in allowing too much chit-chat between appellant and NCDC. We did not sufficiently insist upon one person finishing his evidence before being questioned, and it all sometimes got rather disorderly though never unfriendly. This, I am sure, did not affect the final result, it merely prolonged proceedings a little unnecessarily. Similarly, at the site inspections, we had great difficulty in explaining to appellants that we did not want to discuss the merits of the case at that point, but merely to look at the site.

On one occasion the appellant *was* legally represented; this was a very strange affair. The lawyer spent a great deal of time insisting that we had no jurisdiction to deal with the appeal. Since we had been appointed to deal with the matter, whether we had jurisdiction was not for us to decide, but for someone else, to whom the lawyer ought to have applied. The irony was that, having viewed the site, we had, over coffee previously come to the view that unless the NCDC had some thing very strong and unexpected to say, there could be no objection to the proposed development. However, not having heard the NCDC's case, we could hardly interrupt the lawyer by telling him that his client was almost certainly going to win anyway. The silly chap went on and on. Eventually we adjourned to take legal advice, reconvened some weeks later and found in favour of the appellant. All ended happily for him except that, I imagine, his lawyer's efforts on his behalf must have increased his costs, to no good end, by some hundreds of dollars.

I do not recall any occasion on which we took more than about ten minutes to reach a unanimous conclusion. The local architect tended to take the leading role because details of design and construction were often a predominant influence; I weighed in fairly often about privacy distances and accesses, and the lay Chairman, the nicest and wisest of people, mostly listened, applied lay common sense about the probable results of the development and asked one or other of us clarifying questions about technical points which we had not explained sufficiently clearly.

I am really not sure how well this procedure would work in relation to anything bigger than the very tiny matters we dealt with, and it would certainly in this country be very costly because of the vastly greater number of cases and the improbability of enough people being found who would be willing to give their services for only nominal fees. But there it worked very well.

Suggested improvements to current English system

I believe that the present system could be materially improved without radically altering it; in order to do so I would, in effect, merge the two present systems of inquiries and written representations. As regards the former, I believe that its adversarial style is unnecessarily cumbersome. As regards the latter, I believe that it is wrong for an adjudicator to have to make his determination without an opportunity to question the parties.

In pursuance of this object I would first make it mandatory for appellants to supply a full statement of the case before the appeal is investigated, after receiving the council's statement. Thereafter, I would always have a site inspection attended by the inspector and representatives of both parties at which the inspector could ask what questions he liked, but would confine them to issues of fact rather than of merit. I would then always have a hearing, however brief and informal, in tiny cases no more than twenty minutes over drinks at the nearest pub. In more important cases I would retain the present procedure of using a hall (perhaps better not the council offices if avoidable). I don't see why there should be any set procedure invariably followed. The procedure appropriate to a particular case depends upon its nature, complexity, the fulness and competence of the statements of the case and to some extent on the person-alities involved. There ought not to be any legal limitation on representation but I am not persuaded that legal representation of either side is very often worth while.

The inspector might often begin by reciting the issues as he saw them, invite each side to comment on his statement and to put to the other side for clari-fication any conflict over facts. No more than this might often be necessary in order to inform the inspector sufficiently to make a decision, but, equally, there would often be occasions on which the inspector was doubtful about the tech-nical soundness of some of the evidence on one or both sides and would find it useful to conduct a conversation with, rather than an interrogation of, the person concerned. No doubt, usually, he would think it right before closing down to give each side an opportunity to make a brief closing statement of clari-fication, rebuttal or amplification of points discussed. Needless to say, with this procedure, the inspector would need to be a person of real weight and character and a chartered town planner.

What about third parties in such a procedure? I am not persuaded that in a well conducted appeal system third parties have a useful part to play. The council is elected to serve everybody and, in refusing an application, should clearly have taken into account the probable or possible detrimental effects of the proposed development on neighbours. If the councillors are not doing a good job it is for the electors to replace them at the next available opportunity. The DoE are also there to ensure that the council is doing its planning job adequately and to serve as a check that in a particular case the council is applying its policies sensibly and without bias. Impliedly, in our system, the DoE are possessed of higher wisdom than that of the council, which is why it is particu-larly important that inspectors should be persons of sound and weighty judge-ment. But third parties, as neighbours, are, out of the whole population of the world, the people least capable of taking an unbiased view of what is proposed. Neighbours seldom want anything to be changed, unless it be the removal of a particularly horrible eyesore, though even that may be represented by some of them as a cherished landmark and ecological reserve. They are usually incapable of taking or putting a balanced view. It does not much matter whether or not they are heard so long as weight is only given to their opinion if that opinion is backed by good evidence. They waste time. I should like to see them eliminated, but it would take a brave government to legislate for their elimination from appeal proceedings. What can and should be done is to encourage inspectors not to allow them to waste time with irrelevances.

6

Representation at appeals

Anyone taking part in an appeal has the right either to represent himself or to be represented by anyone he chooses. Dealing first with inquiries, the kind of representation which is often adopted for important appeals is to employ a barrister. As most people know, it is only possible in this country to employ a barrister if one first employs a solicitor, through whom the barrister is employed. This adds a great deal of expense for the appellant. It adds less to the expense of a council, who have plenty of solicitors available to perform that function. Almost invariably an expert witness will also be needed, except for third parties, who may feel able to rely on the evidence of the witnesses on the side which they are supporting. Expert witnesses are also expensive (except for councils, who of course employ their own in the form of planning officers) but they are not as expensive as barristers or solicitors. One or more lay witnesses may also be needed to speak to facts. How much it will all cost depends upon the eminence of the persons employed, the extent of their acquisitiveness, the amount of preparation needed, including the number and length of conferences with counsel, and the time the inquiry takes.

If such an arrangement is thought too grand to be necessary or too expensive to be tolerable the barrister is dispensed with and a solicitor may be used on his own, but solicitors in private practice are by no means all keen to take on the job of advocate; it is hard and demanding work and some solicitors feel they do not want to expose themselves to the criticism of clients if they perform poorly or unsuccessfully; they prefer to let a barrister take the flak. My own experience has been that solicitors who are not good at advocacy are absolutely terrible, but that the best are as good as anyone. This is especially so with solicitors employed by councils; the poorest are so dreadful that one wonders how they have the nerve to draw their salaries, but the much more numerous good ones are excellent; they know the locality and local personalities and facts far better than can any barrister brought in just for a particular case, and sometimes make deadly use of this knowledge. As a witness for appellants I have found some council solicitors the most formidable opponents of all.

The next economy, a big one, is to dispense with lawyers altogether and to employ a town planner both as witness and as advocate. This is a bold thing to do, but it saves a lot of money and may produce better results. I have never personally found it necessary to charge more for acting as advocate and witness combined than for acting only as witness: the time-consuming, irritating and often futile conferences with counsel are saved and one does not have to educate a solicitor and barrister (sometimes separately) about technical matters or scribble frantic notes at the inquiry, directed at getting the professional advocate to ask the right follow-up questions during the course of cross-examining an opponent.

Nevertheless, an appellant needs to be cautious in choosing someone to act as advocate and expert witness combined. It is a task of which it is all too easy to make a monumental mess; yet, given plenty of technical knowledge and experience, a good measure of confidence and some prior study (listening to good planning advocates is the best) a chartered town planner should be able to perform very satisfactorily. Members of other professions concerned with the use, management and direction of land may also do quite well in simple cases which relate strongly to their professional field of expertise, but are unlikely to have a sufficiently broad and balanced view and knowledge of town planning.

It is generally unwise for anyone to act as an advocate-witness in a case in which large numbers of witnesses are going to give evidence on either or both sides. The effort needed to keep a grip on the whole situation is too great; two people are needed, one to do the advocacy and keep track of the relationships between the different parts of the mass of evidence offered, spot the weak points, make his own points and exploit the opposition's weak points, the other to concentrate on putting over the planning evidence in favour of his party as effectively as possible. It is hardly possible to give a definite indication of where the point comes at which the combination of the roles of advocate and witness becomes impracticable, but it is wise for a potential advocate-witness to draw the line conservatively, not to bite off more than he is likely to be able to chew. Nevertheless, it should be borne in mind that what matters most is securing the right decision, not putting up an elegant performance. Elegance may have little effect on the mind of the inspector or the DoE (see Ch. 11).

The cheapest way of all for the appellant is of course to conduct his own case (though, of course, he may in the long run lose money by losing his case). There is no reason why a sensible, confident and articulate lay person should not conduct his own case if it is very simple, but he would find it extremely helpful at least to get some general advice from a town planner about the town planning issues which are involved, for the council's statements will not necessarily bring them out, and a poor inspector may then also miss them. Yet they may be the very things which could clinch the case in favour of the appellant.

People who do not have the confidence to conduct their own cases and are without sufficient means to employ professional help may be able to obtain 'planning aid'. They should consult the Royal Town Planning Institute, 26 Portland Place, London W1N 4BE, Tel. 01-580 2436 or the Town and Country Planning Association, 17 Carlton House Terrace, London SW1Y 5AS, Tel. 01-930 8903.

I do not want to give the impression that professional advocates are nearly always unnecessary. The skills of a good advocate are very great. If the issue is an international airport, a power station or a proposed huge mineral working, the large number of different but interwoven issues, the large numbers of witnesses needing to be called by both sides and the fairly numerous points of law which may arise in such cases compared with most ordinary planning appeals, combine to render the professional advocate's role of overriding importance. Heaven help anyone except a professional advocate who tried to conduct a case of that kind.

There is also the question of professional integrity. Professional advocates are not concerned with the rightness of the cause which they support. There is widespread lay misunderstanding of this. It is quite common to brand barristers as hypocrites. 'He can't possibly believe what he's saying', is a frequently heard comment. This is to misunderstand the professional advocate's role entirely. He is there to present his client's case in the most effective possible way. It has cynically been said that the advocate's role is to mislead without actually telling lies, but this is indeed an unduly cynical view. The advocate has certain facts and opinions to play with, and his skill is to deploy these as powerfully as he can. In doing this he does his best to destroy the credibility of the opposition's case. I have no doubt that advocacy may often exceed reasonable limits of seemliness and decent behaviour but that is another matter.

The position of the chartered town planner acting as advocate-witness is entirely different. His professional integrity demands that his case is technically reasonable. He ought always to be able sincerely to end his submission by saying 'I therefore believe that this appeal should be allowed', if he is acting for the appellant. If he cannot do this he should not take the case on either as advocate or witness, let alone both. If he does, the client is not getting the best help. He needs to find someone who can make such a statement with conviction.

My own experience as an advocate began in the army, acting from time to time either as prosecuting officer or defending officer at Field General Courts-Martial. In straightforward cases of absence without leave, refusal to obey an order and so on, I found no great difficulty in making submissions or bringing out the evidence of my witnesses. But when it came to cross-examination it was very different. Though, as we shall see in Chapter 7, one can to some extent prepare oneself to carry out cross-examination by compiling a list of likely questions in advance, when it actually comes to it the mind tends to go entirely blank or, even worse, one begins to think, 'this chap's evidence is absolutely right, what can I possibly find in it to quarrel with?' Experience quite soon overcomes the worst of these dreadful feelings, which I fancy are common to everyone. I think it is likely that chartered town planners will increasingly find it desirable to act as advocate-witnesses whether on behalf of councils or appellants, and it would be a very good thing if more planning schools held more mock planning appeals at which students could gain some experience.

To continue with further experiences which in the light of recent events may be of some special interest, when I was working as a planning officer for the Kent County Council in the 1940s it was common form for planning officers in Kent to be asked to act as advocate-witnesses at simple appeals. It was a satisfactory arrangement. The atmosphere was far less intimidating than that of a Field General Court-Martial and the work of preparation was much lightened by the absence of a professional advocate; one's performance, judging by results, seemed to be reasonably satisfactory. At the first appeal at which I conducted the council's case I was confronted by a barrister with a local reputation for extreme ferocity, but, perhaps because he had never before been confronted with an amateur opponent, he was on that occasion remarkably mild. On another occasion the only people in the room were the inspector, my opponent, who was a local estate agent, and myself, not even the appellant being present. This was remarkably satisfactory; the whole proceedings took about an hour and a half during which my opponent and I fully set out our cases and attempted to destroy the other's. It was about the location of a house in a rural area and for a case like that I cannot think of a better way of doing the job.

Later on, as a consultant, I was fairly often asked to take on the role of advocate-witness and did so with, I think, reasonable success judging by the results. As already noted, although doing this means working much harder on the day than if you are merely acting as a witness, the preparation is much less tiresome. One client, now alas dead, encouraged me in this role, and had the endearing habit of writing out the cheque for my fee while I was making my concluding statement.

In the 1960s a new factor appeared on the scene when the Town Planning Institute was applying for its charter. It became known that the grant of the charter would be influentially opposed unless it contained words which precluded chartered town planners from acting as advocates, and such words were inserted. As a member of the Town Planning Institute Council at that time I said that I thought to do so was immoral and monopolistic in tendency.

Of course life is full of absurdities, but this was an absurdity so monstrous that it should not be allowed to be forgotten, even though it has since 1982 been put right. Anyone has always been allowed to be, at law, a representative or advocate for anybody at a planning appeal. This item in the charter meant that chartered town planners were picked out as a unique class among the whole nation as not allowed to fill this role. On almost any assessment they were, however, apart from professional advocates, far more likely to be good advocates than any other group of people. I regarded the prohibition inserted in the charter as so immoral and so totally contrary to good sense that I declined to be bound by it. I happily continued to act as an advocate whenever asked to do so until my departure to Australia in 1968. Had I been challenged and threatened with expulsion from the Town Planning Institute I should have conducted a vigorous and embarrassingly public defence. Apart from citing the items already mentioned here, I should have said something like this: 'I am a chartered surveyor as well as a chartered town planner. Do you seriously expect me to lower my standing at appeals by only mentioning that I am a chartered surveyor and not, much more importantly, a chartered town planner?'

An alternative, aggressive line of defence, or an additional one, might have been, 'You say I can't act as an advocate, I won't then. From now on I will simply present evidence, and when the council put their case I will simply say I want to ask a few questions to make sure that I know what the opposing evidence means.' I think that would have been a watertight defence and indeed it came very close to the style in which I have habitually conducted planning inquiry cases. In fact the issue never arose, and in 1982 the Council of the Town Planning Institute very laudably succeeded in having this restriction removed from the charter. Nevertheless, the effect has been bad. I gather that a good many chartered town planners have been deterred from conducting appeal cases by that provision in the charter. They must now make up for lost time.

The position with regard to written representations is rather different, though the general principles of what I have been saying apply. Having looked at a very large number of written representations I feel safe in saying that the majority of well prepared statements on behalf of councils have, from internal evidence, clearly been prepared by planning officers rather than by lawyers. As regards those submitted on behalf of appellants I find it possible to draw up an order of merit. Chartered town planners draw up by far the best representations, followed at a considerable interval, but quite ably, by chartered surveyors. Next, by a long distance, come architects, whose skill seems to reside far more, as a class, in the drawn line than in the written word. After that come what I feel bound to call disparagingly the 'scrub' professionals or sub-professionals, who habitually waffle lengthily, irrelevantly and illiterately. Last of all, surprisingly and regrettably, come solicitors. Many do little more than translate their clients' opinions into stiff and rather pompous legalese without attempting to make any real case. Such statements often have an oddly old-fashioned ring as if they had been written in the 1930s.

7

Preparing and conducting an appeal

Involvement in an appeal can range from writing a four-line letter of objection as a third party to being involved from start to finish: first advising an applicant whether and in what form to make an application and seeing him right through subsequent refusal and appeal, finally, perhaps, analysing the precise meaning and implications of conditions attached to the appeal decision. For the sake of completeness and simplicity we will assume the latter case in this chapter.

A planning officer's work is much the same as that of an applicant's adviser, except that instead of considering how best to make an application, he will be considering what report and grounds of refusal or conditions, if not an unconditional permission, to recommend to his committee; or to give, if the power of making the decision has been delegated to him. For further simplicity we shall consider only the case of a refusal, not onerous conditions or failure to determine. The best way to do this seems to be to take an imaginary example which brings in a fairly wide range of factors to consider without being confusingly complicated.

The town of Urton in the County of Wheatshire is a pleasant small town with a population of about 8000 people. There is an approved structure plan for Wheatshire but no local plan for Urton. However, there is a very ancient approved town map for Urton (see Fig. 7.1). The applicant, Mr Hardbrick, is a builder who has an option on about 5.25 ha (13 acres) of land at Oatley Farm. It was not allocated for residential or any other kind of development in the town map. It has access to Trame Road. Other sites which we shall hear about are: land at Quince Farm, which was allocated for residential development in the town map, but which is very steep and rugged; land at Gage Farm not allocated for development in the town map, but which rather mysteriously received planning permission for housing in the early 1970s before the Urton District Council came into existence; land at Pippin Farm and at Gote Farm has obvious attractions as land for housing because of its position and physical characteristics, but has not yet in either case been the subject of an application for planning

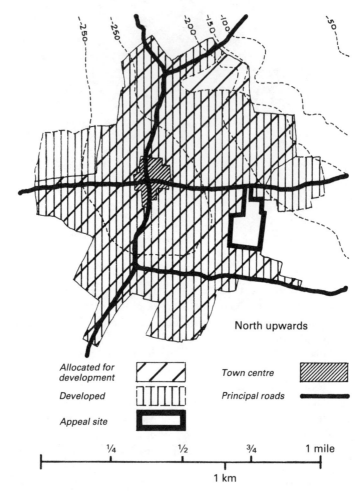

Fig. 7.1 Urton town map

permission; land at Peartree Farm received planning permission for housing a few years ago as the result of an appeal and has now been developed; finally, land at Cherry Farm has an attractiveness similar to that at Pippin Farm and Gote Farm. The town centre, though picturesque, is very congested; since Urton is a 'crossroads' town all through-traffic has to pass through the town centre.

Mr Hardbrick asks Ms Southbank, a planning consultant, whether he should apply for planning permission for housing now and what form the application should take. Ms Southbank advises him to apply at once; the town seems buoyant, there seems no advantage to be gained by waiting – since the land is not allocated in the town map for development and since there is no sign of a local plan being adopted and a refusal is likely, followed by an appeal, which will take months to determine – the sooner the better. There are no special characteristics attaching to the site which might make it advantageous to submit

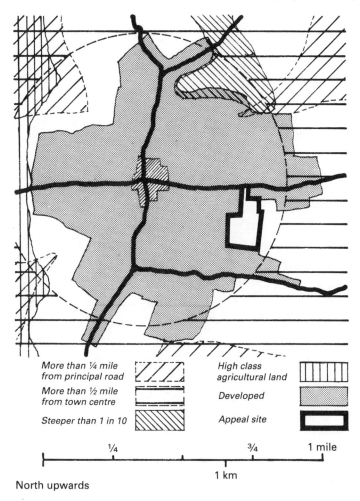

Fig. 7.2 Urton survey

a detailed application, and an outline application will of course be much less costly to prepare. So they decide to put in a simple 'red-edged' application supplemented by a very rough layout plan (not reproduced here). Better also give an indication of density in case there is any niggling about that; what does Mr Hardbrick have in mind? Mr Hardbrick is not sure; after discussion they decide on 'about 25 dwellings per hectare' (10 dwellings per acre), a total of about 130 houses.

Ms Southbank accordingly puts in an outline application. This, after a few days, arrives on the desk of Mr Gloscat, the local planning officer. He is neither surprised nor pleased. He has not been with the council very long and he is far from being ready with the district plan which he has it in mind to prepare. The structure plan seems to him, so far as it affects this application, to be both vague and too restrictive. He does not understand why it should have prescribed

51

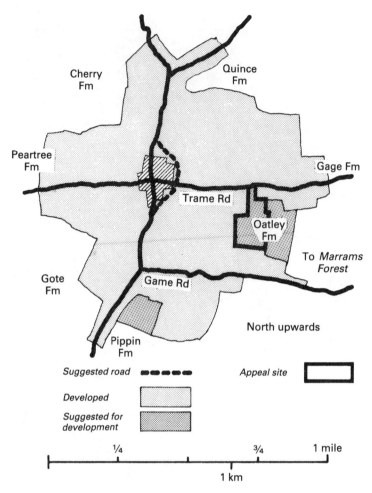

Fig. 7.3 Ms Southbank's suggested outline plan for Urton.

'limited growth' for the town, nor what 'limited growth' means in this context. He does not understand the reasons for the land allocations in the town map nor the permissions given for land at Gage Farm and Peartree Farm. Probably the original reason for them is that Quince Farm is such an unattractive site and pressure for housing was such that something had to give somewhere. But in that case why not have allocated Oatley Farm? It seems an obvious choice. He discovers that influential residents just to the west of Oatley Farm opposed its allocation as land for development in the town map because of 'the view'.

He is in a difficulty. If he recommends permission for the application in disregard of the town map, will that open the floodgates and be followed by applications for development of most or all of the sites mentioned above? If that were to happpen and they were all permitted, then the town would really be getting much bigger, and perhaps local services and facilities would be swamped. The town centre would certainly become badly congested and the principal roads of the town uncomfortably so, at least at times.

In a cautiously worded report to his Planning Committee, Mr Gloscat advises refusal. They agree with him rather more enthusiastically than he altogether likes; the people who live just to the west of Oatley Farm are still influential. Accordingly the following decision is made and issued.

The Urton District Council refuses planning permission for residential development of land at Oatley Farm, Urton, for the following reasons:

'1.   The proposed development lies within an area defined in the structure plan for Wheatshire as one within which only limited growth is to be permitted and in which new development should therefore be confined to that needed in connection with local employment. The proposed development is not necessary for that purpose.

'2.   The land is not included for development in the Urton town map and is not likely to be so included in the local plan for Urton at present under preparation.

'3.   The proposed development would have an injurious effect on the view of Urton from the East, as seen from the vicinity of Marrams Forest.'

Mr Hardbrick is anxious that, if possible, the delay and expense of an appeal should be avoided, so he urges Ms Southbank to go and have a talk to Mr Gloscat. She, having weighed up Mr Gloscat's probable thoughts pretty accurately, is not hopeful that this will be useful, but of course complies. Ms Southbank and Mr Gloscat know and respect each other (indeed there is perhaps a certain *tendresse* between them). They have an agreeable and frank talk, but neither undergoes a change of opinion and no acceptable compromise presents itself. So Ms Southbank promptly lodges an appeal on the formal ground that

'the proposed development is entirely consistent with the intentions of the structure plan for Wheatshire. The site should have been included for residential development in the town map for Urton and ought to be so included in any local plan for Urton. The proposed development would not have an injurious effect on the view of the town from the East'.

Ms Southbank and the council are invited by the DoE to agree to the appeal being dealt with by written representations. The council immediately agree. Ms Southbank checks with Mr Hardbrick, who, having been assured that an inquiry will cost him little more than written representations and that the chances of success, though not perhaps very great, are greater if an inquiry is held because of the fuller exploration of the issues which is possible, authorises her to opt for an inquiry. He is a bit apprehensive about the possibility of needing to give evidence, but Ms Southbank assures him that this is unlikely, and in any case she will look after him. In due course the council's Statement arrives. This is the gist of it.

'1.   (Formal history of application – i.e. site, development proposed, date of submission, date of refusal, grounds of refusal).

'2.   As regards the first ground of appeal, paragraphs 4.10–4.13 of the approved Structure Plan for Wheatshire deal with a number of areas within the County, of which Urton is one, in which only limited growth is to be permitted and development is intended to be confined to comparatively small-scale development within urban and the larger rural centres to an extent which is compatible with but not greater than that needed to meet local employment needs. Paragraphs 4.11 and 4.12 state that housing development in Urton, among other places, will normally be limited to infilling of partly developed front-ages and to such sites as are already substantially closely impinged upon by urban development. In the opinion of the Council the appeal site does not fall within either of these categories.

'3.   As regards the second ground of refusal the appeal site was not included as land for development in the Urton town map, which was approved in 1965 and remains the basis of development control in Urton pending the adoption of a local plan for Urton. In the town map the appeal site lies within an area of 'white' land, that is to say an area in which it is expected that existing uses will for the most part remain undisturbed.

'4.   The preparation of a local plan for Urton is under active consideration, but due mainly to the need for extensive consultation it is not expected that such a plan will be adopted for at least two years from now. It is, however, not anticipated that the appeal site will be included in an area for future urban development in the plan.

'5.   As regards the third ground of refusal the Council take the view that the proposed development seen from the east, especially in the vicinity of Marrams Forest, would substantially damage the very pleasant rural view at present enjoyed therefrom. In addition the Council believe that they have a duty to protect the very pleasant views out of the town, towards the east, at present enjoyed by residents immediately to the west of the appeal site. These views have been enjoyed for a very long time and any detriment to them would substantially reduce the pleasing character of houses on the eastern outskirts of Urton.

'6.   The Council acknowledges that in recent years there have been some developments in the vicinity of Urton which have not been wholly in accord with provisions of the town map, but are on that account all the more anxious that further infringement should be resisted. They therefore confidently urge the inspector to dismiss this appeal.'

Ms Southbank responds as follows. (Words in square brackets are notes she makes for use at the inquiry.)

'*Statement of Case for Appellant by Susan Southbank, Chartered Town Planner*

'1.   (Preliminaries similar to those given by the council in their Statement.)

'2.   I have been engaged in the practice of town and country planning for the last twelve years, partly in the service of local planning authorities and partly on my own account. I have had extensive experience of the problems of towns such as Urton.

'3.   I consider that the development which is the subject of this appeal is wholly consistent with the natural controlled growth of Urton and that the Council were quite wrong to refuse permission for it.

'4.   The first reason for refusal relates to statements in the structure plan for Wheatshire. It will be well within the inspector's knowledge and experience that many of the state-ments in structure plans are exceedingly vague, capable at best only of very general and uncertain interpretation. I do not know what "needed in connection with local employ-ment" means, nor, with any certainty, what "local employment" is. I find difficulty in interpreting "in connection with" and am far from clear about the relationship between "needed" and "necessary for that purpose". [No doubt, one way or another, Mr Gloscat will in due course enlighten me.]

'5.   Looking at the Council's first ground of appeal, it appears to me that what the County Council have tried to do is to indicate that they don't want enormous growth in Urton, growth which might swamp local services such as schools, shops, public open space and the road system and might transform the character of Urton and exacerbate its problems. I think they may have tried to say that, but they have mistakenly tried to put the boot on the other foot. What they say is that they only want development "needed in connection with local employment". That, I submit, is the wrong way round. It suggests that the people who will live in these proposed houses are to be regarded simply as potential recruits to local industry and that we mustn't have too many of them in case there aren't enough jobs for them in local industry.

'That is a totally wrong way of looking at it. Many of these "potential inhabitants", as I may call them, are likely to work quite a long way away, in Somodàh for example, where there is so much industrial and commercial activity related to the salt industry, but where, because of what I would regard as an unduly restrictive conservationist policy, there is so little housing land. They will spend here much of the money that they earn in Somodah. That will stimulate employment here in shops and similar places. There will be more children to teach, more clothes needed for the children and their teachers and so on. Builders will thrive, initially in the course of building the houses, later, much later, in the course of repairing and maintaining them. The idea that one should plan so as to limit the population of a place to a number which will match the planned number of directly productive jobs, is dead. No one now tries to plan for a specific number of directly productive jobs. What makes sense is to permit residential growth to occur, in accordance with demand, subject to an orderly sequence, up to the town's geographical and infra-structural limits. It may be a pity that regional planning is not conducted on some less crude basis, but in practice, despite the fine words of structure plans, it is not.

'What my client proposes is wholly in accordance with the principle I have just suggested and wholly in accord with any sensible interpretation of the structure plan.
'6.   The second ground of refusal is, if anything, even less defensible than the first. It is notorious that the old town maps were practically worthless. Most town maps allocated land for development far too conservatively, and few of them allocated it rationally. The Urton town map is no exception. Although it obviously didn't include enough land for housing it managed to allocate some, at Quince Farm, which no one has wanted to build on, and no wonder. Instead, the Council allowed unallocated land to be built on at Gage Farm, not very sensibly I think. That spread the town out quite unnecessarily. It took the efforts of the SoS to secure development of Peartree Farm, since unaccountably the Council wouldn't give permission for it. Oatley Farm is very similar, I suggest, to Peartree Farm. [Fortunately in this case, the SoS won't have to be troubled, since the responsibility for determining this appeal is transferred to the inspector..]
'7.   I am surprised that the Council have not yet prepared a local plan for Urton. After all, they and their predecessors have had a clear duty to plan Urton ever since 1943, if not before then. One would think that everything that needs to be known in order to do a proper plan for Urton has long since been discovered. Knowledge and memory about local planning didn't disappear in a flash when the very wrong conclusions of PAG (Planning Advisory Group) were adopted and everyone seemed to be advised to start again. Nor did they disappear when local government was re-organised in 1974. There was continuity in the storage of information, continuity in the recording of ideas, continuity in many cases in the identity of the planners concerned [though I don't suppose Mr Gloscat was here before 1968]. I'm quite sure that if Mr Gloscat were put to it and turned loose, as it were, he could produce a sensible, up-to-date plan for Urton by next Tuesday. I certainly could and I don't know as much about Urton as Mr Gloscat does. In fact I attach to this Statement a plan for Urton which I'm sure could temporarily serve well, supported by simple survey data. (See Figs. 7.1–7.3.)
'8.   The third ground of refusal is, if possible, even flimsier than the others: the view from the east, from Marrams Forest. The inspector will see what that is like, except that he won't unless he trespasses or gets permission from the farming owners. From the only public right of way which crosses Marrams Forest, for a distance of about 2 km, the appeal site can only just be seen for a total distance of about 50 metres. I have walked it and checked that. My client has erected a pole 10 metres high, about ridge level of the proposed houses, on the highest part of the site, and I could only see it for 50 metres of my 2 km walk. Even if this were not so, even if the public could see the appeal site from many points in Marrams Forest, there would still be no slightest reason for refusal. When this development is completed the eastern urban edge of Urton, a much cleaner, sightlier urban edge than exists now, will have moved about 100 metres closer to

Marrams Forest: 100 metres out of about 2000: an imperceptable bagatelle.[Nothing like Birnam Wood and Dunsinane.]

'9.   I formally object to the second limb of the third ground of refusal, brought out in the Council's Statement, the alleged effect on the view to the east. It is a totally different issue to the view *from* the east and an illegitimate afterthought to the grounds of refusal. It is not only procedurally illegitimate, it is intellectually indefensible. When people buy houses they do not buy the right to a view from them; if they could and did, there could seldom be *any* urban expansion allowed. If you want to buy the view, you have to buy the land of which the view is composed. There are only rare exceptions to that and this is not one of them. [However, Mr Swiyne is evidently here to speak about the imaginary right to a view, and I don't suppose you will prevent him from speaking, so I shan't press my objection.]

'10.   There can, I suggest, be no reasonable doubt that the appeal site ought to be developed for housing and developed as soon as possible. I'm never sure to what extent inspectors are likely to be interested in layout plans in connection with an outline application. In case the inspector *is* interested, a possible layout is shown on Plan D, (not reproduced) but in case she is not interested I've done it quite roughly to save my client expense.'

The great day dawns. The appeal is held in the Urton Council Chamber. The inspector is Miss Hardicanute. The council's case is presented by a solicitor on the council's staff, Mr Speakwell; Mr Gloscat is his only witness. A local solicitor, Mr Swiyne, is there to represent the well-to-do residents immediately to the west of Oatley Farm. Ms Southbank knows that he is aptly named, and her scalp tingles pleasantly in anticipation of having a go at him. There are a few members of the public scattered around but they have not indicated that they wish to make representations.

After the usual preliminaries, Miss Hardicanute invites Ms Southbank to present her case, and she begins: 'You already have a copy of my Statement and so have the council. I have enough further copies for most people here, perhaps I should hand them round.' (Much murmuring, 'please', 'thankyou', 'most considerate'.) 'There are some plans attached to the Statement; I've made transparencies of them. I have an overhead projector and there's a screen up there. If you are agreeable I will display the plans on the screen at appropriate times.' (More appreciative and affirmative murmuring.) 'I imagine that as there are members of the public present you would like me to read my Statement?' (Affirmative nod from the inspector.) 'It may help Mr Speakwell if I say that I am not distinguishing between evidence and argument in my Statement and so I shall be happy to be questioned on all of it.' (Appreciative nod from Speakwell, scowl from Swiyne.) 'As I have indicated, Mr Hardbrick is here to answer questions if necessary.'

She reads her Statement, adding an occasional afterthought or ad lib.

Mr Speakwell rises to cross-examine her. He is quiet, pleasant, respects the old maxim that if a witness seems to have talked sense but not to have done you too much harm, it's best not to spend too much time on cross-examination.

Q.   Ms Southbank, you don't think very much of the Wheatshire structure plan?
A.   No.
Q.   Nor of the Urton town map?
A.   No.
Q.   But they are all we've got, aren't they?

56

A. No.
Q. No?
A. No; you've got the skill, knowledge and experience of your planning office to produce a proper plan.
Q. A local plan?
A. Yes.
Q. But not to put too fine a point on it, the DoE aren't exactly hurrying councils to produce local plans, are they?
A. No, unfortunately.
Q. And the DoE do what the SoS tells them?
A. Notionally.
Q. Well, that's a matter of opinion. At least you're not suggesting that there's anything especially bad about the Urton Council's performance?
A. No, just ordinarily awful.
Q. You've produced a plan which, you suggest, would do very well as a local plan for Urton. How many people did you contact before producing it?
A. No one.
Q. No one? That doesn't say much for public participation, does it?
A. Public participation goes on all the time. There was a public inquiry into the town map. It happens whenever you consult residents about an application. It happens every time there's an appeal. It's happening now.
Q. Not quite what the DoE mean by public participation?
A. I can't help that.
    (*'Leave it, leave it,'* says Speakwell to himself, *'or it may go on for ever.'*)
Q. Now, the grounds of refusal, Ms Southbank. You say that the parts of the structure plan the council have quoted are virtually meaningless. I put it to you that they are quite clear and meaningful: you just don't like the meaning?
A. I can't agree.
Q. At least can you go with me as far as agreeing that they suggest comparatively small growth for Urton rather than large growth?
A. Yes.
    (*If you've got to admit, do it readily; that may throw him. It does, slightly.*)
Q. Thank you. And would you call 130 houses 'comparatively small growth'?
A. Yes.
    (*'Damn,' Speakwell thinks, 'where have I got to? Nowhere much.*)
Q. Well, we shall have to disagree on *that*. Now, you've suggested I think, that Urton might be allowed to grow with less restriction?
A. Er, yes; not quite in those words, but yes.
Q. But if there were demand for a lot more development, isn't it rather odd that Quince Farm hasn't yet been developed?
A. No, it's a perfectly dreadful site; terribly expensive to develop; steep slopes, broken land, I don't think in ordinary circumstances anyone would want to try to develop it.
Q. Well, we shall see what my witness has to say about that. Turning to something else, Ms Southbank, you said a good deal in your Statement about the proposed development generating employment: you didn't mention people taking in each other's washing?
A. No, there's not much of that done now.
Q. But the way in which that expression is commonly used is to illustrate an obvious economic fallacy, is it not?
A. Yes.
Q. Into which you've fallen.
A. Well . . .
Q. Thank you, Ms Southbank. You don't live in Urton, do you?
A. No.

Q. I'm referring now to your outline plan. Would you care to tell me how many hours you spent in Urton while preparing this?
A. I don't know; there were two or three visits. About 10 hours in all, I suppose.
Q. And you seriously suggest that is long enough to enable you to prepare a sound plan for Urton?
A. Yes. It's only an outline plan; that doesn't need a great deal of site survey. There are ordnance maps too, you know. They give a lot of information.
Q. Coming now to your evidence about the third ground of refusal. Are you seriously suggesting that the addition of 130 houses on the east side of Urton is not going to change the view from the east?
A. Not appreciably. I think I've already explained that. The edge of the town will not appear perceptibly closer than it is now, there will be few places along the public right of way from which it will be visible . . .
Q. But people might picnic at those places?
A. They might, but I had not finished my answer.
Q. Sorry.
A. And the edge will be a better looking edge than it is now.
Q. Ah, your layout plan?
A. Yes.
Q. In which you're not very interested.
A. *I'm* interested, I'm not sure whether the inspector is.
Inspector: Yes, I am interested, but perhaps not overwhelmingly.
Q. Thank you, Ms Southbank.
    'Damn,' thinks Ms Southbank, 'I let him jolly me on at the end; I could have made more of that. Still, not too bad; now for Swiyne.'

Inspector: Do you want to say anything by way of re-examination, Ms Southbank?
A. No thank you. I don't think there are any points that need clarifying (*Implication: there wasn't much to it.*)

Mr Swiyne is now invited to question Ms Southbank.

Q. As you have anticipated, Miss Southbank, it is about the interests of the residents to the west of the appeal site that I am concerned. Do you recognise the rights of property?
A. It's not for me to recognise them, the law does that.
Q. Nevertheless, you recognise that property owners have rights?
A. Same answer.
Q. I see you're unwilling to answer.
A. I have answered.
Q. I shall put it another way. Town and country planning law is designed to protect the interests of owners and occupiers of land, is it not?
A. Not principally, the main purpose . . .
Q. Never mind whether the purpose is primary, please answer the question.
A. (She thinks, 'No more mucking about, I must stop this now.) Mr Swiyne, you ask the questions and leave the answers to me, and don't interrupt.
Q. Really, this is outrageous, the witness must be amenable . . .
Inspector: All right Mr Swiyne, just a minute. You did interrupt; the witness must be allowed to answer in her own way. But Ms Southbank, not quite so sharp, please.
A. All right.

It would be painful and paper-consuming to set out the rest of this cross-examination in detail, for it takes a long time. Mr Swiyne's only real point is that his clients have a nice view, have had it for a long time and ought not to be deprived of it and the provisions of the town map ensure that they won't.

Ms Southbank unswervingly points out that a town cannot grow except at the expense of the views of at least some of those who, theretofore have been at the edge of the town, that the town map is inadequate and out of date, and that the appeal site is an admirable choice for Urton's next piece of housing. They snarl at each other a bit more, but not very much; the inspector's sensible and soothing intervention has had its effect.

Once more Ms Southbank is invited to make a statement by way of re-examination but once more declines.

Inspector: I have just one question, Ms Southbank. I'm not clear how you've determined which are the principal roads. Are they classified roads?
A. No, they are the ones which are shown as the principal roads of the town on the town map and my ten-hour inspection of Urton confirmed that as a suitable choice.
Q. Anything arising from that that you want to put to Ms Southbank, Mr Speakwell? (*The inevitable precautionary invitation, almost invariably, as in this case, declined.*) Is that your case, Ms Southbank? (*The necessary reminder that now is the time to get in anything that has been forgotten.*) Mr Speakwell.
Q. Thank you Madam. I will call my first and only witness, Mr Gloscat. Mr Gloscat, I think you have been Principal Planning Officer with the Urton District Council for the past two years?
A. Yes.
Q. And you are a chartered town planner?
A. Yes.
Q. Would you read as your evidence the relevant parts of the Council's Statement?
(*He does so, well enough, perhaps not quite so well as Ms Southbank did because he is not very happy; he thinks he is likely to win this appeal but knows he has a doubtful case. When he finishes Mr Speakwell says:*)
Q. A few questions arising from Ms Southbank's evidence, Mr Gloscat. I do want the Inspector to be clear about this. Is it right that in the case of the Gage Farm housing, on land not allocated for development in the town map, permission was given for that before the creation of the Urton District Council in 1974 – so that the present council has no responsibility for that?
A. Yes, that's right.
Q. And in the case of the Peartree Farm development, the council couldn't help that either?
A. No, it was allowed by the Secretary of State after an appeal against refusal.
Q. So the Urton District Council have not so far themselves permitted any substantial departure from the town map?
A. That's right.
Q. Now, turning to another matter (*'Crikey, will I get away with this,'* he wonders, *'It got left out of the Statement.'*) What effect on traffic do you think the proposed development would have?
Ms Southbank leaps to her feet.
Ms Southbank: Really, Miss Hardicanute, this is extraordinary. There is nothing about traffic in the council's grounds of refusal or their Statement, and I was certainly asked no questions about it. I must protest most strongly.
Mr Speakwell: (*Thinking: 'No such luck.'*) But Madam, Miss Southbank has herself, in the plan that she submitted, drawn attention to the matter of traffic, by indicating on the plan the principal roads of the town, to one of which the proposed development would connect. Surely ....
Inspector: No, Mr Speakwell; you can't do that. If you wanted this matter brought out you should have asked Ms Southbank questions about it.
Ms Southbank: Thank you, Miss Hardicanute, but, with respect, it's not quite as sim-

ple as that. The issue of traffic has now been implanted in your mind. I really must have the right to uproot it, if I can put it like that.

Inspector: Yes ....?

Ms Southbank: I could of course ask for an adjournment in order to consider the position (*a shudder runs round the room*) but I should not like that to happen (*general relief*). I should like to withdraw my objection; and I think I can deal with the matter adequately by questioning Mr Gloscat about it and by referring to it in my closing statement. (*She doesn't think there's anything much in this; 'useful little bit of aggro, though; now let it run.' General murmur of 'yes', 'fine', 'excellent idea'.*)

Inspector: Very well, that's how we'll proceed; Mr Speakwell.

Q. Now, Mr Gloscat. (*Mr Gloscat recalls himself with a jerk; during the last exchanges he has been lost in a pleasant fantasy. He and Ms Southbank are snowed up in a log cabin, the flickering firelight plays upon her ...*)

A. Yes.

Q. Mr Gloscat, I want to step very carefully here. Is it a fact that the proposed development, if carried out, would cast considerably more traffic upon Trame Road?

A. Of course.

Q. And what effect would that have upon the town centre?

A. It would make it more congested.

Q. Thank you. Now, one last thing. Ms Southbank was very definite that the Quince Farm area was quite unsuitable for development; what do you think?

A. I think she exaggerated; it's not without its difficulties, I accept, but I think very good housing could be built there.

Q. Thank you.

Inspector: Ms Southbank?

Q. Mr Gloscat, I'm not going to try to persuade you into agreeing with me about exactly what the implications of the structure plan are for the growth of Urton, but at any rate you may be able to agree with me that if there is to be any appreciable further growth (*Damn, I'm waffling*) of Urton, the appeal site would be a good place for it.

A. Quite good.

Q. Any better places?

A. Well, there's Quince Farm.

Q. Yes, Quince Farm. Do you know that on the part of Quince Farm allocated for development in the town map there's an average slope of 1 in 8.3?

A. No.

Q. No; I take it you've not done any measurements there.

A. No.

Q. Well, I have. Will you accept my figure of 1 in 8.3?

A. Of course.

Q. And will you further accept it if I tell you that there are several 150 metre squares within which the average gradient is 1 in 6.2?

A. Yes.

Q. Well, I do so tell you. Do you think these are good site characteristics for housing?

A. With careful siting and sensitive design it could be very attractive.

Q. Even if most of the land also has an aspect between north-west and north-east? Very cold and bleak?

A. I agree that's a disadvantage, but we have central heating nowadays.

Q. A disadvantage that doesn't apply to the appeal site?

A. That's true.

Q. Any other candidates? Pippin Farm?

A. It's too far out.

Q. Cherry Farm?

A. Road access might not be possible.

Q. Gote Farm?

A. That has high agricultural value.
Q. Thank you. Now as to traffic. How would you describe Trame Road?
A. It's just an ordinary road.
Q. No special problems with bends, gradients or narrow bits?
A. No.
Q. So if there's going to be more housing in Urton that might be quite a good road for it to use?
A. There's the town centre; a lot of it would go that way; there's congestion there.
Q. Which needs to be relieved, doesn't it? Anyhow?
A. Yes.
Q. And I show a relief road for the town centre on my plan, don't I?
A. Yes.
Q. Anything wrong with it?
A. No, but it might not be built for a long time.
Q. Like any other road?
A. Yes.
Q. Mr Gloscat, I don't want to push you too far, but the appeal site isn't a bad site for housing, is it?
A. No, it isn't.
Q. Thank you. (*Leave him alone, that's fine; he's gone as far as it's fair to ask him to go.*)

Mr Swiyne then tries to question Mr Gloscat. The inspector says: 'No, Mr Swiyne. You are obviously on the same side as Mr Gloscat, I can't let you cross-examine him.' After a bit of huffing and puffing and *sotto voce* rumblings by Mr Swiyne, the inspector says: 'Now, Mr Swiyne, will you make your submission; I gather you are not calling any evidence.'

Ms Southbank takes the hint. After Mr Swiyne has uttered a few sentences, she points out that he is really giving evidence. Will he be willing to submit to cross-examination? Mr Swiyne indicates indignantly that he will not. Ms Southbank then, reasonably enough, points out that evidence not tested by cross-examination is worth very little and the inspector tactfully indicates that she will bear Ms Southbank's comments in mind. We need not reproduce Mr Swiyne's Statement. There is nothing in it except constant reiteration that his clients' marvellous view ought not to be damaged. He rambles on for quite a while to appreciative nods and becks from his well-dressed clients, but bores all others out of their minds. Mr Gloscat's erotic fantasy returns.

Inspector: Mr Speakwell, do you want to wind up on behalf of the council?

Mr Speakwell winds up very briefly. He says that no convincing evidence has been produced to suggest that further development of Urton cannot await preparation of a local plan and indeed that is what ought to happen. Ms Southbank is also then invited to sum up and she says; 'I will be even more brief than Mr Speakwell. I am satisfied, Miss Hardicanute, that you have heard everything you need to hear in order to reach a right decision and that when we have made the site inspection you will also have seen everything you need to see.'

The inspector then closes the inquiry and makes arrangements for the site inspection. This is attended by Ms Southbank and Mr Gloscat as well as the inspector. Mr Swiyne cannot of course be bothered, but two or three of his clients turn up and make a bit of a nuisance of themselves. The inspector, Ms Southbank and Mr Gloscat combine in repelling them and insisting that they do not make comments about merit. They don't last out the 2 km walk along the right of way, and Ms Southbank, uninterrupted, is able to indicate the, indeed, very short stretches from which the pole erected by Mr Hardbrick can be seen.

As they left the Council Chamber the participants mused as follows:

Mr Speakwell: 'OK, not bad. Gloscat did well, what a silly chap Swiyne is. Sue Southbank's good, but I don't think she did quite enough to win; don't think Hardicanute has quite got the bottle to uphold her. Silly case, what the hell does it matter? A bit more development would pep us all up. Off to squash.'

Mr Gloscat: 'Did OK. Still don't much like it. Silly structure plan, absurd town map. Speakwell ought not to have raised that traffic thing; embarrassing; I told him not to. Sue was good, but pity about that bogus economics. Wish I could do a *real* plan for Urton.'

Mr Hardbrick: 'Knocked 'em all over the ground. Bloody marvellous; well done Sue.'

Mr Swiyne: 'Oh well, clients liked it. Bloody women. Bloody planning. Bridge now!'

Ms Southbank: 'Not bad. Fixed Swiyne. Bet we lose.'

Miss Hardicanute. 'Good, got it over in a day.

Miss Hardicanute does not find the decision letter an easy one to write. She is bound to take account of the structure plan policy. If the proposal is definitely in conflict with it she must dismiss the appeal unless some specific reason can be found to demonstrate that it should be overridden in this particular instance. Vague though the wording of the structure plan is, it certainly puts fairly strong restrictions on the growth of Urton.

The town map is absurd and the permissions given for developments outside its allocations are confusing. No help to be had from the decision letter in the Peartree Farm appeal. The administrator who drafted it wrapped everything up so much in 'ifs' and 'buts' that it gives no lead to follow. (Cunning administration, bad planning.) The Quince Farm land is virtually undevelopable; Gloscat ought to have admitted that. The appeal site is much more suitable. However, so is land at Cherry Farm, Gote Farm, Pippin Farm, and, come to that, apart from the mere question of amount, there's no reason why development of the appeal site shouldn't later continue eastwards, at least as far as the present eastward limits of Urton along Trame Road and Game Road. If *all* that happened, and, if she allows this appeal, it might happen, then indeed there would be a much bigger Urton: the need for a bypass would become more urgent, the town centre would become intolerably congested and need redeveloping, and so on. A good thing too perhaps; why shouldn't Urton expand? A nice little place, but rather 'one horse'. But that would clearly be in conflict with the rather silly structure plan.

The 'view' objections, whether from east or west, are clearly specious. Ms Southbank did a good job on those, a pity she went in for all that simplistic economic argument. Better if she'd just said that people are much more mobile than they used to be.

There is nothing in the traffic point; that was naughty of Speakwell; that's the way to the High Court if you're not careful! Must be sure she makes clear she hasn't taken it into account. A pity she can't write the decision letter in simple straightforward terms but must make it 'proper' and 'dignified' and avoid saying anything too general which might seem to commit the SoS.

Shorn of descriptive material and bureaucratic trimmings, Miss Hardican-ute's decision letter addressed to Ms Southbank as the appellant's agent, comes out like this:

'From my inspection of the site and surrounding area and from the representations made, it appears to me that the main issue to be determined here is whether the proposed development would be unacceptably in conflict with paragraphs 4.10–4.13 of the approved structure plan for Wheatshire and with the approved town map for Urton, at present used as the basis for development control in Urton, pending the preparation of a local plan.

'If it were decided that there would be no such conflict the question would also arise whether the proposed development would have an unacceptably injurious effect on the view of Urton from the east or the view eastward from the present eastern edge of Urton. Having carefully considered the evidence given and having viewed the site from all relevant places, however, I do not consider that there would be sufficient detriment to amenity caused by the proposed development to justify its refusal on that account.

'During the course of the inquiry a further issue was raised regarding the possible traffic congestion which might be caused by the proposed development. I was not convinced by the evidence given that sufficient congestion to justify dismissal of the appeal would be likely to be caused by the proposed development and, in reaching my decision, I have not therefore taken this possibility into account.

'There can, in my opinion, be no doubt that, however else the relevant parts of the structure plan are to be interpreted, they are intended to apply restraint to the growth of Urton. Primia facie, therefore, in considering applications for residential development in Urton, applications in respect of land not allocated for development in the town map would be likely to be refused. But clearly, there have been certain anomalies. It is difficult to reconcile the permission given for development in the vicinity of Gage Farm with either the structure plan or the town map. My colleague, Mr Upsidaizey, in recom-mending that the appeal in respect of land at Peartree Farm should be allowed, indicated that he regarded that proposed development as a very special case. Nonetheless, the development that has followed has obviously constituted an appreciable expansion of Urton. It appears to me that the land allocated for development in the town map at Quince Farm is hardly capable of economic development. Nevertheless the town map was approved and that land was allocated for development.

'It is not easy, in these circumstances, to arrive at a just determination. In the end I conclude that, if this appeal were to succeed, not only would the consequent devel-opment in itself constitute an expansion of Urton hardly compatible with the structure plan, but would inevitably provide almost irresistible arguments in favour of giving permission for the development of much other land, almost, if not quite, as suitable for development, the development of which would materially alter the character and scale of Urton and cast severe strain upon public and private services and facilities.

'I have taken account of all other matters raised, but do not find them sufficient to affect my decision.

'For the above reasons and in exercise of the powers transferred to me I hereby dismiss this appeal.'

Let us look briefly at all this with a Godseye view. Of course the appeal should never have been necessary. Long ago there should have been a proper town plan prepared for Urton, something like an old style town map, but rather more detailed, regularly reviewed and revised, accompanied by a detailed programme map to indicate the order of release of sites for development and supplemented by local plans with the order of detail of what used to be called supplementary town maps. (See Chapters 2–5 of *Town Planning Made Plain* for detailed exposition of this subject.) The failure to produce plans of this kind is indeed the worst failure of British town planning.

Many readers may have been left with the impression that the disputants never really quite got to grips, that there was more sparring than infighting. (Ms Southbank was only asked one question, about her sieve map.) That is quite true, and it is quite typical of planning appeals; somehow the realities don't get fully debated. Ms Southbank tried to get them fully debated (the futility of the structure plan and the town map) but had no luck. Mr Speakwell didn't think it necessary for the success of his case to do so; for Miss Hardicanute it was pure poison; to tangle in that would be to get involved with matters which everyone has always told her are none of her business. It is very hard indeed to get such matters seriously debated in an appeal inquiry; somehow it is always plausibly argued that the proper forum for that is some other forum (and at the other forum, that it is yet another forum). Nevertheless, Ms Southbank might well have mentioned in a final address that her suggestions for selection of land for development in Urton had not been seriously challenged. However, she decided, perhaps rightly, that omitting a final address would have a better effect on the inspector.

Apart from that, Ms Southbank did a good job; maybe her economics were simplistic, but what she said needed refutation or confirmation and got neither. Again, it was not necessary for Mr Speakwell to take this on to win his case and poison for Miss Hardicanute to tangle with. Note that neither party brought up land supply statistics. How wise: it is almost impossible to defend them or attack them decisively.

Ms Southbank set a good example by behaving in straightforward, courteous but non-deferential fashion. This rubbed off on everyone except Mr Swiyne. Mr Speakwell did a thoroughly competent job; as we have noted earlier, it is not his job to ensure that right prevails but to present the case handed to him as competent as possible. Mr Gloscat also did a good job; as we have seen he had some misgivings about the case he was supporting but he acted correctly, competently and honourably. Mr Swiyne made his clients happy, but his initial advice to them should have been to try to find a planning consultant who felt able to make some genuine points on their behalf.

Miss Hardicanute: given the formal importance attached to structure plans, it's difficult to critise her for dismissing the appeal. It was probably the wrong decision, but her job is not to alter the planning system, her job is to exercise her expertise and judgement as fully and justly as possible within the framework of that system. Perhaps she might have said that the structure plan needed reconsideration because there was no apparent reason for drastically limiting the growth of Urton, that a local plan ought to be adopted very quickly, that she believed it ought to allocate the appeal site and other land for development and that this would necessitate proposals being included for town centre re-development, a town centre relief road and probably for a bypass. But inspectors are not, one believes, encouraged to say that kind of thing in their decision letters. Perhaps this is reasonable; to make such statements would to some extent usurp the role of the SoS. The blame can only lie with Secretaries of State for not obtaining better planning advice, with their advisers for not giving it and with the planning profession for not unceasingly besieging and berating successive Secretaries until they perform better, especially by insisting on the production of more definite structure plans, the rapid production of local plans, and the application of much stricter technical criteria in determining appeals. For more about this see Chapter 10.

Inevitably there has been a touch of caricature in this account. Statements in structure plans are seldom *quite* as opaque and silly as the one with which we have been concerned, town maps are not often quite as inadequate as the one discussed here. Dialogue does not flow as crisply as portrayed here: verbatim transcripts in real life tend to be very long and boring. Mr Speakwell would probably not have totally ignored Ms Southbank's sieve map, but would have tried to knock it in some rather meandering fashion, but I hope that all in all the account contains the truth that often resides in caricature. It is a naturalistic rather than a realistic account.

If, instead, the appeal had been dealt with by way of written representations, the council's initial Statement would no doubt have been much the same and Ms Southbank's response would have been the same as her initial Statement; similarly, Mr Swiyne would have dreared on paper exactly as he dreared verbally. The council would then certainly have put in a response to Ms Southbank, bringing in the content of the questions which were in fact put to her in cross-examination, and she would have responded in terms similar to her response to the cross-examination. In that response or in her initial Statement she would also, depending upon when she received a copy of it, have dealt with Mr Swiyne's statement. That would probably have been that until an almost exactly similar site inspection had taken place and an almost exactly similar decision letter had been sent. However, almost certainly, there would have been even less direct argument and clash of ideas than occurred at the inquiry, and Miss Hardicanute might well have got a less clear picture of the issues than in fact she did. Mr Hardbrick, though he lost, had a better chance of winning by opting for an inquiry.

An inquisitional type inquiry (see Ch. 4) might have been much more satisfactory, but for it to have been so Miss Hardicanute would obviously have had to feel much less inhibited in her questioning than, as has been suggested a little earlier, inspectors now are.

Would the council have been better served by using a barrister; would Mr Hardbrick have been better served by using a barrister and/or solicitor? Surely not; no one could have done more than Mr Speakwell or Ms Southbank did. There are plenty of Mr Speakwells up and down the country and plenty, at least potentially, of Ms Southbanks, though they have been held back too long by the purported restrictions of the Town Planning Institute charter for many yet to have emerged. As already suggested, the objectors would have been better served if they had been represented by a Ms Southbank (if they could have found one to support them) instead of by the egregious Mr Swiyne.

One interesting point remains. Would the council have been as well or better served if they had been represented solely by Mr Gloscat, and had not troubled Mr Speakwell? In this particular case, probably not, because although Mr Gloscat had recommended refusal, he had done so with considerable mental reservations. These would matter little to a professional advocate but might well damage the performance of an amateur advocate rather badly. How that kind of rather subtle distinction, and decisions based upon it, can in practice be made in a district council office is rather a problem.

Preparation, presentation and tactics

Everyone has an individual specific pattern of thought and action. It is difficult, therefore, to give detailed advice which will suit everyone, but the following might perhaps suitably be followed by most people.

The first thing to do when getting involved in an appeal, whether as advocate, witness or advocate-witness, and whether for council, appellant or third parties is, having obtained copies of the essential documents, to decide what the nub of the case is. What points are likely to be uppermost in the mind of a competent tribunal? Next, or at the same time, have a good look at the site and as wide a surrounding area as seems relevant. Then, decide whether you can conscientiously support the side you have been asked to support. Do the points in favour of your side amount to at least 51 per cent and the points against not more than 49 per cent? If not, withdraw as gracefully as possible. If they do, prepare your case (in whatever form) as soon as possible to leave time for second thoughts and refinements.

It is unlikely that the documents initially received will give all the information needed; if not, the next thing to do is to consider what further information is essential and get it. It is useless to be too perfectionist in this regard. There are, for example, huge amounts of useful, relevant information held by public bodies, but they may be reluctant or slow to provide it, or if they do, may not provide it in usable form. It is necessary to use the best that can be obtained quickly, even if it is imperfect, and useful to use information provided by the opposition if it is not too grossly imperfect; it will be difficult for them to disavow their own material. To give a very simple example, Ms Southbank used the council's own set of principal roads for one of her maps. In fact it suited her purpose rather better than possible alternatives.

Ordnance Survey maps, at various scales, provide immense amounts of information if skilfully interpreted. In many appeals, the amounts and disposition of steeply sloping land are of great importance. For most town planning purposes these can be worked out easily and in sufficient detail from contour lines on ordnance maps. (Evidently, from her statement, Ms Southbank did rather more than that. She seems not to have produced her detailed slope analysis, but would obviously have done so if challenged. No doubt she is a dab hand with a clinometer.)

Existing use surveys of small towns and of town centres can be done very quickly, in sufficient detail for planning appeal purposes. Sunday morning is a very good time for these, when pedestrian and vehicular traffic is likely to be slack. (Obviously, if traffic patterns need to be studied, that is the worst time!)

The best presentation of graphic material, especially maps, presents problems. The first is whether to try to cram everything onto one map, which reduces cost and prevents confusion of one piece of paper with another, but increases the likelihood of confusion in trying to understand the one piece of paper; or to follow the principle of a different map for each subject, which reverses the advantages and disadvantages and may have the additional disadvantage of hindering comparisons, e.g. between high value agricultural land and steep land.

Produce lots of copies of everything (except hand coloured maps, because of cost). Somehow, one more copy is always needed; parsimony attracts criticism, liberality enables *you* to criticise the more effectively any harmful parsimony to which you are subjected. As an extreme example, one has known the council advocate and the planning officer to have to share a single copy of the appellant's statement of evidence, to their evident and justified discontent: how can two people make notes on the same paper at the same time?

It is quite unfair to third parties and members of the public if they do not have the same graphic information as the principal parties, and if they do not they can legitimately complain and seek an adjournment for the lack to be remedied. Transparencies and overhead projectors (as used by Ms Southbank), or slides, can be a great help, and ought to be used more often than they are. Above all make sure that the inspector has a copy of everything he is likely to need. As an inspector settling appeals by written representations I was often surprised at the failure of *either* party to supply a simple existing land use plan of the area surrounding the appeal site, even when the land use pattern was of the essence of the appeal. It is not much fun doing one's own survey in the depths of some hellish industrial town, with darkness and snow falling together, and it is the parties' fault if, in those conditions, some item important to one of them is missed.

Photographs are splendid *aides-mémoire* for inspectors, so are aerial photographs if suitable ones can be obtained at reasonable cost. Sieve maps, if carefully and clearly presented, can summarise an argument better than thousands of words. While black and white presentation must, because of cost, be the norm, touches of colour to emphasise especially important items vitalise a drawing and should, when possible, be added at least to the copies for the inspector, the opposition and oneself.

The written content of evidence is, of course, immensely important. It must be comprehensive, but it should be kept as short as reasonably possible, otherwise there is the danger of important points being lost in the swamp of words. Paragraphs should be numbered for ease of reference during cross-examination and for the notes the inspector will take. Keep sentences short or understanding may falter. Avoid officialese and jargon, or if jargon is absolutely unavoidable, explain what it means. Especially avoid impersonal passive forms such as 'It is considered that . . .'. (*Who* considers it? The witness, the council, the SoS, all decent people?) If the appeal is to be dealt with by way of an inquiry it is important to frame Statements so that they can easily be read aloud without sounding confused or silly. Otherwise there is no reason to write a statement of evidence in any way different from any other piece of decent English. The plainer the better; Orwell rather than Lawrence Durrell should be the guide.

Some people favour a standard format for statements of evidence, with headings always in the same order: 'grounds of refusal, development plan provisions, site and surroundings, views of third parties, refutation of grounds of refusal', etc. Well and good perhaps, but it tends towards a boring, wooden effect, and subject-matter varies so much from appeal to appeal that a standard format may often damage rather than assist clarity and impede the development of a smoothly flowing argument. Certainly, though, a steady movement from the general towards the particular is desirable unless there is some special reason to proceed otherwise.

Care needs to be taken regarding 'holding back reserves' and dealing with weak points in one's own case. Entrapment of the opposition *can* be brilliantly effective when successfully carried out. One leaves an obvious gap in the evidence apparently to avoid a weak point, or rather clumsily glosses it over. But it is not a weak point; it is a strong one, and when the opposition gleefully seizes on it in cross-examination, wham! They are hoist with their own petard. But this is a dangerous ploy. It is not unknown for the opposition to decline to cross-examine, or they may simply not notice the trap, or they may detect it as a trap. Better not try to be a Perry Mason.

Real weak points in one's case are a different matter. If it is not a very damaging point the best thing is to acknowledge it in the statement of evidence and explain that it is not of much importance and should not affect the result of the appeal: 'The junction of Love Lane with Fair Street is undoubtedly poor, but the proposed development will cast very little additional traffic on it and the junction already carries so much traffic that its improvement is in any case urgently needed.' However, if the point is a very serious one, better leave it alone in the statement of evidence for an inquiry and work out beforehand how to deal with it as well as possible under cross-examination which, astonishingly, may not come.

With written representations there has to be a fine judgement whether less harm will be done by ignoring the point than by setting out an inadequate reply and thereby drawing attention to it. There is no obligation to volunteer anything except what is in one's own favour.

Speaking evidence is much like any other kind of public speaking. It is essential to be heard and understood, and that means speaking more slowly than novices think can possibly be appropriate. There are many good books about public speaking, which novices should study. A special, not very easy skill which is very necessary is to read without seeming to be reading; failure to do this is very soporific. There are many hints available: mark pauses in your copy of the 'script'; white-out all the commas in it, which will produce some hesitations and stumbles – not as silly a suggestion as it sounds; write in a few 'ad libs' – very helpful, but don't put in too many or inspector and opposition may ask you to stop while they make notes of them; best of all, practise, practise, practise.

Being cross-examined is not a very relaxing activity; nor should it be. The responses made may largely determine success or failure. Don't be hurried, think before answering, refuse to answer more than one question at a time. It is a favourite advocate's device to shoot several questions in succession, pick out the answer that seems most helpful and pursue that, while ignoring the less helpful answers. This is unscrupulous, unfair, confusing; don't wear it.

Keep answers as short as possible, but refuse to give anything less than a complete answer; interrupting the witness when the answer begins to sound unpromising is another advocate's dirty trick. Continuing trouble of that kind is best dealt with as Ms Southbank dealt with it: 'You look after the questions and I'll look after the answers.' Never lose your temper except on purpose and when it seems worth while to do so. If a damaging answer has to be given, give it cheerfully and willingly, don't force the opposition to drag it out; that emphasises the effect, a quick casual admission minimises it.

Of course it is easy enough to write this; it is a different matter when Sir Arbuckle Quelquechose is looming over you with a voice of thunder, beetling eyebrows and crimson, quivering dewlaps. On such occasions visualise how absurd he would look if he were standing there without his trousers. One thing not to do is to try to be defiantly funny under attack; this is meat and drink to bullying advocates and if you try it you will disappear within a second down Sir Arbuckle's gullet. In my view advocates ought to protect their witnesses from bullying more quickly and more often than they do, and inspectors should more quickly do the same for all witnesses. The witnesses who get bullied are always those who most need protection; bullying advocates seldom try it on with people of their own weight, or not for more than about five seconds.

The amateur advocate should have little trouble of this kind; if he hasn't enough confidence to deal with bullies he shouldn't be acting as an advocate. The thing to remember is that (as emphasised in Chapter 6) there is no compulsion to behave like a mouse or like a conventional picture of a witness. Temperaments, of course, differ greatly, but for some a good way of coping would be to say (not too soon): 'Now listen to . . .' 'No! *You* listen to *me*. I will not have you speaking to me, – DON'T INTERRUPT – to me like that. From now on unless you address me with reasonable courtesy I shall only answer questions if they are put to me through the inspector.' There is not much he can do about that; he will look an awful fool if you insist on him putting his questions through the inspector, and the inspector could hardly refuse you if you did. (MPs, Ombudsmen, High Court loom).

Let us not get things out of proportion; one might go through a hundred appeals without serious trouble of this kind, but we all owe it to each other to smash it when it crops up.

Being re-examined, in my experience, is horrible and best avoided. Even the best advocates seem to find it difficult to put questions in re-examination which one can understand. The use of re-examination is to try to repair damaging admissions made under cross-examination; the advocate is not allowed to ask leading questions, that is questions put in a form which suggests what the answer might be or what answer the advocate would like to get. It may be a perilous fishing in the dark. Here is one advantage the advocate-witness has. If he thinks it worth while he can make a statement by way of re-examination and, of course, knows what he wants to say. But, even so, it is seldom worth while. Unless the damage done can be completely repaired the statement may do more harm by drawing attention to the damage than it does good by repairing it.

Something has already been said about cross-examining in Chapter 6. I think that it is, more than any other aspect of appeal fighting, a gift. At mock appeals carried out by students I have heard very able cross-examinations conducted by students who had had no previous experience at all. Those of us who are less gifted can still do quite well, especially after some practice; student mock appeals, where everyone can happily make a fool of himself, whether as witness or as advocate, without dire results are admirable training; there should be many more of them.

The golden rule is not to try to be too clever and, of course, not to try to imitate Sir Arbuckle Quelquechose, whose behaviour is improper, and whom you couldn't effectively imitate anyway. Once more, temperaments vary and dictate different styles. The main thing, I think, is not to try to behave like a lawyer, but to be oneself. Just as there is no need for a witness to behave like the conventional picture of a witness, so there is no need for an advocate to behave like the conventional picture of an advocate. Ms Southbank was perhaps a little nervous and therefore unnecessarily formal with Mr Gloscat. Here is a brief sample of how a genuinely informal questioning might go.

Q. *Mr Herriot-Watt,* I shan't keep you long, but there are four matters in your evidence that puzzle me a little, and I should like you to clarify them. First, you told Mr Certiorari that the factors I had chosen for testing the suitability of land for development were 'not necessarily the most suitable'. Is that right?

A. Yes.

Q. Well could you tell me which factors I have chosen wrongly and any others I've not used which would be more suitable? Let's take the first to begin with. Which factors have I used that I shouldn't have used?

A. I don't think distance from the town centre is a suitable factor but there are others.

Q. Let's take that one first, shall we? What's wrong with it?

A. It doesn't take account of current dispersal of services.

Q. You mean into sub-centres?

A. Yes.

Q. But the town centre, in this town at any rate, is still much more important than the sub-centres, isn't it? Have you tried buying a suit in a sub-centre? Sorry, two questions.

A. It's all right. That's true to some extent, but most day-to-day purchases now seem to be made in the sub-centres. If someone needs to buy a suit and has to go to the main centre, he really doesn't mind whether it's a mile or two miles away. He may only need a suit every five years.

Q. Quite, but . . .

And so on.

70

Final statements. Don't make them unless you feel you simply must or that your client will feel let down if you don't. Ms Southbank was quite right when she said that if she hadn't got her points over before then she was unlikely to succeed with a final statement. The inspector's tired too – how lovely to get away just that little bit earlier.

Site inspections. Make sure the inspector sees and identifies everything necessary. Never say anything that even touches upon merit; if someone else does, only protest to an extent which helps relieve the inspector of embarrassment; he's probably crosser about it than you are. Don't greet the inspector at the site, however old a friend he may be, with 'God, Jim, it's good to see you again; goodness, you were sloshed last time I saw you!' He won't like it.

Decision letters. If it's unfavourable, don't start thinking about whether there's any way of getting to the High Court. Try to work out why you lost, how you might have won if you'd proceeded differently and whether the wording of the decision offers hope for the success of a slightly different application.

A final point for appellants. Inquiries usually take place on the council's home ground; the Council Chamber or a committee room. Some councils try to exploit this, for example by trying to ensure that the light will be in the opposition's eyes. To do this they put documents on the tables and chairs which back onto windows. They do this early in the morning, then nip off for a quick coffee. Appellants who discover this ploy should remove the documents to the other side of the room, appropriate the places sought to be reserved and meet protests with the old maxim 'It's bums that reserve places, not books.' Any attempt at officious behaviour by council staff should be met by 'This room is the DoE's today, not yours. I'll do what the inspector tells me, not what you try to tell me.' Similarly, it is sometimes very important to insist on having enough room and proper table space. Of course it's not wise to be too pernickety, but you are entitled to as much room as you reasonably need to deploy your papers. It is often hard enough to keep them in order in even the best of conditions. Especially, you are entitled to as much room as Mr Snarler, Sir Arbuckle Quelquechose, Mr Swiyne, Sir Drabface Chillihand and the rest. Insist on it.

8

Legitimate and illegitimate reasons for refusal and imposition of conditions

Terms more generally used than those above are 'valid', 'invalid', 'enforceable' and 'unenforceable', 'reasonable' and 'unreasonable'. I shy away a little from these because their exact meanings are rather shadowy, especially the difference between 'invalid' and 'unenforceable'. Moreover, the legal situation is shadowy. I begin with a discussion of general points which seem to be generally agreed and which would probably be upheld if they came before the courts, though as always there has to be the caveat that no two cases are exactly the same, and quite small differences in the circumstances or the nature of the site might well produce different judgements.

Most people would agree that the reasons for refusal or the imposition of conditions must, to be legitimate, relate to land use planning, not to other aims, however worthy. It would not be legitimate, for example, to refuse planning permission for a pub on the grounds that drunkenness is a social evil which needs to be diminished, and that the proposed development would tend to increase rather than diminish drunkenness. If it seems improbable that anybody would think otherwise, take a look at the *Hampstead and Highgate Express* of 12 August 1983 according to which, at an inquiry into a planning appeal against a refusal of permission for 'a high-quality amusement centre', it was urged by one representative of third-party objectors that to give permission would 'lure young gamblers'. Another is said to have admitted that although the case against the centre was 'weak on planning grounds', he hoped 'the volume of public protest would sway the decision'. But of course it was a planning inquiry. No *volume* of objection, however large, should have had the slightest influence on the result; it was the *quality* of the *planning* evidence that mattered.

The practical effect of invalid reasons for refusal is, if they are wholly invalid, simply to turn the subsequent appeal, in effect, into an appeal against a failure to determine. The appellants might simply suggest that the council had better keep quiet if there were no planning reasons for refusal. But note that the appellants would not then necessarily be home and dry. The inspector would be entitled to consider whether he thought there were planning reasons for refusal, even though the council had not expressed them, and to find against the appellants if he thought there were and that they were sufficiently strong to justify refusal.

Invalid conditions are a different matter. There can be no doubt that the preposterous example given in Chapter 2 about making permission conditional on the appellant's wife sleeping regularly with the Chairman of the council, is utterly invalid as contrary to the law of the land and public policy and irrelevant to land use planning. It could safely be ignored by the applicants. But what of less extreme conditions which *seem* to be invalid but might not be? It is hardly safe to ignore these; if one ignored them, one might be faced with an Enforcement Notice from the council. It would only be prudent to appeal against such a condition and fight the appeal on the basis that the condition is invalid and (if the facts warranted one's doing so) in any case unreasonable and unenforceable. It would be wise in such circumstances to insist upon an inquiry rather than having the matter dealt with by written representations, since a very good case would lie for claiming costs and these cannot be claimed where written representations are relied upon.

An example of such a condition would be one that 'all reasonable steps shall be taken to ensure that large numbers of people do not assemble in the street upon which the site fronts'. There are no steps the appellant could take to prevent people, in whatever numbers, gathering in the street outside the site: use of the street is for everyone, and it is for the police, in extreme circumstances, to regulate its use. Anyhow, what are 'large numbers'? Ten, twenty, fifty, a thousand? Nevertheless, it is necessary to be careful; though I am in no doubt that such a condition is invalid, it would be wise to get a legal opinion before acting on that belief. While, as I have earlier suggested, there is no point in involving lawyers in planning matters unless they can be useful, there is every reason to do so when they can. The cost of a lawyer's opinion on a point like that is likely to be much less than the cost of fighting an appeal against an Enforcement Notice.

The example of a condition seeking to control the assembly of people in a street offends against five of the acknowledged canons of development control regarding conditions:

1. It seeks to apply conditions to land outside the appellant's control, i.e. the street.
2. It is vague.
3. It is unenforceable.
4. It is unreasonable.
5. It tries to apply planning control to matters which can be dealt with by other means, in this case police control of crowds.

Reasonableness, enforceability and vagueness

These merit further discussion. It is generally recognised that it is not reasonable to impose conditions which have the effect of virtually nullifying the permission given, e.g. as an extreme, 'the shop shall only be opened between the hours of 3 p.m. and 5 p.m. on Tuesdays'; 'instruction shall only be given to titled people'; 'the external walls of the premises shall be resurfaced monthly to the satisfaction of the Council, with 18-carat gold'; or, a little less remote from the boundary of reasonableness: 'all grassed areas shall be mown daily during the months of April to October inclusive'.

As regards enforceability, a useful example is: 'No one but a full-time employee of the applicants shall be allowed to park a vehicle on the premises.' Unless a council employee spent the whole of his life outside the premises and asked and received answers from everyone entering the site with a vehicle whether he was a full-time employee of the applicants (and he might well be told by most or all to mind his own business) there would be no possible way of enforcing such a condition. Its only probable effect, if imposed, might be to deter subsequent prospective purchasers of the property. It is this effect which makes it important not to acquiesce in unreasonable conditions, rather than the likelihood of being inconvenienced by attempts to enforce them.

The classic example of vagueness is 'the site shall be kept tidy at all times'. What does 'tidy' mean? Whose opinion about tidiness is to be taken as authoritative?

In summary of this part of this chapter, it may be said that the supposed invalidity of a refusal of planning permission will not usually exert direct influence on the course of events but will add fuel to the flames of appeal. Invalidity of a condition had better not be relied upon in the absence of specific legal advice thereon, but, again, can be heavily relied upon when appealing against it. Unreasonableness, unenforceability and vagueness of conditions are seldom capable of being relied upon with absolute certainty without testing the matter at appeal. Unless they are of special importance the test may well be left to await the service of an Enforcement Notice and pursued to appeal thereafter, unless the possibility of re-sale of the premises, referred to a little earlier, makes it desirable to clear the matter up at once. The only danger of simply awaiting an Enforcement Notice is that the council may suggest at the subsequent appeal that the appellant acquiesced in the condition and only challenged it when subjected to enforcement procedure: a good inspector, however, would not take much notice of that.

Behaviour

There are other important factors which affect the legitimacy of refusals or conditions. Contrary to many emotive statements, town planning is about land, not directly about people. The idea is to control the use of land so that people can occupy and use it more safely and comfortably than otherwise, not to control their behaviour. Indeed, it is another well respected general principle that planning conditions must not seek to control people's behaviour. That statement needs a small modification; to impose conditions regarding the hours of work carried out on premises may be perfectly reasonable and that is in a sense to control people's behaviour. It is perhaps difficult to make the distinction with absolute precision. It would not be legitimate to impose a condition that 'employees shall not sing or shout when entering or leaving the premises'. Perhaps one can come a little closer if it is said that conditions governing conduct are only legitimate if they relate to conduct directly connected with the operations for which permission is being sought and, moreover, conduct which can lawfully and reasonably be regulated by an employer.

Continuing with the matter of behaviour, when considering whether to permit or refuse some kinds of development the only sensible and practicable test is to consider whether ordinary, decent people occupying and using the site in accordance with the proposed development would be likely to cause such detriment to neighbours as to render refusal or the imposition of some very special conditions (e.g. screening, restriction of hours of work, etc.) reasonable. It is inherently unsound, in argument or in consideration of an application, to assume on the one hand that the people concerned will behave like angels or on the other hand that they will behave like unmitigated villains. Angel-like behaviour might render almost any use acceptable almost anywhere, at least as regards its impact upon neighbours, while undilutedly villainous behaviour would render any imaginable development unacceptable. For example, no house could be built anywhere near another house on that assumption. Nor, except in the very rare circumstances where a permission can appropriately be limited to a particular person or persons rather than given for the benefit of the land, can the exemplary character or behaviour of present or known prospective occupiers or users be properly prayed in aid. They may be replaced by other people of quite a different kind at any time without notice or permission. In order not to get into a hopeless tangle on this subject it is necessary to think of everyone as being like the legendary 'man on the Clapham omnibus'.

Need and harmlessness

One test which it is useful to apply to any borderline case, and I am not sure that planning officers apply it as often as they should, is to ask, 'What harm could it possibly do?' If the answer is 'absolutely none' a permission must surely follow. This is not to suggest that the harm likely to be done by a permission has to be immediate, local or obvious for refusal to be justified. It is not justifiable to give permission for a shop merely because it can be seen that it will do no harm locally, if it will prevent or discourage, even to a small extent, the concentration of shopping facilities in an area. Indeed, it is frequently a powerful reason for refusal that a proposed use, though in itself harmless, will prevent or discourage concentration of the same or similar uses in the best possible location from the point of view of accessibility, traffic safety, etc., at a site or sites specifically allocated for such purposes.

The question of need or the lack of it for a particular building or activity often arises in considering an application for permission. 'Need' is one of the vague words which bedevil planning. What is need? The lack of something without which life cannot be comfortably carried on? Then what does 'comfortably carried on' mean? Lord Denning once made life a little more difficult for planners, especially for inspectors, by drawing a distinction between 'necessary' and 'essential'. But it has become firmly established that lack of need is not a good reason for refusal, while on the other hand great or exceptional need may properly override some minor planning objection.

'Prematurity'

To refuse an application permission on the grounds that it is premature, can, it seems to me, very rarely be justified in the 1980s. Ever since 1943, local authorities covering the whole country have had planning duties and planning powers, and many had them long before then. As has been pointed out earlier, planning knowledge and planning experience are not obliterated each time the local government system or the development plan system is changed. There is simply no excuse now for any local authority not to have plans in considerable detail to cover all parts of their area in which change is happening or imminent. Usually, therefore, an allegation of prematurity because of lack of planning proposals is simply an admission of failure of duty. It is, of course, otherwise if something unforeseen and unforeseeable has arisen, such as a proposal for a new airport or the exploitation on a large scale of a mineral hitherto undiscovered or underesteemed.

Prematurity may also be fairly claimed if development would be dependent upon a new road or sewage works not yet undertaken or finished. Even in such circumstances intending developers could frequently with justification say 'get a move on then!' when confronted with lack of plans or lack of facilities as a reason for refusal and, in the former case, cry 'what about this for a plan then!' waving a plan showing how the proposed development would fit in well with response to the unforeseen contingency. Of course it might be cogently argued by the council concerned that such a plan had not and could not have taken into account all the factors necessary to ensure its adequacy and correctness, but one wishes that the chances were greater of such a plan being effective in winning the day.

Personal permissions and time-limited permissions

These impose restrictions on the identity of the people who may occupy or use a site and restrictions on the period for which a site may continue to be used for a particular purpose or a building to exist. Both are imposed by means of conditions attached to planning permissions, are sometimes useful and legitimate, but are both capable of abuse. The latter, especially, is frequently abused.

Personal permissions

The justification for 'personal' permissions arises in three cases. The well-known 'agricultural condition' is applied when permission is given for a house on a site where an ordinary house would not be permitted, but which it is deemed necessary to site there for occupation by an agricultural worker for operational reasons. Permission is then usually made conditional on the house being occupied by a person employed in agriculture, or, to cope with retired people, 'one whose last occupation was in agriculture'. The second case is when a building has been illegitimately constructed or is being used for some illegitimate (in planning terms) purpose by a 'poor old soul'. Permission is then sometimes given for the occupation or use to continue, but only by that particular person. The third case relates to an activity which is harmless where it is and carried on as it is, but which might be quite harmful if carried on by some other organisation even though, in terms of development control, the two might be indistinguishable.

Time-limited permissions

These can reasonably be given in order to avoid excessive compensation when an area is in the course of change and what is sought to be done is incompatible with a better future arrangement of uses, but compatible with present conditions. A time-limited permission may occasionally also justifiably be applied to a use which a planning officer or committee regard with some suspicion, but for which there also appears to be some need or justification. It is then imposed on a 'let's see how he gets on' basis.

Occasionally, a time-limit is applied when a building is thought to be constructed out of materials which are likely to be short-lived. It is usually expected in such cases that renewals of the temporary permission are likely to be sought and given until such time as the building begins to be an eyesore. I think this is a clumsy device and that such a situation is usually better dealt with by imposing a condition regarding maintenance of satisfactory external appearance. Nor do I like the 'let's see how he gets on' method. It is part of the job of planning to look ahead imaginatively and to enable developers and and users to look ahead with confidence. All temporary permissions impart uncertainty. They may also be nugatory permissions because the risk of having to demolish even a comparatively cheap building before it has 'paid for itself' may well deter an intending developer. It introduces too much of a gamble into his calculations.

Mixed areas

Great care needs to be taken not to get confused where questions of 'nice' and 'nasty' areas and uses arise. It is a betrayal of planning principles to proceed on the assumption that 'nasty' uses are all right in a 'nasty' area but not in a 'nice' area. It is the duty of every planning authority to turn all their 'nasty' areas into 'nice' areas as fully and speedily as possible.

There are of course areas in which the mixture of uses is so great and so well established that the prospect of sorting them out satisfactorily is so remote that a continuation of the mixture may simply have to be tolerated, but this should be rare. From the point of view of improving all unsatisfactory areas an application can best initially be considered by deciding whether it is well located in relation to the planning proposals for the area and, in detail, whether it is likely to have an unfavourable impact upon adjoining uses. A very useful test is to ask: 'If you were designing this area afresh for new development or comprehensive development, would this proposal be acceptable as part of your design?' It is a very good test, but of course it has to be applied with discretion. A proposal might quite often not be fully acceptable with such a stringent test applied, but none the less acceptable in relation to a pattern unlikely to be capable of being changed for many years.

An argument which should *not* be used to justify development is: 'It won't be as bad as what's there now.' This is often urged as a test, either crudely or subtly, and it is quite invalid. If there is sufficient impetus, financial or otherwise, for some change to be brought about, there must almost certainly be the possibility of making it a change of a kind which is acceptable in town planning terms. If, exceptionally, that is not so, far better to leave the existing unsatisfactory situation until change to a use acceptable in planning terms becomes practicable. To allow a change from an unstable, unsatisfactory situation to a stable, unsatisfactory situation, which is the likely result of allowing such a proposal, will make the situation worse, not better.

Illegal uses

Finally, there is the rare, but, when it arises, exceptionally difficult problem of how to deal with illegal or 'immoral' uses. Presumably an application to use a site for cockfighting would be invalid; cockfighting is illegal, so no permission given could be legally implemented. A sensible council would simply ignore such an application and if the applicant had the temerity to make an appeal against failure to determine, what would happen? I think the DoE would simply refuse to entertain it. If however they did, the council would presumably decline to offer evidence, would decline to have it dealt with by means of written representation, and would simply appear at the inquiry and ask for costs to be awarded against the appellant. No doubt this would be done. Splendid. But what about applications relating to uses of dubious legality? Here we enter the murky world of sex shops. I am not at all sure that local authorities are wise to try to use planning powers to deal with these. In terms of land use, are sex shops likely to pose problems greater than those of ordinary bookshops or grocer's shops? It is not clear to me that they are, even if I do not much like them.

This leads us inevitably to brothels. They are at present clearly illegal. At least one local authority which has been troubled by them has tried to deal with them by tinkering with planning powers. I do not think that this can be the best or most effective way of dealing with the matter. Planning action is inevitably slow. Stop Notices are an exception to this, but because of the compensation implications, councils are very naturally chary of using them. Enforcement Notices may be effective in the end, but appeals against them take a long time to determine, and in the absence of a Stop Notice (terribly difficult, one imagines, to use on a brothel or suspected brothel because of the difficulty of framing a Stop Notice in suitable terms) distress may continue for those affected pending determination. Police action or invoking the law of nuisance are, surely, preferable alternatives.

Here is a problem to whet the appetites of those addicted to crunching the minutiae of law. If someone submitted an application for permission to establish brothels in various places in an urban area and accompanied that application with, first, a skilfully prepared analysis of demand, catchment areas and suitable sites related to these in terms of minimum impact upon adjoining property, and said in a covering letter that he was aware that at present what he proposed was illegal but anticipated that in view of current opinions in and modes of government, it would shortly become legal and wished to get into the market in good time, what ought the planning authority to do?

9

Third parties

Third parties may be defined as those other than councils or appellants, who, in relation to a particular appeal, think they will be affected by its outcome. In different countries and at different times, third parties have been and are treated very differently. In this country, at present, virtually everyone who thinks he may have an interest in the outcome of an appeal has an opportunity to have his say, so long as he hears about it in time.

The appeal will be advertised in various ways according to the particular circumstances. If it is to be dealt with by way of an inquiry, there will, apart from anything else, be a notice about it placed on the site well in advance. If it is to be dealt with by way of written representations, residents within an area which the council think is large enough to cover all likely to be directly affected will be notified by letter. In either case there are also likely to be advertisements in the local press. It is not very likely that anyone with a strong interest will be left uninformed. At an inquiry the question of whether third parties will be heard and in what way and to what extent is theoretically at the discretion of the inspector. In practice he will hear anyone and to almost any extent desired. In the case of written representations there is no way in which third parties can be prevented from writing in with their opinions and these are supplied to the inspector.

So far and to that extent, very good. In Australia, and especially in Queensland, for example, matters are quite otherwise. The situation there is bizarre. Within the City of Brisbane, third parties who object to a proposal have the opportunity of saying so officially, of thereby precipitating an appeal to a court and of presenting their objections to it. In the rest of Queensland the situation is quite different. There, in an area roughly the same size as Western Europe, they can only participate if a council proposes to approve the application. If the application is refused they have no right to take part in a subsequent appeal. This gives rise to peculiar and not very agreeable happenings. On one occasion permission was sought to erect a large motel. The application clearly had its merits but was not without aspects which might be regarded as injurious to neighbours. The council concerned favoured it, but refused permission. At the subsequent appeal they were therefore able to put up a designedly weak case against it and there was no opportunity for the aggrieved third parties to state their objections. Nasty fiddling, contrary to natural justice.

A long, cool look needs to be taken at the whole subject. Few if any would dispute the propriety of the opinions of third parties being given opportunity for expression. The question is how much time should be allowed to be taken up in the expression of these opinions and how much notice should be taken of them. I say in advance that my opinion is that the time allowed for their expression should be limited fairly severely. Third-party objections ought not to be allowed to 'hog the microphone' to the extent of unduly increasing the costs through increased attendance time of the parties. As to the influence they should have, I think that they should be judged entirely on their merits. The last thing that should be encouraged is a counting of heads. An ill-founded objection backed by a thousand people should have much less weight than a well-founded objection backed by only one person. Unfortunately the DoE and inspectors are not sound on this. 'Absence of any strong local objection' and 'very strong local objection' are quite often used in justifying appeal decisions, either, as in the first case, to justify allowing an appeal, or in the latter for dismissing it. The only legitimate way of taking account of such expressions, in my opinion, would be to say in the one case: 'Very well-founded and expressed third-party opposition assisted me in arriving at my decision to dismiss this appeal' or 'The local opposition expressed was not well reasoned, so I have not taken account of it in reaching my decision'. This avoids the ambiguity of 'strong'.

The proper role of planning committees also needs cool appraisal. They are democratically elected to decide, *inter alia*, planning applications. To do this they are assisted by the advice of their planning officers. They have, or should have, though often they do not (see p. 64), a plan which gives the answers to all applications except those which affect the 'fine grain' of local development.

What do they gain, or might they gain, from obtaining the views of local residents on a particular application? Very little, one believes. For a start, local residents, out of the whole human population of the globe, are those least equipped to give a fair and impartial view of local proposals. They are likely to entertain exaggerated hopes of a proposal or, more often, exaggerated fears. It is very unlikely that they will have the knowledge and experience to understand the probable impact of an application if it is given permission. Planning officers can understand it because that is their trade, and longstanding members of planning committees may also begin to do so if they listen attentively to the advice of their officers. But local residents simply do not understand the proper limits of what is amenable to planning action. Their arguments are frequently *ad hominem*: 'Mr X has been nothing but a nuisance ever since he started his grocery business and certainly should not be allowed to expand it. What is more, his son has a prison record and his daughter has two illegitimate babies.' Or alternatively, but no more valuably: 'Mr X is a pillar of the local community; his generosity and kindness to children, especially at Christmas time, are notable.' Anything more than the bare consideration, on its merits, of local objection leads logically and inexorably to going the whole hog and deciding every application for planning permission on a head count of local opinion. But that would be no way to secure satisfactory or consistent planning results. Local opinion is highly susceptible to the 'at least it will be better than what's there now' fallacy, commented upon in chapter 8. Local opinion cannot visualise the true impact of a proposal, the limits of the scope of planning powers or the futility of hand-to-mouth, temporary, partial solutions.

Looking back at all the appeals I have determined one way or another I can recall very few cases in which the expressed views of third parties have affected or ought to have affected my opinion to an extent sufficient to change the decision I should otherwise have arrived at.

More often I have picked up a few useful clues and hints which have suggested that an approach a little different from that of either the council or the appellant might be appropriate. Just once in a while, as I have suggested in Chapter 6, a suitably advised third party may be able to save the day by taking over the case against an application from a weak or unwilling council; but that is about the limit of usefulness of third-party representations.

10

Implications of structure plans and local plans

The very technical subject of development plans is dealt with extensively in my *Town Planning Made Plain*, especially in Chapter 5 and, less comprehensively, but in greater technical detail, in Chapter 4 of my *Principles and Practice of Town and Country Planning*. There are not many other critical accounts of the system, but plenty of explanatory ones.

The essence of the matter is that in considering applications for planning permission, councils must have regard to the provisions of the current development plan for the area concerned as well as to any other material considerations. The current development plan consists of the relevant structure plan approved by the SoS, and of any local plan adopted by the council. Local plans do not normally have to be approved by the SoS but there has to be full public consultation and investigation of them before formal adoption. In the absence of an adopted local plan, any town map approved before 1968 (when the new system of structure and local plans came into existence) remains the basis for development control, as in the case of Urton (see Ch. 7).

Structure plans are prepared by county councils and local plans by district councils. Structure plans usually contain very little except motherhood statements and diagrams expressing facts and intentions in very general terms. The form and content of structure plans are governed in very general terms by the Town and Country Planning (Structure and Local Plans) Regulations of 1974 (SI 1974 No. 1486). The most noteworthy item in these is the extraordinary provision that structure plans must be accompanied by a key diagram, but that this must not be on a ordnance map base. This kind of thinking has been in vogue in parts of the planning world for quite a long time. The reputable or comparatively reputable basis for it is that planning authorities, in doing regional 'strategic' plans, ought to feel free to express their policies in as general a way as they think fit and not be pinned down to specific boundaries for areas allocated to particular purposes or subjected to particular restrictions. This idea was contained in the perfectly honest, but naive and misconceived *The Future of Development Plans* produced by the Planning Advisory Group in 1965. Unhappily, it has been distorted and perverted to provide an excuse to get right away from town planning as design and to regard it as an administrative exercise.

The regulations could easily be avoided by a determined county council which insisted on doing good town planning. All they would have to do would be to put national grid lines on the diagram, or, if even that were deemed to be putting it on an ordnance map base, to leak to the local press the scale of the map, and anybody could then quickly transfer the diagram to an ordnance map, though why people who want to make useful and constructive criticisms and suggestions about a structure plan should be put to such trouble is a mystery. The whole thing is an insult to the public, resulting in less informed and useful comment than would otherwise be possible.

This is bad enough, but some county councils, unaccountably, have not merely omitted the ordnance map base and any statement of scale from their key diagrams, but have much distorted the shape of the diagram. One such diagram is for a country which has a good deal of coastline. This is drawn in straight lines running directly up and down and across the sheet. I do not think that anyone, if the place names which are shown on the diagram were omitted, would be able to work out what part of England it related to. This extraordinary distortion, bizarre though it is, would not matter so much were it not that the diagram shows a large number of sinuous shapes which relate to land restricted in various ways. There are a Green Belt, a Local Green Belt, a Coastal Protection Belt, High-Value Agricultural Land, Areas of Outstanding Natural Beauty, a Regional Park, a Nature Conservation Zone, a Special Landscape Area and Sites of Special Scientific Interest. Many overlap each other. It is fair to assume that many of the boundaries of these areas relate to contours, ridge lines or water courses, but no one could, from this distorted diagram, transfer them to ordnance maps. Without doing so, how could anyone say whether they were sensibly drawn or foolishly drawn? But to decide that must be one of the most important objects of public scrutiny.

What is the use of having such areas unless one can tell whether a particular piece of land is inside or outside one or more of them? If the land is inside, one or more particular restrictive policies applies, if outside, not. Written statements vary enormously in their nature and scope, but bear a family relationship to those encountered by Ms Southbank in Chapter 7. The system reduces the graphic content of planning almost to nil and increases the written content almost to totality. In practice nearly anything that anyone wants to do can be deemed to be a violation of one motherhood statement or another, or, from the opposite point of view, capable of being brought within an exception or reservation to a motherhood statement. That leaves the unfortunate inspector at an appeal to choose his own interpretation.

Structure plans have a further disadvantage which also applied to the county maps which preceded them. What is the use of having about seven different kinds of restriction upon a piece of land when each of them is designed simply to prohibit or frown severely upon most kinds of development? What town planning should do is to prescribe certain limited areas for urban and village development and to prohibit general development elsewhere, prescribe sites for airfields, country parks and so on and allow, in most places, only buildings needed in connection with agriculture, forestry, etc. A proposed development is not seven times more unsatisfactory if it has seven kinds of restrictive provision ruled over it than if it is simply in an area not allocated for general urban or village development. In fact these massive and complex prohibitions and discouragements have a reverse effect elsewhere. They suggest to an ignorant Minister, administrator or inspector that the ordinary 'white' areas of the countryside, areas (to quote a familiar definition 'in which it is expected that existing uses will remain for the most part undisturbed'), are to be regarded as vulnerable, as perhaps eligible for development, unless there is some strong definite planning reason against it, compared with the total ineligibility of the specially protected land. This is a terrible error. There is, no doubt, a great deal more ordinary 'white' land in the country than specially protected land, but it should be regarded as prima facie just as ineligible for development as the specially protected land.

Local plans are of three kinds: district plans; action area plans; and subject plans. They, too, consist of written statements illustrated by maps and diagrams. The regulations provide that they shall be accompanied by 'proposals maps' for areas in which development is definitely expected or intended in the fairly near future and that these shall be drawn on ordnance maps.

District plans vary a great deal. In some places they cover extensive areas, including open countryside, small towns and villages, or they may cover only a single town or a part of a town. Many are town centre plans, and very useful they are. Action area plans are usually for quite small areas, and are intended for places where extensive development or redevelopment is intended to take place in the near future. Subject plans deal with only a single aspect of planning, such as transportation or recreation. Some district plans include village envelopes, i.e. areas within and adjoining villages in which development will, prima facie, be favourably considered.

Perhaps all this sounds fairly good, except for the structure plans, but there is at present very incomplete coverage of the country by district plans and no strong urging by the DoE to councils to prepare them quickly so as to cover all areas in which anything considerable is likely to happen in the near future – which is a crying need. Moreover, many district plans are pitifully skeletal. However, there is nothing to prevent district councils from showing proposals on any kind of map they choose as a basis for development control, and a good many use quite detailed but informal maps.

A further important snag in the system is that there is no obligation on local authorities to review and revise structure or local plans at regular intervals, or indeed at all. This matters a great deal as regards structure plans, since however out of date they may get they still have semi-sacred status. Inspectors have no mandate to override what a structure plan says; at most, if they think an appeal should be allowed, even though the proposal is not in accord with a structure plan policy, they may be able to find a good reason for regarding the particular case as exceptional in some way, or so slightly in conflict with the structure plan as not really to damage its policies, or only doubtfully in conflict with the structure plan.

In the absence of a system for revision and review, good inspectors may increasingly have to rely on finding such formulae, but they are rather miserable devices, the dubious devices of diplomacy, not the proper application of planning principles. A better device for an inspector who wants to do the right thing may be to dismiss an appeal because of conflict with the structure plan, but to draw attention in doing so to the defects of the plan. That may set local opinion going and put pressure on the council to make an amendment. If that happens, justice has been delayed but not frustrated.

Local plans are different; they have no such semi-sacred status. The highest status that can be accorded a local plan is to say of it: 'The SoS didn't think this plan was so bad that he was justified in using his powers of intervention to overthrow it.' Not much of a status. Clearly, therefore, inspectors are fully justified in allowing appeals for development which contravenes local plans if they think the proposal contravened is a bad one. Yet this is unfair on a good district council; it puts them at the mercy of an ignorant inspector. They are at peril every time an appeal is made and can only pray they will get good inspectors.

It is inherently unsound for the testing of plans to consist of determination of appeals against refusal of permission for development which allegedly contravenes them. Something is almost certain to go wrong at some stage, and there is the ever-present temptation for councils to urge and inspectors to accept the argument that plans should not be altered bit by bit by individual appeal decisions. Under the old system, when reviews nominally had to take place every five years, there may have been some justification for this argument; there can be none now. It is therefore very desirable that appellants and councils should, at all appeals where it is at all appropriate to do so, put forward their own 'district plans' where none exists or they regard it as defective. If this were done often enough, inspectors would find it much more difficult to brush such plans aside than they do now. This would be much better than the exchange of fusillades of motherhood statements and arguments about their precise meaning, and might help towards a return to a genuine debate about physical planning merits at appeals. This is no place to embark upon any long discussion of planning principles, but any plan put forward on one side or the other must be helpful if it demonstrates that a particular kind of development on a particular site will or will not:

- Be consistent with maintaining compactness and good levels of accessibility for the settlement concerned.
- Fill a gap in the accessibility pattern of a service or facility for the settlement (e.g. local shops, filling station, pub.).
- Maintain appropriate separation of incompatible uses and association of compatible uses.
- Be the best of the feasible alternative uses for the site.
- Be, in terms of physical characteristics, a suitable use for the land and as

suitable as or more suitable than other possible sites.

- Block the route for a necessary future road.
- Be compatible with the maintenance or promotion of a good town or village silhouette.
- Help to prevent the merging of settlements which it is desired to keep separate.
- Promote a better balance of dwelling types within a town or a particular part of it.

Such demonstrations ought, I think, to be common form. Unfortunately, cases like that of Urton, discussed in Chapter 7, may not be greatly helped either way by such demonstrations because the debate there was not so much about which land ought to be developed as whether there ought to be any appreciable further development of the town at all.

Since there has been a virtual breakdown of regional planning, it is absolutely essential that this sort of impasse should be resolved. If there are not going to be regional plans of a kind which, even within fairly wide limits, set down the proposed population size of every town and village, there really must at least be plans which show, in detail, land for which planning permission for general development is to be regarded as prima facie obtainable, and, where there is a good deal of this, an indication of the order in which it will be released for development to avoid spotty development. It is hardly realistic to assume that no more development will ever be allowed in a town or sizeable village, yet present planning policies often seem to get very close to saying that.

11

The mind of the DoE and the
mind of the inspector

One was tempted to call this chapter 'The mind of the Ministry and the instincts of the inspector'. But that would not be accurate. Inspectors also have minds and Secretaries of State also have instincts.

I want to make it quite clear that in this chapter I am not 'blowing the gaff' on anything or anyone. I emphasise this because for two years recently I was a part-time *ad hoc* planning inspector for the DoE. In the course of that work I occasionally acquired bits of information not generally accessible to the public; nothing dramatic, certainly nothing in the least scandalous, still, it was confidential, and however 'open' government ought to be, I think there has to be some element of the confidential in it. I do not believe that all the processes of government can best, or even practicably, be carried on in a goldfish bowl. Let me therefore say emphatically that there is nothing in this chapter, or indeed in this book, which embodies any such information.

The DoE

To begin at the top, it is a long time since there has been a Secretary of State who displayed any considerable knowledge of, or interest in, town planning. This is unfortunate, because the special nature of town planning makes it necessary for the Ministers who deal with it to understand it well. Its benefits take a long time to show through; this is true even of direct physical benefits. The very important social and economic benefits also take a long time to take effect and have the additional disadvantage of being, to a considerable extent, concealed. Town planning is highly controversial; even the best planning decisions and policies attract opposition. It is rather subtle; the soundest planning policies sometimes have the unfortunate characteristic of not, in ordinary common-sense terms, *seeming* the most suitable (housing density is the prize example of this). It is essentially an idealistic and radical activity. If done with any seriousness it seeks to make physical conditions *much* better than they are now, not just to keep things in equilibrium or achieve modest improvements (in fact in many planning matters, such as the planning of central areas, any *real* improvement in the physical nature of things can only be a big improvement).

The public have only the vaguest idea of what town planning is all about, and it has a bad name. 'Planners' are thought of either as faceless bureaucrats, there to stop people doing what they want to do, or as dreamy Utopians; sometimes both at the same time. Moreover, 'The Planners' are frequently blamed for things for which they have not the slightest responsibility, such as closing schools or hospitals, and even for things which they have opposed and sought to prevent. Thirty years ago, town planners worth their salt were already emphasising the absurdity of building large numbers of tall blocks of flats, for economic, social and traffic reasons. They were laughed to scorn. Today the absurdity of building these is widely acknowledged, but 'The Planners' are still blamed for tall flats.

All in all it would not be surprising if most ambitious politicians regarded being appointed Secretary of State for the Environment as entry into a political minefield rather than as reaching the fulfilling summit of a political career.

Much the same attitude is probably prevalent among senior civil servants; however, I shall not speculate about this but shall argue that influential positions in town planning within the DoE are totally unsuitable for unspecialised civil servants: mandarins. The main characteristic of mandarins is to think they know much more than they do, and therefore to proceed with confidence towards near-disaster or complete non-achievement, being careful to cover tracks so as to be able at the end of the day to regret, with a sage and wistful shake of the head, the folly of others which has produced such a sad state of affairs. They have a certain scorn for mere technical expertise. The 'new' 1968 development plan system and housing density are striking examples of this. Housing density is quite a tricky subject in a small way; it is by no means as simple as a cursory approach to it may suggest. It is doubtful whether any mandarin has recently fully understood it or listened closely to an explanation of it. DoE policies and exhortations have therefore been consistently wrong; earlier, regarding tall blocks of flats and now, regarding what is known as 'high density, low rise', which has little to commend it as a generally used form of housing. It slightly reduces the amount of residential land needed, but greatly reduces the variety and general pleasantness of the local physical environment.

A good deal has already been said about the 'new' development plan system. Here, one wishes to emphasise a somewhat different aspect of it from those previously discussed. The naïve but well-meaning PAG report sought means of producing better conceived and more effective development plans more quickly than under the previous system. The mandarins not only, one believes, swallowed the naïve reasoning of the group's report, but saw in it a means to get away from unpalatably unambiguous maps which committed, or were thought to commit, the SoS when he approved them. But the 'new' system has in fact produced less well-conceived and less effective plans more slowly than the old ones, accompanied by a stifling fog of bureaucratic requirements. It all reminds one of the apocryphal wartime story of the mandarin attempt to produce more staves for Home Guard pikes more cheaply and quickly which, after immense thought and effort and many committee meetings, resulted in fewer being produced more slowly and more expensively.

In brief, better town planning will not be done until those most influential in the DoE are people who know a good deal about town planning and really want it to succeed. This means employing experts for the most senior jobs. Sir John Hoskyns, in an admirable article in *The Guardian* of 30 September 1983, entitled 'How to galvanise the moribund' describes current civil service thinking as 'shallow, conformist and lacking in rigour'. He speaks of 'institutional timidity', '. . . the officials' fear of having their advice rejected by Ministers. When advice is accepted, you score a mark. If it is rejected, you lose face. So the official either seeks to get his way by guile, or he tailors his advice to suit his Minister.' Later, Hoskyns suggests that among various drastic changes needed '. . . it must be possible to bring adequate numbers of high-quality outsiders into the civil service'. All this applies, perhaps with special force, to the DoE, an organisation with quite inadequate concepts for the inspiring task calling to be done.

Nevertheless, below the highest level, there is much competence in the DoE. The circulars it produces, though one may deplore the haziness and occasionally even the wrongness of the policies they set forth and explain, are usually set out clearly and well. In recent years, unfortunately, the haziness has become thicker and some earlier, better, circulars have been cancelled, but there is a strong impression of competent brains thinking clearly within the constraints of dubious premisses.

These premisses become more and more dubious. As I shall argue in Chapter 20 and have already argued in Chapter 2 of *Town Planning Made Plain*, there is a very great need in town planning to formulate objectively valid standards, especially space standards, to be firmly, though not rigidly applied: standards which would replace the kind of unverified, though very likely sound 'seven acres of open space per thousand people', 'seventy feet between facing windows', 'twelve houses per acre', standards which have been generally applied for more than half a century. Unfortunately, DoE policy for the last two decades has pointed in the opposite direction. As regards housing density policy, having in the past favoured excessively high, specific densities, the tendency now is evidently to favour high but vague densities. 'Ten to fifteen houses per acre' is quite a usual specification of the permitted density of an area to find in a local plan. This is hopelessly vague for town planning design purposes though convenient for those who neither understand nor favour technical or intellectual rigour and wish to maintain what amounts in practice to an almost infinite flexibility. Similarly, floor space indexes and plot ratios, promising if crude instruments for measuring and controlling non-residential densities, instead of being refined and improved have been pushed quietly into the background, as have daylight indicators, not nearly so crude, but requiring a certain sober application of technical understanding for their use. Of course, councils remain free to use whatever technical methods and standards they think fit, but they are discouraged, too easily discouraged, by ministerial discouragement, especially if they find these methods and standards disregarded when appeal decisions are made. As we shall see a little later, inspectors are not immune from such influences, indeed they must not be.

An example of the tendency to ignore technical considerations may be useful. In the 1960s, I was giving evidence for an appellant at an inquiry against refusal of planning permission for some houses within a large village. The application had been refused on a number of grounds, but the crucial one was that the proposed development would cause danger and congestion in the local road system. *Roads in Urban Areas* had recently been published, and I made use of Fig. 10.1 therein, which gives acceptable amounts of traffic at T-junctions in various circumstances. While, unfortunately, it is seldom possible actually to *prove* a planning case, I came as near to doing so as is possible by demonstrating that the road system was not currently overloaded and could not possibly become overloaded through the addition of traffic produced by the proposed development. My evidence on this was not challenged by the council, nor did the inspector ask me any questions about it. Nevertheless, in his report, he said that he was '*not convinced*' by my evidence and the Minister did not dissent from him in making his decision. 'What do I have to do to win?' I might well have cried (and did). It is this kind of thing which causes justifiable concern about the appeal system. Before a judge, there could hardly have been any doubt about the result; evidence so relevant and important and unchallenged could hardly have failed. I should not in the least like our appeal system to be changed so that judges determined appeals, as I have made clear in Chapter 3, but such ammunition should not be given to those who would like them to do so.

What can have been in the mind of that inspector? (to anticipate a little the second part of this chapter). It is very hard to say; I suspect his thoughts went something like this:

It's quite a lot of houses (about twenty) to add to even a large village. It's not the sort of thing that often gets allowed. Councils don't like it. I don't like it. I don't think the mandarins will like it and I've already been overruled twice this year. The other grounds of refusal collapsed; I can't find any holes in Keeble's figures but they're only figures based on assumptions. The mandarins don't like figures. I'll just say I'm not convinced by them; after all, the onus is on the appellant in this sort of case, and if I haven't been convinced, that's it.

To return to the main theme: as well as reluctance to encourage, rely on and support standards, there is evident reluctance in the DoE to enunciate general planning principles sufficiently explicitly. In the previous chapter I set out (p. 86) a list of considerations which, expressed graphically, ought to help greatly in determining an appeal decision. I now restate them more succinctly: *Town planning should seek to promote accessibility and safety, maintain urban and village compactness, separate incompatible uses and juxtapose compatible and complementary uses, secure appropriate intensity of land use, promote economy in use of resources and conservation of resources, secure good appearance.*

Most of these are implicit in DoE circulars and in the quite good *Development*

Control Policy Notes issued from time to time. But they are insufficiently explicit and not bound together to constitute the sort of received planning orthodoxy which we need, at least as a foundation upon which to build detailed arguments, justify exceptions or use as a point of departure from which to promote rival theories.

Further down the line there is much excellence in the DoE. I have already mentioned the virtual infallibility in arranging that inspectors arrive on the right day, at the right time, in the right place. The care and courtesy with which arrangements are made and agreed for inquiries is beyond praise. The very occasional mistake and its consequences only underline what chaos there would be if the organisation were not almost perfect. A telephone enquiry to the DoE at Marsham Street, London or Bristol produces remarkably swift, courteous and good response. If it is an enquiry about a specific matter in a specific place, one must accept that it will probably be the third extension to which one is transferred that will be able to give the answer, but that is quite unavoidable.

The main 'nuts and bolts' criticism of a serious kind which can be levelled against DoE is the continuing appalling slowness with which appeals are heard and determined. To this nobody seems to have any effective answer. The institution of advance notice of decisions (at the time of writing used only in respect of the small minority of appeals dealt with by means of inquiries) merely nibbles at the edge of the problem. One suspects that a good many more inspectors and more clerks are needed to get through the work more quickly, but this is hardly a solution likely to commend itself to the Government at present. One also suspects that some files simply 'stick' through human error, in trays which are not emptied often enough. It is virtually certain that far too many consultations are undertaken with bodies which could only have a remote and minimal interest. This is a fault which is certainly also endemic in local government. One fancies that, currently, many distribution lists might as well simply be replaced by OUTCAA (Old Uncle Tom Cobley And All).

In fact, speed and playing safe are incompatibles. Since playing safe is a strong and in many ways admirable characteristic of the civil service, substantial increases in speed are unlikely to be secured without some substantial relaxation of meticulous care. There is much to be said for this being done, for, beyond a certain point, extra care produces rapidly diminishing returns and even negative returns, as the following story illustrates. It is said that a high-minded author and firm of publishers resolved to produce a book which contained no misprints whatever. They laboured long and hard to produce this result. To celebrate, a statement was printed at the front of the book, which said that colossal efforts had been made to produce a book without misprints, and they thought that they had succeeded. Unfortunately, though the book itself was indeed clear of misprints, there was a misprint in that statement.

The irremovability of human error, and the phenomenon of 'the fiend in the typewriter' are well illustrated by both the following. In an appeal in which I gave evidence for the appellants, I thought we had done very well and would win. It was not a 'transferred' case. The inspector's report was admirable. He detected all the errors in the council's and third-party objectors' cases and appreciated all the strong points in our own. His report led up to a splendid climax at the bottom of a page. The next page was obviously going to contain the recommendation. It did, 'I therefore recommend that the appeal be dismissed.' Incredible. Fortunately the accompanying decision letter overruled the inspector's recommendation. What had happened? It must have been that the inspector, more used to writing the word 'dismissed' than the word 'allowed' had written the wrong word. The report had gone through sieve after sieve, one feels sure, but only the last one had spotted the error. What a pity, that inspector was among the best of inspectors; surely at some point someone should have asked him: 'Didn't you mean "allowed" instead of "dismissed"?' Similarly, but fortunately less seriously, I once wrote a decision letter and sent it off to be typed. The typist failed to include the word 'not'. I did not detect the error, nor did any of those who subsequently checked the letter. It went out with a sentence in the middle which, without 'not', meant absolutely nothing. Fortunately the sentence was not a crucial one.

To sum up one's impressions of the DoE, it seems to have good middle management, a good rank and file, but inappropriately chosen topmost management.

Inspectors

It must first be emphasised that although full-time planning inspectors are civil servants, they are by no means ordinary civil servants. It is not experience in government or in departmental administration that matters for them, but expertise and experience in town planning and a well developed sense of impartiality and justice, especially of that very important, but not easily defined concept, natural justice. As we have seen in Chapter 3, they must logically be regarded as expert tribunals, otherwise any reasonably intelligent and literate layman picked up off the street would do almost as well. He would not know the conventions of departmental modes of expression, the relevant law or ministerially approved planning policies, which any regular inspector obviously needs to know but a little tactful vetting of his decision letter would be easy and sufficient if the letter had displayed ignorance of such matters.

How much about town planning does the current inspectorate in fact corporately know? The short answer, I think, is 'quite a lot but not nearly enough', to which it may be important to add 'and what they do know they do not seem much encouraged visibly to display'. It seems that about half the present full-time inspectors are chartered town planners (only about 10% are women). Unsatisfactory, indeed ludicrous as this is, the position is probably slowly improving. What makes stark figures unreliable is that they cannot take account of changes in recruitment policy by the DoE, influenced, one fears, more by the need to adjust numbers in different parts of it and to keep down overall numbers that by desire to have the finest possible inspectorate. The picture is also blurred by the fact that there is an appreciable number of inspectors who could readily have become chartered town planners if they had sat the necessary exams and who would have done so if that had been a condition of continued employment or of promotion.

It is fair to say that to be a chartered town planner (or before the granting of the charter, a corporate member of the Town Planning Institute) can never have loomed large enough in the mind of the DoE as a requirement when recruiting inspectors. In the past, many local government officers who, similarly, had not been sufficiently impelled to obtain a planning qualification, left the rigours of local government for the easier, if somewhat lonely, life of an inspector. Most of these came from council planning departments in which architectural, engineering or surveying qualifications were considered sufficient and so, possessing one of these, could be said, in a rough sort of way, to know a bit about town planning; the very process of working as an inspector, given some basic knowledge, must have caused them to learn some more. Moreover, the professions of architecture, surveying and civil engineering each overlap planning a little, enough at least to suggest a plausible if thin, generic kinship.

In the mid 1960s, displaced colonial administrators came over in a wave and some of them found re-employment as planning inspectors. This produced a new crop of inspectors whose qualifications and antecedents had no connection with town planning at all. A few years later came prematurely retired soldiers, sailors and airmen, lawyers and others. Some of these were part-time, some full-time. Some of the qualification letters which followed the names of some of these were utterly unfamiliar.

Finally, there has been employment of a sort of mobile reserve of consultants, ready and willing to step in to deal with those sudden increases in appeals which come in surges. Of these, it is said, about half are chartered town planners. Why are they not all? As I emphasised in Chapter 3, *every* inspector ought to be a chartered town planner except in those rare cases where the subject-matter is very specialised.

There is now the unsatisfactory situation that there are at least three different kinds of inspectors: chartered town planners, whose knowledge should be fully adequate; members of related or 'relevant' professions, who may or may not have adequate knowledge, and others, few if any of whom can have adequate knowledge of town planning. That the quality of decisions given by such a mixture could be uniformly high is very improbable. It is certainly not that, but varies widely and, I think, roughly in conformity with the relevance of inspectors' qualifications. Unfortunately there is detectable also a positive correlation between ignorance and over-confidence, architects pontificating happily about social matters, engineers about aesthetics, soldiers about almost anything: a fault of which chartered town planner inspectors are less often guilty.

To create so heterogeneous a body when a fair degree of homogeneity is clearly needed, appears to me a grievous error of logic, symptomatic of the shallow thinking, lacking in rigour, of which Hoskyns complains.

It is of course virtually impossible for anyone to prepare an appeal case likely to convince a particular kind of inspector, especially when the identity of the inspector may only be known well after most of the work has had to be done. Even if that were not so, it would still be difficult to know what line of argument would appeal most to a wholly ignorant inspector.

Leaving out of account extremes of competence and incompetence, however, there are characteristics found in a large proportion of inspectors which it will now be worth examining critically to see what they add up to:

- Inspectors are not young; they are not appointed when young; this is no disadvantage, experience is a valuable attribute for inspectors.
- Inspectors are not usually very creative; it is not a job which much calls for creativity; creative-minded inspectors are therefore most likely people who have fallen into the job more or less accidentally rather than having aspired to it.
- Inspectors are not usually rebellious, radical-minded types. If they were, they would hardly find the job tolerable.
- Inspectors are quite incorruptible.
- Inspectors are kind and patient people; they need to be.
- Inspectors are neatly dressed.
- Inspectors are sometimes women, especially the good ones.

This may have sounded a little frivolous, but it is not intended that way. Those are indeed the characteristics of inspectors which most prominently present themselves, and which, as I will show, influence their decisions and the ways in which they express them.

I must have sat under about one hundred and fifty different inspectors, perhaps more, and I think it is a tribute to them as a class to say that one was manifestly off his head and should not have been out, two were rude and biased to an unpardonable extent, and two were pompous fools: $3\frac{1}{3}$ per cent complete duds; there are few professions or callings which could claim so low a rate of inadequacy. The rest, though I may occasionally have felt critical about the way they conducted inquiries and sometimes doubted their knowledge and judgement, were, at the lowest estimate, tolerable. It is this kind of record which should be borne in mind if some of my criticism seems incompatible with the high regard for the inspectorate which I have also expressed.

Some of the characteristics mentioned display themselves so consistently that it is impossible to believe that they are not to some extent acquired rather than inherited characteristics. That is to say, the DoE obviously trains and requires inspectors to behave and express themselves in certain ways rather than others. This is inevitable; without it there could be no consistency in appeal decisions and some consistency, as a matter of natural justice, is essential. It is hard to be sure whether constraints applied to inspectors by the DoE are excessive, insufficient, or about right. I think that they are probably about right, but tend a little towards the excessive. It can be no violation of confidentiality to say that out of the two hundred or so appeals I decided for the DoE there was not a single case in which it was suggested in any way that my decision ought to have been different. Since I am not a particularly orthodox person and a few of my decisions were probably not the same as a very orthodox person would have given, this is a useful piece of testimony in favour of the requirements being about right. Nevertheless, looking at the whole range of inspectorial performance since inspectors' reports began to be published, it is difficult not to believe that consistency has been bought at the cost of excessive woodenness and stolidity and playing safe. It would, I think, be necessary to wade through a very large pile of reports and decision letters before coming across any of the following, much though they need to be said:

- The council have acted irresponsibly and in disregard of their duty to prepare proper plans for the area.
- There is no conceivable planning justification for the proposed development and the evidence put forward in favour of it was derisory.
- The council treated the appellant shamefully by denying him information which he needed and to which he was entitled and by needlessly delaying a decision on the application made.
- The appellant evidently did all he could to confuse and mislead the council without actually telling lies.
- Mr Clott's evasive answers under cross-examination emphasised the unreliability of his evidence.
- It is with regret that I have to find in favour of the appellant/council since his/their case was ill-stated and left out of account many important considerations. Nevertheless on a true assessment of merits, he/they must clearly succeed.
- I consider that the accessibility diagram produced clearly demonstrates the need for a group of shops at or near the appeal site.
- Neither council nor appellant troubled to provide me with such obviously needed information as an existing land use map of the vicinity of the site.
- The development plan is so hopelessly out of date that it provided me with no useful guidance in determining this appeal. The suggested plan produced by the appellant seemed to me perfectly sound and was not challenged by the council who, indeed, did not seem at all clear why they had refused the application.
- The northern elevation of the proposed building is eight metres too close to the southern elevation of 'Strangeways' for the latter to continue to receive sufficient daylight.

The sort of statements one would find in profusion, relating to situations similar to those listed above, are:

- I note that a local plan for the area of which the appeal site forms part has not yet been prepared.
- It is difficult to see the planning justification for the proposed development, and I was not convinced by the evidence advanced in its favour.
- I can readily understand your client's dissatisfaction with the treatment he received from the council. Nevertheless . . .
- I was not convinced by the evidence given for your client.
- I accept that the case presented by the appellant/council was not entirely complete. Nevertheless . . .
- From the evidence produced it appears that there may well be a need for

shops in the general vicinity of the appeal site . . .

- Although the information with which I was provided did not include . . .
- I note that the relevant development plan was approved in 1960 and that inevitably it is not now an entirely reliable guide to development control. In these exceptional circumstances, therefore, I have felt able to take some account of the 'suggested plan' submitted on your client's behalf. (But probably he crosses out that last sentence as a bit dangerous and writes instead: 'In all the circumstances, therefore . . .' and doesn't mention the suggested plan.)

Everything is damped down and made comparatively non-committal. Hard technical evidence is ignored or referred to obliquely. Once more there is, of course, a touch of caricature in the above and diligent search would certainly produce exceptions, but it is true in spirit; it expresses the habitual difference between what one is sure must be in the thoughts of a good inspector and what he writes.

This is a great pity. It is difficult enough to express town planning ideas clearly and without veiling one's thoughts: the veil does more than veil, it often blacks out.

Why has this habit grown up? Quite simply, it must be because, although an inspector's role is closely analogous to that of a judge or arbitrator, he is, formally, a civil servant; civil servants express themselves quite differently from judges and arbitrators, very well for some purposes but not well for judgemental purposes. Yet there can be little doubt that apart from the frequently proclaimed and perfectly genuine principle that in transferred appeal cases the decision is for the inspector and no one else to make, the ethos and ambience of inspectors is of civil servants rather than judges. The introduction of consultants from outside the civil service as part-time inspectors may help to remedy this, but conformity is easy, non-conformity difficult. The tendency to conformity is so strong that as regards some matters it operates to make it almost impossible for an appellant to win. As noted in Chapter 10, green belts have been defended with such fanaticism that it has been exceedingly difficult if not impossible to develop at a green belt edge, even when the boundary of the green belt has undoubtedly been drawn inappropriately by mistake.

More generally, there has been a tendency for inspectors, particularly those with a local government past, to assume that no local authority would refuse planning permission unless it 'had good reason to do so'. Of course this is not true; local authorities quite often have fits of irrationality and refuse permission for no reason at all, let alone a good reason. Every inspector ought to make allowances for that; but I don't think they do so sufficiently. Except in a few kinds of appeal where no policy issue can possibly be involved, I feel certain that many more borderline appeals are dismissed than are allowed, simply because of the weight of conformist thought. I am the more certain because I have in mind not only the cases I have lost for appellants which I am sure should have been won, but the cases I have won for councils which after the lapse of years, I find myself surprised to have won. I am not surprised to have won any that I won for appellants. Let it be emphasised, by the way, that however hard one tries to exercise unbiased professional judgement, the moment one enters an appeal from one side rather than the other one is at least a little biased in favour of that side, however unwillingly or unwittingly; but the bias wears off after a time.

One year, by an odd coincidence, I found myself giving evidence for four appellants in widely separated parts of the country before the same inspector (and with the same deeply respected and much liked barrister on my side). The inspector was an ex-local goverment person; his whole demeanour, everything that he said and later wrote, suggested that for him a council could do no wrong. We lost all four. We had a good case each time. The subject-matter of each case was different from that of the others. We were not therefore bumping up simply against an isolated patch of prejudice but a huge frontal system of prejudice.

Another deadening factor is fear of the courts, MPs and ombudsmen. Being 'taken to the High Court' is not of course an experience which any inspector could be expected to welcome. Nor is it likely to be welcomed by his bosses. It will involve his decision letter being taken apart word by word and any ambiguity, contradiction or ultra-virility (if there is such a word) being merci-lessly exposed. As the money that hangs on appeal decisions increases year by year, the greater the likelihood is of appellants trying desperately to find some defect in the decision letter to justify going to court, even though this will not produce a reversal of the decision, but at best allow them to go back to square one. I think that to worry about this danger is much like worrying about being struck by lightning when setting out for a walk on a clear day; it might happen, but it's unlikely if you've been reasonably careful, and there's not much you can do about it.

Unfavourable and uncomfortable comments from MPs and ombudsmen are other hazards. Ordinary common sense ought to avert ombudsmen, while MPs are likely to take up issues for political reasons rather than town planning merit. One of my decisions as an inspector drew great wrath from the local MP. Since it was a decision in which I regarded the merits as being about 9 to 1 in favour of my decision and could be fairly sure that about 90 per cent of inspectors would have come to the same conclusion, I lost no sleep.

There is known to be a hierarchy within the inspectorate. Desire for pro-motion is natural; in many fields, the prospects of promotion are advanced more by a reputation for safeness than for initiative. Perhaps the DoE need to shift a little towards favouring initiative

Suggestions and conclusions

Almost everyone who has had considerable experience of the working of the appeal system recognises its merits despite its imperfections. Lay people who attend an appeal inquiry for the first time are often deeply impressed by the decency, fairness and friendliness of the proceedings, which they had not previously expected in something run by 'The Man from the Ministry'. They also often go away with much friendlier feelings towards the council than they had previously entertained. To the profession the defects are nevertheless apparent and substantial.

What can and should be done about these defects? As regards speed, as already suggested, a stoical attitude towards occasional errors should, I think, be adopted. Errors will occur anyway; if they are going to occur it is better for them to occur quickly than slowly and I doubt very much whether encouragement towards speed, combined with a reasonably wary look-out for gross errors would result in many more errors than already occur.

Unfortunately, one improvement which I believe needs to be made, strikes directly against greater speed. During 1983 there was a widespread, growling protest about the inadequacy and undue brevity of decision letters. I think it was justified. Letters determining an appeal dealt with by written representations probably average about one-and-a-half sides of paper. Where the appellant or the council has no case at all, this is enough, but in many cases it is quite insufficient. I think that anyone who puts forward a well considered, well reasoned, thorough argument on either side, is entitled, if that argument is not to prevail, to have the deficiencies that the inspector finds in it analysed with equal care and thoroughness.

This would often need a decision letter six or eight pages long. Eight pages would obviously take much longer to write than one and a half pages. The reasoning would also necessarily involve some general statements about town planning principles which, from their virtual absence from decision letters, one deduces the DoE does not like, as tending morally to commit the SoS and other inspectors either to agreement in comparable decisions or to explicit and embarrassing inconsistency. It would also be necessary to spend much more time checking decision letters to detect libels, improprieties, ultra-virilities and violations of policies.

For all that, I would favour the use of longer decision letters. It would encourage the production of fully reasoned cases, would discourage the brushing aside of powerful evidence and would provide unsuccessful parties with clear leads about where they had gone wrong. It would make it harder for inspectors to write shallowly conformist decision letters and, best of all, force the development of rational planning theory.

I think the DoE (quite contrary to its present line) should let it be known that councils are expected to have available proposals in graphic form, approved by the council, to support appeals in urban and village areas, that these will be given full regard, but that, in their absence, every appeal will be determined strictly on its planning merits, irrespective of motherhood statements.

More generally, if development plans are to be genuine guides to development control, it is essential that there should be an obligation to review them regularly and frequently, reducing the procedural ritual which has habitually surrounded such exercises. It is also essential that, to restore town plans to the status of works of planning design which they need to have, all areas likely to be needed for development in the visualisable future should be shown on them, but carefully staged so that including land in an area for ultimate development provides no excuse for trying to get permission to develop it now. Given such plans, I think that there would be fewer appeals than there are now and that there would be a clear and legitimate case for charging costs against appellants who sought to violate thorough, detailed, well-considered plans. No such case now usually exists.

I should very much like to see a move by the Royal Town Planning Institute to urge every chartered town planner involved in an appeal to protest to the DoE if it is being dealt with by someone who is not a chartered town planner, except of course in those rare cases mentioned earlier, where the skills of a chartered town planner are clearly not needed.

The chief planning inspector, fortunately for public confidence, has usually been a person of manifest distinction and ability; it is good to be able to say that the current holder of that office has those qualities and is also both a chartered town planner and a woman.

Part II

Examples

12

Introduction

It may be well to summarise some of the most important conclusions reached in previous chapters.

Appeals, as we have seen, are often really, in effect, belated substitutes for development plan inquiries. An appeal against a refusal of planning permission may in fact often be the only practicable way in which to get a planning dispute settled, and it is often necessary to insist with some force that this is so; that neither council nor DoE is entitled to shuffle it off on the excuse that a decision should wait upon a development plan review. It follows that only in quite exceptional circumstances can prematurity legitimately be prayed in aid as a reason for refusing permission. It may therefore often be necessary both for the appellant and, though this is perhaps insufficiently frequently recognised, for the council to put forward as part of their case detailed planning proposals considered suitable for a sufficiently large area around the appeal site to demonstrate that the satisfactory detailed planning of the area either is or is not compatible with the proposed development. If, over the years, DoE and councils had recognised this need and met it with detailed plans, many appeals would have been avoided.

On the other hand, it can seldom be profitable to attack the wisdom of planning policies incorporated in an approved structure plan, vapid and useless though these may often be. An appellant needs to be able to demonstrate one or more of three things: that the plan proposals are manifestly out of date to such an extent that it would be unfair to make appellants wait for the elephantine process of review to take place before being given permission; that, on any sensible interpretation, the proposed development accords with policies in the plan; or that it is so triflingly out of accord with them that, having regard to the demonstrable benefits and advantages of the development, the conflict should be disregarded.

No such status is enjoyed by local plans. As has already been said, all that can be said for sure of a local plan is that the SoS has not thought it so bad that he felt it necessary to intervene and prevent it coming into operation.

Attacks on the merits of local plans are therefore perfectly admissible, whatever form they may take and appellants should be remorseless in insisting that this is so and that the inspector should have no initial bias in favour of such a plan. Councils should equally be conscious of the need to defend a plan at every appeal and not rest on their oars.

Precedent, however, inevitably gathers some weight, and if a particular provision in a local plan has been consistently either upheld or rejected, by six different inspectors after six different appeals, it would be necessary, in order to obtain a decision going in the opposite direction, either to demonstrate convincingly that all six inspectors were wrong (a difficult task) or that circumstances had changed so markedly that quite different considerations, leading to a different result, must be held to apply. This may sometimes be possible.

Unfortunately, precedents have a cumulative effect. In a case of the kind described, the first inspector to determine an appeal may well have been wrong, at least marginally, and the second inspector, in doubt which way he ought to go with his decision, went the same way as the first in the interests of consistency. It then became progressively harder and harder for the third, fourth, fifth and sixth inspectors to go the other way, however much their expertise and experience suggested to them that they ought to. This is perhaps one of the unavoidable defects in our system. One believes that inspectors, caught in the difficulty of an obligation to uphold consistency or a manifestly wrong plan policy or proposal, should always make it clear in their decision letters that they believe reconsideration to be necessary. The problem for an inspector who feels he must get out of the snowball of accumulated precedent is perhaps more difficult. If he does break the mould, he risks exposing the council to another wave of applications from previously disappointed appellants, and has, possibly unfairly, discriminated in favour of the latest. Here again, compliance with precedent as regards the actual decision may be the most just thing to do, but reference to the need to reconsider is especially necessary for justice to be done.

The need for attack or defence in depth needs stressing. It is not wise for a council to rely on a single ground of refusal if there are other grounds which they believe would also justify refusal. The inspector may not agree with them on the main ground, and may not even become aware of the other grounds unless they are pointed out. Similarly, appellants are unwise to rely upon a single justification for permission, overwhelming though it may seem. Any legitimate additional reasons should always be included. On the other hand, and this is a fault frequently committed both by appellants and by councils, makeweight evidence which is not really relevant or weighty, is much more likely to weaken a case than to strengthen it. Referring back once more to Chapter 7, the landscape objection to the proposed development surely amounted to nothing at all, and might justifiably have led the inspector to wonder whether the main case could be very good if the council had thought it necessary to bolster it in this way.

The examples given in the following chapters are all based on real life appeals. In order to avoid any possible embarrassment to anyone, I have made sure that, nevertheless, they are unidentifiable. I have also taken steps to conceal, in all but a very few, what part, if any, I personally played.

Appeals fall naturally into broad categories, and even into sub-categories, but every appeal is distinguishable from every other appeal in some way, quite often in a way which will lead to a decision different from that given, properly, in an apparently identical case. This is what makes it so important for discussion of most appeals to be carried on with an appropriate site plan in front of the participants. Never, as witness or advocate, allow yourself to agree with the comparability of an appeal and the appropriateness of the decision given upon it in relation to the one under discussion without having the opportunity to look at an adequate plan dealing with the alleged comparable case.

The examples given do not of course, include an example of every kind of appeal. This would have made the book much too lengthy.

13

Is it development?

This subject has already been discussed at some length in Chapter 2, but will now be exemplified in relation to two matters which blanch the cheeks of anyone who has to do with them in connection with town planning: horses and boats.

Horses

A useful word, 'horsiculture', has been coined to express the confusing relationship between horses and agriculture in connection with town planning. Brief reference has already been made to this in the judgment discussed on pp. 15 and 16. One starts with the definition of agriculture in the Town and Country Planning Act 1971, section 290, dryly referred to by Lord Donaldson as 'somewhat indigestible':

'Agriculture' includes horticulture, fruit growing, seed growing, dairy farming, the breeding and keeping of livestock (including any creature kept for the production of food, wool, skins or fur, or for the purpose of its use in the farming of land), the use of land as grazing land, meadow land, osier land, market gardens and nursery grounds, and the use of land for woodlands, where that use is ancillary to the farming of land for other agricultural purposes, and 'agricultural' shall be construed accordingly.

From a welter of arguments and counter arguments of a complicated kind, put forward at various times by various people, the following seems to emerge as good sense:

1. If horses live on land to become meat, or are used to draw ploughs, carts, etc., then so long as the land is used for agriculture and is an agricultural holding of more than one acre, the horses are part of the agricultural scene and do not need planning permission to live there.
2. If horses do most of their eating on the land, the land is being used for agricultural purposes, even though the horses do not live there all the time, but work, and even sleep, elsewhere.

3.   If horses do not spend most of their time on the land or work agriculturally on it, but, e.g., are used for riding lessons and only eat there because they can't be prevented from doing so, then they are not 'agricultural horses' and their presence on the land may well need planning permission.

Put a little differently, if the horses eat a large proportion of their food from land, the land is used agriculturally, whatever else the horses do. They are 'consumer agricultural horses'. If they work as agricultural workers on the land, they are 'producer agricultural horses' whatever and wherever they eat (they may well indeed, be both consumer and producer horses, and most are). If the horses neither eat to a substantial extent on the land nor work on it at agriculture they are not agricultural horses at all ('play horses').

The question might well be asked whether anybody cares about this, and the answer is that many councils do. If horses are used for riding, whether solely on the land concerned, or simply using the land as a base, and being ridden elsewhere (i.e. as 'vehicles'!) they may have very substantial effects on the surroundings: noise, mess, smell and traffic congestion caused not only by themselves on the site and on the roads and bridle-ways they traverse but by the vehicles of those who come to ride them and so on. There is in those circumstances a business use which certainly needs permission and may well, in many locations, merit refusal of permission.

There are all kinds of complications which may render the admirable advice to planning officers to use common sense difficult of application. *De minimis* is in this connection a worrying term. The occasional brief ride by a farmer's daughter for fun on one of the farm horses is hardly likely to attract the unfavourable attention of a council. But where does legitimate concern begin?

Consider the following case. In the lush West Country is a farm (or farms? No one seems to be quite sure which). The farmhouse is occupied separately by two different branches of the same family. No one seems to be sure which branch does what, agriculturally, on which land. One branch evidently gives riding lessons on the farm (which is a perfectly genuine farm, many different kinds of animals live there in profusion, including horses, which indubitably eat a lot there). The council dislike this for a number of the reasons mentioned a little earlier and say that they are considering taking enforcement action.

Meanwhile a member of the other branch of the family applies for planning permission to use an existing building on the farm for the stabling of six horses. He does not make it clear where the horses are coming from, but says they will be used to provide riding instruction. He does not say where this instruction will be given. He does not apply for planning permission to use land as a riding school. One wonders why he has applied for planning permission. Perhaps the council inspired him to; if so they have attracted a good deal of trouble to themselves.

There is no question of the fairly old building having been erected in breach of planning control, and no question even of it needing to be altered. The necessary stalls are already in place and have evidently been there as long as the building has. They are currently occupied by a surprising variety of animals, including a duck, a goat and a horse. The council refuse planning permission on the grounds that the site is unsuitable for use as a riding school. An appeal is made. The reader is invited to consider the following questions:

1. If the building in respect of which the application was made were to be occupied by horses which already lived on the farm, even though not previously occupied by them, would planning permission be needed? If so, why?
2. If not, does it make any difference to the legitimacy of the use of the building if the horses that sleep in it (and live and eat on the farm) also carry learner riders on their backs from time to time? Is that not a separate issue?
3. If the council inspired the application, what public good did they hope to achieve?
4. If the application was not inspired, but was made 'voluntarily' what good did the applicant hope to do himself?
5. If you had to determine the appeal, how would you determine it?

Boats

Boats are vehicles just as horses sometimes are, but unlike horses they may also be thought of as structures or erections. Appalling doubts, rising like mists off an estuary, surround their liability to planning control. Up in the north-east of England, further north than one would think there would be reasonably clement weather for most of the activities to be described, there is the wide river Pribble, with an island of several acres on which is an old and charming house, occupied by a four-person group who have spent much time and effort in restoring the house and grounds to a beauty and order from which they had some time before fallen. In this particular case I shall disclose that I acted as advocate-witness for them, as the style of narration would otherwise become stilted and cumbersome. I had also better say that the four are close friends of long standing. Figures 13.1 and 13.2 set the scene.

The four own a couple of vessels which they tie up at various points around the peninsula from time to time; a couple of friends who own a rather picturesque old houseboat asked if they could tie up there too. Consent was readily given. Then, drama!

In November 1979 the group received a letter from the local council which said that it was proposed to carry out a survey in accordance with the provisions of section 280 of the Town and Country Planning Act of 1971. In doing this, the council were apparently responding to a letter written to them by the Water Authority as long before as August 1977. The council's letter enclosed a notice requiring certain formal information to be given. The survey took place and the council's planning officer wrote and said: 'My records show that my assistant enforcement officer called on your clients on the morning of 12 February 1979 and advised them that permanent moorings for a vessel needed to be the subject of an application to the local planning authority and the appropriate forms were

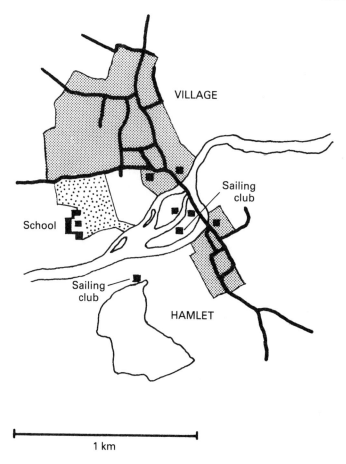

VILLAGE

Sailing
club

School

Sailing
club

HAMLET

|———————————————————|
1 km

Fig. 13.1 The boat case. Location plan

left with them for completion and submission.' He went on to say that no application for retrospective planning permission nor for an established use certificate had been received. One of the group then promptly applied for planning permission for 'the mooring of an old college barge converted into a houseboat in 1940, for weekend and holiday use only'.

Long out of time, the council issued a notice of refusal of planning permission, on four grounds. The first related to planning policy regarding the concentration of development in certain selected areas. The second referred to the permanent mooring of a houseboat as being contrary to council planning policy, and said that proposals for additional moorings would be resisted to safeguard and maintain the character of the river environment. The third alleged that the 'proposal' would lead to the establishment of a unit of residential accommodation in an isolated rural location. The fourth referred to the lack of adequate facilities for the disposal of sewage and refuse and said that the permanent mooring of a houseboat represented an intrusive form of development.

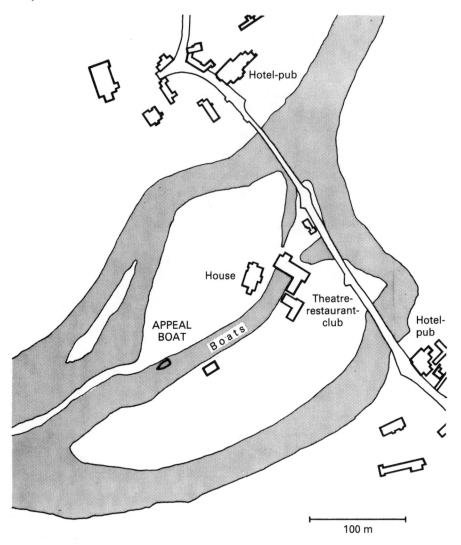

Fig. 13.2   The boat case. Site plan

Soon after this, the appellants got in touch with me. I told them that it would have been better not to have made an application for planning permission, as in my opinion no development was involved, that they should appeal and that the matters involved were too complicated to be dealt with satisfactorily by means of written representations. They accepted this advice, and an appeal was made.

While a date for the inquiry was being arranged, the council issued an Enforcement Notice in respect of the boat. I appealed against this as well. Unfortunately the council found that the Enforcement Notice they had issued was defective on technical grounds and had to amend and redistribute it at what must have been substantial expense. I appealed against the new notice.

The council's Statement arrived in due course and revealed that the survey which had been carried out had not only stemmed from the letter of the Water Authority written two years and four months earlier, but that the relevant parish council, having been consulted, had made the remarkable observation that if the boat were moved nearer the house it would be shielded from view from the opposite side of the river, but that such repositioning 'would of course make it more objectionable for the yacht club.' Much was later heard at the inquiry about how objectionable the noise from the yacht club was to occupants of the house on the island. One was reminded of the man who complained that he had been hit savagely on the fist by someone's jaw.

Other diverting titbits in the Statement were that while the Middle Pribble branch of the River Pribble Society did not object to the mooring of the boat, the Upper Pribble Branch did object (via its grandiloquently titled 'Area Planning Officer'). The Water Authority was quoted as saying a number of things in the Statement, but in the end did not seem to mind the boat, even though it had started the whole thing off!

The Statement thundered on for several pages, under the heading of 'Planning Merits'. It quoted the County Structure Plan as proposing that most housing developments should be 'steered to a limited number of areas' but that elsewhere, 'a policy of general restraint' should be applied and that in rural areas such as that in which the appeal site lay, new development should 'generally only be permitted to satisfy some particular local need'.

Perhaps the only truly relevant statement was: 'If developments were permitted to be dotted all over the place and strung out along roads, rivers and canals, the face of the countryside and riverside, et cetera would be undesirably changed. In the local planning authority's opinion this applies as much to developments for weekend and holiday purposes as it does to permanent residential accommodation.' Undoubtedly this is a sound statement if applied to the right target and where development is in fact involved. It is at least doubtful whether the boat was a right target, and as to development being involved, what the Statement said about this was that: 'the District Council considers that the mooring of a boat (other than in the course of navigation) on land covered by water, requires planning permission. They are convinced of the need for planning permission to be obtained when boats are moored permanently to the river bank and used, albeit at weekends and holidays, for residential purposes.' In the following paragraph, they 'drew attention' to a number of allegedly comparable cases.

To return to the question of whether the boat was a suitable target for attack on policy grounds, let us consider Fig. 13.1 in some detail. It will be seen that to describe the appeal site as being 'in an isolated rural location, detached from an existing settlement', as the council did in their third ground of refusal, is to strain the meaning of words a good deal. Not more than 500 metres away is the core of a large village on one side and even closer on the other side a sizeable and fairly compact hamlet. Next door to the appeal site (taking the island as the 'planning unit' – and whether it was or not was a matter hazily argued but never resolved during the course of the appeal) is a building used for the combined purposes of theatre, restaurant and club. On the same side of the appeal site and also adjacent to it there is a sailing club with a substantial club building and, associated with it, all the boats and noise mentioned a little earlier. About 200 metres from the site, one on each side of it, are two large hotels-cum-pubs. Less than 200 metres away is the village church, and the playing fields of a public school extend to within 300 metres of the appeal site. In summary, were the appeal site not liable to flood, part of it at least would have to be seriously considered as suitably located for village housing!

As soon as possible after receiving the council's statement, I sent the DoE and the council copies of a Statement of my case (as advised as desirable in Chapter 7). The following is the gist of it. A good many of the matters discussed in Chapter 2 come into it.

'This appeal is important for several reasons. Local planning authorities should not try to exercise powers which they do not possess and they should not exercise such planning powers as they do possess in an overbearing and unnecessarily tiresome and trivial way. Councils are there to serve those who elect them, and though this service, as regards town planning, necessarily means exerting authority over those who elect them, it is service rather than the exercise of authority which should be dominant in the minds of councils. They should not interfere with the actions of people in their exercise of planning powers unless there is a clear and unmistakable need to do so in the public interest. This is not only important from the point of view of individual welfare and freedom, but less directly, because of the need for town planning authorities to have a good reputation. Town planning is an activity of great social importance, capable, if rightly conducted, of achieving great improvement in our physical environment, but it cannot succeed unless it has public support; inappropriate behaviour by planning authorities does not attract that support, rather it alienates it.

'I do not believe that the Council has legal power to interfere with the mooring of the boat which is the subject of this appeal, as I shall presently argue in detail, but even if it has, it is not, as I shall also argue, a power which ought to be used.

'My case is divisible into four almost independent components:

(i)   No operation or change of use amounting to development is here involved.
(ii) If that argument does not prevail, then, at most, what is involved here is permitted development.
(iii) If that argument does not prevail, then, on merit, there is the clearest possible case for giving permission.
(iv) If that argument does not prevail, there is an established use here which puts it outside the control of the Council.

For this appeal to fail all four of the above arguments have to fail; if only one succeeds the appeal to be allowed.'

(i) Is development involved?

Though I am in one sense delighted that a barrister should have been chosen to act as inspector at this appeal, because of the special knowledge, wisdom and experience possessed by many lawyers, in another sense I am not pleased because the essence of the matter is that whether something does or does not constitute development is a matter of fact, not of law. By analogy with court proceedings it is a matter for the jury rather than the judge. Without any discourtesy being intended towards the inspector, I therefore say that I hope he will feel able to regard himself as jury rather than judge in considering this issue. To complicate the matter further, I shall be referring to decisions made by several eminent judges on what does or does not constitute development, but I think they were doing this as experienced and sensible people rather than as lawyers. It is noteworthy that some of them, notably Mr Widgery and Mr Bridge, as they then were, had had long experience of the sharp end of planning inquiries up and down the country.

'The only reason, I think, for judges to have to give decisions about whether something does or does not constitute development is if applicants take the opportunity of bypassing ordinary planning procedure by making an application for a judicial declaration instead of making an application under section 53 of the 1971 Planning Act to the local planning authority to determine whether what they want to do amounts to development.

'For something to amount to development there has to be an operation or a material change of use or both, and one is immediately faced with the problem of deciding what is an operation and what is material.

'Section 22 of the 1971 Act, as is well known, defines development as " ... the carrying out of building, engineering, mining or other operations, in, on, over or under land, or the making of any material change in the use of any building or other land". It would be possible to suggest that sticking a bean pole in the ground was a building operation since this produces a structure or erection, and every time you sink a spade in the ground it could be thought of as an engineering operation, but most of the time we call these activities gardening. Here, we have a boat which, the last time I saw it, was secured by a rope and a chain to a telephone pole at one end and to a small post at the other end. No suggestion has been made that the telephone pole is an unauthorised structure or erection, and the post is no taller or stouter than the kind of thing normally used in a gardening operation, so really one wonders whether the issue is simply about a piece of rope and a piece of chain.

'I can think of no way in which change of use might be thought to have taken place. Here we have a house and garden alongside which boats of various types have obviously tied up since time immemorial. The boat of the friends of the owners has been singled out as having, if we are to consider that a change of use might be involved, brought about a material change of use.

'I really wonder whether it should be necessary to say any more to ensure that this appeal is allowed, but then it has from the start been a mystery to me why an application for planning permission should have been solicited, made or refused. I want to re-emphasise a very important point. Whether something is development is a matter of fact and degree not a matter of law. In some cases the Minister or inspector or both have obviously mis-directed themselves about this. They sought legal advice or gave opinions 'subject to the law'. They should not have done so; they should have applied their minds to the facts and drawn their own conclusions. Nevertheless, some persuasive and helpful statements have been made from time to time which can reasonably be used for guidance.

'In Circular No. 67 of 1949, the then Minister of Town and Country Planning gave some help in referring to the fact that the word "material" had not been included in comparable legislation prior to 1947 and said: "the effect of the new definition is to make it clear that a proposed change of use constitutes development only if the new use is substantially different from the old. A change in kind will always be material, e.g. from house to shop or from shop to factory. A change in the degree of an existing use may be material but only if it is very marked."

'On page 6059 of the *Encyclopedia of Planning Law and Practice* a helpful statement is also made by Mr H. J. J. Brown, who says: "A generally held view is that a material change means a change which is significant to town planning considerations – a change which matters from the point of view of planning requirements, so that a change which is of no such significance will not amount to development."

'Lord Parker has said: "What one is really considering is the character of the use of the land and not the particular purpose of a particular occupier." (*Encyclopedia of Planning Law and Practice*, p. 6061). On the same page Lord Widgery is quoted as saying: "It is not my understanding of the law that, if the activity is exactly the same throughout the relevant period, a material change of use can occur merely because of a change in the identity of the person carrying out that activity." In a paragraph just below this a ministerial appeal decision is quoted which says that a change in the identity of the occupier does not in itself constitute development.

'A particularly helpful clue is provided in XI/18 of the *Bulletin of Selected Appeal Decisions* (see *Encyclopedia of Planning Law and Practice*, p. 5121). This says "The appeal was against the refusal of an urban district council near London to permit the mooring of six houseboats in a canal on the grounds that a satisfactory water supply and sanitary arrangements were not available, and that the proposal would be detrimental to the amenity of the neighbouring residential development.

' "Although the canal was semi-derelict, the Minister understood that it had not been abandoned and that rights of navigation therefore existed. He was advised that in these circumstances the mooring of houseboats in the canal could not be deemed to involve development under the Act, and consequently that no planning permission was required. The Minister made it clear, however, that the decision related only to the mooring of houseboats, as distinct from the construction of landing stages or other associated works, and that any development by way of ancillary building on the bank, such as the construction of landing stages, would require permission in the normal way." That seems to me to be both good sense and very definite.

'In the issue of the *Journal of Planning Law* for September 1963, on page 627, there is a very interesting report which includes the words "In the Minister's view, the anchoring of a boat, as distinct from the laying down of a permanent mooring, does not involve the carrying out of any operations. The Minister has considered whether your proposal will constitute or involve the making of any material change in the use of that part of the river where the houseboat is anchored. He does not take the view, which appears to be one argued by the Local Planning Authority that because a boat is used as a houseboat it is not a navigable vessel, nor does he think that the stationing of a houseboat in navigable waters necessarily involves a material change in the use of land; each case must in his view be looked at on its own facts. If the boat is un-navigable, or is fixed in position in such a way that it cannot be readily moved, it may be that development is involved, but in the present case the type of vessel and the degree to which it will be permanently stationed in the river have not been disclosed."

'If that view is sound we do indeed return to a mere piece of rope and a piece of chain. Though I believe it would be less convenient for the boat which is the subject of this appeal to be anchored rather than tied to the bank, it certainly could be anchored, in which case the only remaining issue between the appellants and the Council must be whether the Council really regards the piece of rope and piece of chain as so obnoxious as to justify them in trying to insist that an anchor be used instead, since, if the Minister was right, they have no control over the presence, as such, of the boat.

'I have real difficulty in understanding what a "mooring" is. Many cases seem to draw a distinction between the mere *act of mooring* a vessel and the *laying down of moorings*. It seems to me that the common-sense interpretation can only be that moorings consist of substantial structures of one kind or another, wharfs, quays, jetties and so forth, which are sufficiently large and substantial as to amount to structures worthy of consideration under planning powers. Surely they do not include mere pegs or posts. As the inspector will be able to see for himself, the shore of the island which is the subject of this appeal is pretty freely sprinkled with objects which evidently have to do with boats. How long they have been there I do not know but it is perfectly obvious that a considerable proportion have been there since before 1964. (The material time for existence of established use rights).

'I now turn to appeal decisions that have been referred to by the council.'

'A. Stationing of a houseboat

The inspector manifestly misdirects himself when it is said that he *"concluded that the legal implications of the facts were matters for the Secretary of State and his legal advisers"*. So far as one can tell from the context the only legal implication about the facts is that facts are facts, to be *determined* by the inspector and/or the SoS without "advice". This is very important.

'The decision letter in that case says: "The submission that navigation of a river was a natural incident of land covered by water and was not a use subject to planning control is not accepted." *Who* did not accept it, and for what reasons? What justification can there be for attaching weight to the opinion, unsupported by reasoning, of the person of unknown experience and attainments, who signed the decision letter? The use of the impersonal passive to give the effect of a declaration from Sinai is very much to be deplored.'

'B. Stationing of houseboats

This was an appeal decided in 1969. Here also the inspector wrongly concluded that "the legal implications of the facts found were matters for the Minister and his advisers". However, sensibly enough, he said "the existing user rights which attach to the sites permit the passage of boats . . . Incidental to the right of navigation must be the right to moor". Unfortunately he goes on to say: "The continuous stationing of houseboats . . . had the effect of preventing the use of the sites for the purpose for which they could be used without the necessity to obtain planning permission.' I can make no sense of that. The thinking expressed by the inspector is not sufficiently clear to justify attaching weight to it.'

'C. A more recent case concerning storage and mooring of a boat

This was determined by an inspector, who did better, but still committed some errors. He rightly says, "The appellant is a riparian owner with a basic right to moor his boat on his land" and rightly goes on to compare parking on a road and mooring in a river. But he quotes various decisions and says: "The essence of those rulings is that the mooring for (sic) a boat used for navigation does not constitute a use requiring planning permission, but one which is used for mooring not in the course of navigation does require permission. This seems in flat contradiction of what he said earlier; moreover he does not seem to realise that these "rulings" are not binding upon him. Later he says "the question of precedent must be considered". True, but in town planning precedents are persuasive not coercive. The SoS is charged, if I remember rightly, with securing consistency and continuity in the use of land. To secure these, some regard certainly needs to be given to previous decisions, and one cannot criticise the inspector for doing this. Nevertheless no SoS (or inspector) would want to go down in history as one who continually and consistently supported bad decisions.

'That inspector worries me because he also says "It is considered that planning permission is required." This wording suggests that he is relying on Sinai rather than himself. By contrast he later says, much more acceptably, "In my opinion . . ." but spoils it by going on to say "the question of whether the mooring of the boat constitutes development relies on the interpretation of the facts in the light of various appeal decisions". That is not right; it was for him to discover the facts and *decide* whether, on the facts, development or change of use was involved. It is his decision that matters; other appeal decisions might legitimately give him some light, but his own reasoning is the main and powerful light to rely on.'

Is it permitted development?

Though I do not think that development is involved here, it seems necessary to consider the possibility that the Secretary of State may take a different view. In that event one has to consider whether it is development that requires planning permission. In my opinion it clearly is not. Regarding the boat now as a structure rather than a vehicle it seems to me clearly to fall under Class I of the exemptions in the First Schedule to the General Development Order of 1977 (SI 1977 No. 289). The third category in Class I exempts from obligation to obtain planning permission 'The erection, construction or placing, and the maintenance, improvement or other alteration, within the curtilage of a dwelling, of any building or enclosure (other than a dwelling, garage, stable, loose box or coach house) required for a purpose incidental for the enjoyment of the dwelling-house, as such, including the keeping of poultry, bees, pet animals, birds or other livestock for the domestic needs or personal enjoyment of the occupants of the dwelling-house', so long as certain limitations on siting, sizes and height are complied with.

'The boat is certainly required for a purpose incidental to the enjoyment of the dwelling-house. It adjoins the garden of a dwelling-house and is occupied from time to time by friends of the appellants, and no doubt by the appellants themselves. To have a boat tied up by one's garden, in which one can sit, doze or fish is a pleasure enjoyed by the occupants of many dwelling-houses who are lucky enough to have a bit of river next to their garden. That the boat happens to belong to friends is irrelevant. It might as well be owned by the owners of the land, who might then allow those same friends or indeed any other of their friends to use it from time to time. The ownership of the boat is in fact absolutely irrelevant. I ask the inspector to dismiss the matter from his mind and to consider whether it can conceivably be regarded as a proper subject for planning control to try to prevent people tying up boats beside their gardens. If it made any difference it is at least possible that arrangements could be made for those of the appellants who own the house on the appeal site to buy the boat from its present owners, but it would not make any physical difference and indeed such a transaction could take place without the planning authority or anyone else except perhaps the Boat Licensing Authority being aware of it.

'The Council make the point in their Statement that the height of the boat above the water line exceeds three metres, thereby removing it from GDO exemption. It may, if one includes in this the height of the open railing around the upper deck. No doubt, if it were really necessary to do so, it would either be possible to remove this railing or to lower the boat in the water by one means or another. But *de minimis non curat lex*.

'It seems to me quite certain that this is permitted development, if it is development at all, and I do not think it should be necessary to proceed further.

'(iii) The merits of the case

I next assume that, somehow, the presence of the boat adjoining the island is something that requires planning permission. If I were a planning officer I should recommend permission, perhaps suggesting conditions that it should not be let out for use for any business purpose. One expects to see boats on rivers, and especially to see boats tied up adjoining gardens. As a matter of fact, I cannot recall visiting any riverside garden which did not have a boat tied up beside it. I suppose one might conceivably recommend refusal if it were an exceptionally ugly boat on the grounds that it had an unsatisfactory external appearance. But this is rather a nice-looking boat. Indeed if it were truly a building one might expect in the present climate of opinion that it would have a building preservation order applied to it, but I do not want to plant ideas in the mind of the Council.

If one takes the curious view that boats are nasty things which should be kept away from rivers as much as possible, then concentration rather than dispersal of boats is clearly preferable. There are two yacht clubs close to the appeal site, a splendid concentration of vessels, avoiding the dispersal which is deplored, and the boat the subject of this appeal forms part of that concentration.

'In advance of cross-examination of the appropriate witnesses I shall make some comments on the reasons put forward by the Council.

'The council say that the boat is particularly noticeable from the tow path both from the north and the south. I do not know why this should be considered a disadvantage, but, if it is, a less conspicuous location could be arranged, though it seems a pity to deprive the public of views of the boat.

'We are told that there is no vehicular access to the appeal site and that no facilities for refuse disposal exist and no main drainage. One had understood from the terms of the Enforcement Notice that the whole of the island was regarded as being the site; I think it is right to do so, and of course vehicular access and all other services are readily available, though they are not available at the point on the island at which I last saw the boat moored.

'As to refuse and sewage disposal, the boat has a chemical closet; the house has lavatories and dustbins which the boat owners are welcome to use. One cannot think of many places in which a boat would be likely to create fewer problems of this kind.

'It is said that the boat "occupies a permanent mooring and is used for residential accommodation, albeit at present only at weekends". And it is then said that the local planning authority, ". . . therefore considers that it is appropriate for the development to be examined in relation to planning policies concerning new housing development'. Really, this is so ridiculous that it almost defies comment. I cannot believe that the inspector will be interested in considering a boat ancillary to the use of a long existing dwelling-house as something which should be examined in relation to planning policy concerning new housing.

'(iv) Are there established use rights?

I have placed this section near the end, although it might have seemed more appropriate to put it at the beginning; I have done so because there is a logical progression. I have suggested first that development is not involved, that there is nothing for the Secretary of State to decide within the context of planning legislation, and have gone on to say that even if there is it is permitted development and continued by saying that even if it is not it is harmless and desirable development.

'If I am wrong about all that and it is rightly to be regarded as objectionable development, then, nevertheless, if there are established use rights there is nothing the Council can do about it. I do not see how it can be denied that boats have frequently and for a long time tied up at various parts of the island. I do not think the council are trying to deny this, though they emphasise an extract from a letter from the Water Authority which says: " . . . it would appear that prior to the commencement of the re-building of the nearby weirs in 1960 a launch used for residential purposes was tied up approximately in the same place as the boat in question and that it had been in that location for a period which I have been unable to determine. However, there has been no use of the land as a mooring since the weirs were re-built in 1960." If by "the land" the writer means the island as a whole, what he says is manifestly wrong. On various visits to the island over the last few years, I have myself seen boats moored at various points around it. There *must* be existing use rights for mooring at the peninsula, and if one is thinking of the things to which boats are tied rather than the boats themselves there must be existing moorings at various points around the island which have been there since before 1964.

'But is it to be assumed that if people sleep on a boat it is different from other kinds of boats and excluded from mooring rights? I cannot think that this can be so. Is it then the Couucil's opinion that houseboats are in a special class if they are specially adapted to sleeping and the emphasis is on sleeping rather than movement? I think this must be so otherwise there seems no possible reason for this boat to be picked out and action taken against it and not against other boats which have been tied up at the island. Yet I can see no good reason in law, logic or planning practice why such a distinction should be made. It does not make any difference to the appearance of the boat that people sleep in it. It does not make any difference to the appearance of the boat that it is stationary most of the time. If it moved away its place might be taken by another boat.

'I do not want to take up time by producing a lot of witnesses to find that their evidence is not contested by the Council. For the moment, I simply say that there must surely have been sufficiently frequent sleeping in boats around the island before 1964, not discontinued long enough to constitute abandonment, for there to be established use rights to cover this case.'

On 14 April 1981 the inquiry was held at one of the large hotel-pubs referred to above in the description of the surroundings of the site. There was some preliminary informal chat before the inquiry was opened. Both the inspector and the barrister who had rather surprisingly been briefed by the council seemed very keen to get the inquiry over that day. Indeed the barrister hoped it might be finished 'by lunchtime' and was very cross indeed when I said I thought it was bound to go into a second day; so was the inspector. I explained that my most important witness with regard to established use rights could not attend until the following day. The inspector then seemed to say that the inquiry could not be held up on that account or prolonged, and I had to make a quick decision. On the one hand, the inspector was obviously wrong and trying to put one over on me. On the other, the established use rights aspect was the one on which I was on the weakest ground for lack of absolutely cast iron evidence. I only had to win on one of the four issues in order to win the case and didn't want to put the inspector's back up too much, so I said I would do my best, but that the time taken depended a good deal upon the extent to which the council pressed their case. We took our seats all bristling a little at each other, but harmony soon prevailed.

I presented my case, based on the Statement of Case I had already provided. It was rather fun laying down the law to two lawyers that the matters at issue were not matters of law. When I had finished my opponent said that he did not want to cross-examine me. My array of supporting witnesses gave excellent evidence, including photographs to show the erstwhile mobility of the boat. Third parties who supported us also performed well, sincerely and amusingly; opposing third parties were so feeble that it was only necessary to ask a few questions in order to demolish them. The young planning officer was admirably frank and honest, and though a little reluctant to give his personal opinion, admitted that he thought the boat would do no harm if it were moved to a rather less prominent position. (Amusing this, in the light of the decision letter, as we shall see.)

Throughout, it was easy and gratifying to be able to say from time to time when suggestions were made about the dire results likely to happen as a result of the boat's presence, 'But it's been there for years, and nothing like that has in fact happened, has it?' 'Er, . . . no'.

In his brief closing statement, my opponent made graceful references to the cogency of my arguments and seemed to rely for success simply on the proposition that a consensus of a kind unfavourable to the appellants had emerged from legal and ministerial decisions and that if that consensus were to be overturned, it should be done by a court and not as the result of a planning inquiry. I think this was a hollow argument. One more court decision could only obfuscate a little more a subject already hopelessly crowded by confused, ambiguous and contradictory pronouncements by judges, DoE administrators and inspectors. What I think is certain is that some simple clarifying legislation is needed to deal with the definition of development as applied to boats, horses and some other very difficult matters not thought of when the definition of development was first written for the 1947 Act.

The inquiry and the site inspection, a jovial occasion, were over by teatime. And three-and-a-half months later, only a week or two less than four years from the first letter from the Water Authority about the matter, the whole thing was over.

It was as well that I had put forward a quadruple case, for we only won on one of the four grounds I had put forward. It was deemed that development had occurred, that it was not permitted development, that existing use rights had not been established, but that planning permission ought to be given, subject to a few trivial conditions and to the boat being kept where it was, not moved to a less conspicuous position!

My friends were delighted, and of course I was pleased we had won; but not so pleased with the inspector's report and the decision letter, which, I think, contained some serious errors.

The inspector's report was seven pages long and the decision letter was three pages long, but they overlapped and even contradicted each other to some extent, and it is very hard to summarise them. The inspector was confident that there was what he called 'a clear distinction' between mooring in the course of navigation and permanent mooring of a vessel without independent means of propulsion. This left in the air what 'permanent' means and what 'independent' means. One would not wish to quibble about the former, since in ordinary language the boat in question was permanently moored, though whether it was moored at a 'permanent mooring' is another matter and one which the DoE and inspector left alone. As regards independent means of propulsion, one wonders what 'independent' means. Independent of what? Independent perhaps of the need to be drawn by another boat or a horse (horses again!). The boat did not have an engine aboard but could if necessary have been propelled by poles or oars and could have had an outboard motor installed. In preparing my case I had in fact been rather keen for this to be done, to arrange for the inspector to arrive at the site inspection to find no boat present, but for it to roar up to the island a minute or two later with flags flying and guns firing. Unfortunately cost and insurance complications prevented this.

What most surprised me was the inspector's statement that 'there is clearly a material change of use requiring planning permission unless such development is permitted'. It seems to me that for there to be a material change of use or indeed any change of use it must be possible to say what the previous use was and what the changed use is. The inspector did not attempt this. The previous use was clearly residential but what was the new use?

The DoE got itself into a logical tangle in the decision letter. Having accepted what the inspector thought about change of use, it seems to have got those words into its mind ineradicably because, in dealing with my submission that any development involved was permitted development within Class I, 3 of the First Schedule to the General Development Order, it said: 'It is not considered that that Class, concerned as it is with operational development, can have any application here.' But the dispute was all about the *stationing* of the boat. Surely that is an operation?

The decision letter also rejected the idea that there was use for a purpose incidental to the enjoyment of the dwellinghouse as such because the boat was owned and principally occupied by 'persons who have no connection with the house other than being friends of the owners'. The entire argument that ownership has nothing to do with planning, a well regarded concept, was totally ignored. The inspector had said:

'It is argued on behalf of the appellant that the use is incidental to the enjoyment of the dwelling-house and that ownership is irrelevant in planning terms. *To some extent that is true* [my emphasis]. But ownership is important because there must be some affinity between the dwelling and the houseboat.' This does not make good sense. It does not deal with my argument that even if ownership were to be regarded as a relevant consideration, ownership could have been transferred to the owners of the house without the planning authority being even made aware of it and without any physical change whatever taking place. Surely that was an argument which deserved consideration, and rebuttal if regarded as unsound, though it is hard indeed to see how it could be regarded as unsound.

There were a number of other points in the inspector's report and in the decision letter which seem to me to be unsatisfactory and indicative of careless thinking, but it would be tedious to pursue them. Had we in fact lost the appeal we should have been entitled to feel very aggrieved because of fairly clear evidence that some of our arguments had either not been understood or not been properly considered.

It seems to me that the whole affair reflects very badly indeed upon the local authority concerned. Spun out over four years, it must have cost more public and private time and money than bears thinking about. If my clients had chosen to go the whole hog, brief counsel through a solicitor and hire a planning consultant, their costs would have been enormous. Indeed it is most unlikely they would have done this, for all the owners of the house were doing was granting friends a small favour, and few people would be willing to spend thousands of pounds to be allowed to continue that. Nor would the owners of the boat have been prepared to spend thousands of pounds; they would probably have preferred to sell the boat.

The council should have been charged with costs. I considered applying for costs, but since it is very difficult to get these awarded on a planning appeal and since the mere raising of the matter casts extra work on an inspector I did not want to prejudice our chances by irritating him.

It was perfectly clear that neither my legal opponent nor the planning officer was eager to win the case; they went through their paces conscientiously and honourably and that was all. Some foolish group of elected members or some less than sensible bureaucrats must, I think, have been the true culprits. I have recounted this case at length because I think it teaches a great many lessons, more lessons than I have ever before seen concentrated into a single case.

14

Housing

In this chapter I shall mostly deal with disputes over housing other than those which relate to whether or not there ought to be any housing at all in the general location proposed and shall leave disputes about general location to be dealt with more fully in Chapters 17 and 18, which deal with development control in the countryside, villages and urban fringes. But there is some overlap and I begin with some very curious cases which do not fit conveniently either in those chapters or in this one. I refer to three cases which have much in common.

In the first, permission for a substantial area for housing was refused, not wholly, but mainly, on the ground that quarrying taking place on nearby land involved the use of explosives and the consequent danger of lumps of rock flying and causing damage to persons or buildings on the appeal site. In the second case permission was similarly refused on the grounds that a large industrial undertaking nearby was liable to allow noxious fumes to escape, to the detriment of anyone who lived on the appeal site. In the third permission was refused because detriment might be caused by smell from a sewage works. These all seem to me clear cases of illegitimate refusals of planning permission, for the quite straightforward reason that it is the duty of all landowners not to allow dangerous things, whether bulls or fumes, to escape from their land. In the first case, which I came across a good many years ago, the subsequent appeal was nevertheless lost, but going through the area by chance a couple of years ago, I noticed with interest that the development sought had now taken place. In the second and third cases the subsequent appeals were won by the appellants. I should think that in at least the first two cases an appeal to the High Court might have been successful, that in all the cases the councils concerned were very incompetent in taking the decisions they did, and that in the first case (decided by the Minister in the days before inspector decisions) the Minister was remarkably ill-advised in reaching his decision. Apart from this aspect of things, however, another rather remarkable principle is involved in all these cases. In the first, it is true that, in the absence of houses, the number of people likely to be walking around the site at the time of explosions would be likely to be very small. Are we then to assume (I think the decision given must have assumed so), that it is all right to put a limited number of people at peril, but not to put a large number at peril? Could there lie the thought behind this that the compensation liable to be paid for killing or wounding a few people would not be insupportably great, but that if the number ran into dozens, it would be?!

In the second case, even this thoroughly disreputable argument could not stand up because there were already something like 2000 people living closer to the source of dangerous fumes than the appeal site was to it. In that case, presumably, the unspoken thought must have been 'at least better to kill only 2000 rather than 2500'. In the third, less dramatic case only about twenty houses were nearer to or about the same distance from the sewage works.

The following cases are remarkable in rather different ways.

In the absence of a clear policy to restrict the development of a particular town it can surely only be justifiable to refuse permission for housing within the urban envelope if there is a clear intention and justification to use the land for public purposes such as schools or public open space. However, some exceedingly odd decisions are made by councils. Figures 14.1 to 14.6 show some of them.

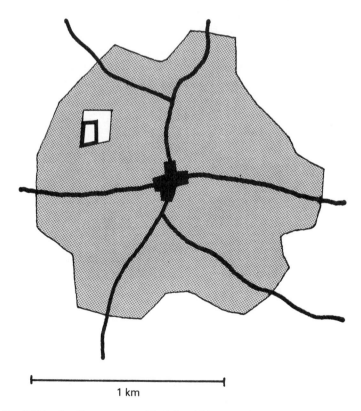

1 km

Fig. 14.1 'White land' unaccountably left within an urban area

In the case of Figs 14.1 and 14.2 the definition of the appeal sites as 'white land' seems to have no justification whatever. In Fig. 14.1 the only reasons for refusal seemed to be, first (unspoken), that it would be rather nice for the people living round about to look out on to an area on which nothing would be happening except a pony or two grazing, and the feeling that this might be rather a good area in which to keep options open; an area which might well in the future be useful for a primary school, a secondary school, public playing fields or a combination of these. This is not fair. Councils must make up their minds. Options cannot be kept open indefinitely. Indeed it is fair to suggest that when a challenge is made minds have to be made up. In that case, incredibly, the appeal was lost, but the inspector concerned was one of the very tiny number of inspectors mentioned in Chapter 11 whose judgement and behaviour were both deplorable.

In the case of Fig. 14.2, where the appeal was allowed, the site was in the midst of a very much larger urban area than in the former case. Unless there was some sort of interested fiddling by councillors, of which there was no evidence, the only possible explanation is that it was omitted from an area allocated for housing by a sheer draftsman's error.

The case in Fig. 14.3 was rather different. Here it was a question of which sites were the *most* suitable for particular purposes and a case for the appeal site being used for housing rather than for a secondary school was presented.

In the case of Fig. 14.4 the argument in favour of allowing the proposed development seems unanswerable. In terms of location and physical character- istics, the site was much better than some of the land allocated for development in the town map. The abolition of the railway line removed any disadvantage of accessibility, and the effect of the view from the 'big house' was simply an extreme example of the 'buying the view' fallacy.

The most common issues in planning disputes about housing relate to: Number of houses; Density; Types of houses; Layout; Access and parking; Acceptability of infilling; Privacy; and these will be considered in turn.

Number of houses

Some very curious arguments arise about this. The inadequacy of either struc- ture plans or local plans as guides to development control have in many areas removed all definiteness from proposals about planned town size and left it altogether vague. The vagueness has been little clarified, indeed perhaps in some ways made worse, by attempts to ensure that a 'five-year supply' of building land for housing is 'available' at any given time. The unit area over which this supply is to be calculated is seldom made clear or related to supply and demand of employment, nor is sufficient account taken of possible popu- lation movements from one 'area' to another. Since 'available' is never closely defined, and since DoE Circular No. 22 of 1980 says that permission should not necessarily be refused for housing on a site because there is a five-year supply

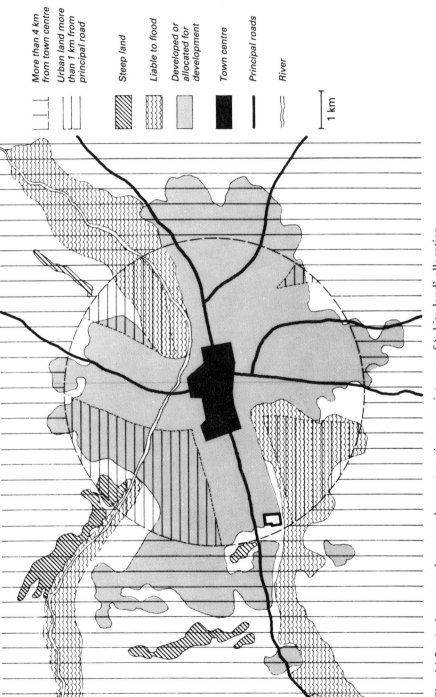

Fig. 14.2 A sieve map drawn to demonstrate inappropriateness of 'white land' allocation

Key (legend):

- More than 4 km from town centre
- Urban land more than 1 km from principal road
- Steep land
- Liable to flood
- Developed or allocated for development
- Town centre
- Principal roads
- River

1 km

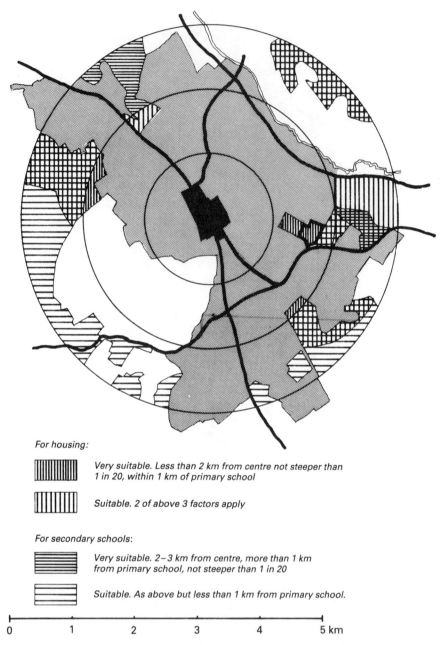

For housing:

Very suitable. Less than 2 km from centre not steeper than 1 in 20, within 1 km of primary school

Suitable. 2 of above 3 factors apply

For secondary schools:

Very suitable. 2–3 km from centre, more than 1 km from primary school, not steeper than 1 in 20

Suitable. As above but less than 1 km from primary school.

0   1   2   3   4   5 km

Fig. 14.3   Analysis to demonstrate suitability of land for housing. The argument was that accessibility of houses to primary schools is an important factor in town planning design and that secondary schools should not therefore be placed near primary schools, because a secondary school occupies a large amount of land which could otherwise be used for housing. Use of land close to a primary school for a secondary school instead of housing therefore reduces general accessibility. In these terms there were some 30 ha specially suitable for housing, of which the appeal site formed part, 224 ha especially suitable for secondary schools because topographically suitable and not near a primary school and 140 ha suitable for either. This seems to constitute an overwhelming case for giving permission for housing on the appeal site.

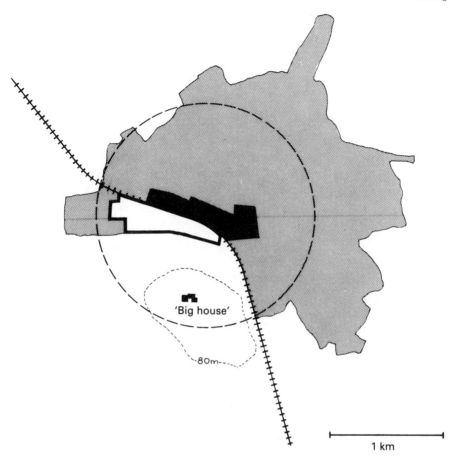

Fig. 14.4 'White land' next to a town centre

available elsewhere, all is chaos. Neither council nor appellant is likely to be able to muster decisive arguments based on this kind of uncertainty.

It is an uncertainty which in one respect at least is traditional. Ever since the Second World War councils have been in the habit of saying that there was plenty of building land available and builders have been in the habit of saying that there was no land available. Of course it depends what you mean by 'available'. From the point of view of a town planner, land is available for building if it is suitably placed, of suitable topography, can obtain road access and has the necessary piped and wired services nearby. To a builder it has to have these characteristics, but it is not available unless someone is also prepared to sell it to him at a price which he is able and willing to pay.

I do not think that there can be any escape from this impasse until councils prepare plans which show with precision land allocated for housing development and the order in which they are prepared to release different sites for development. Figures 14.5 and 14.6 show other curious cases of this kind.

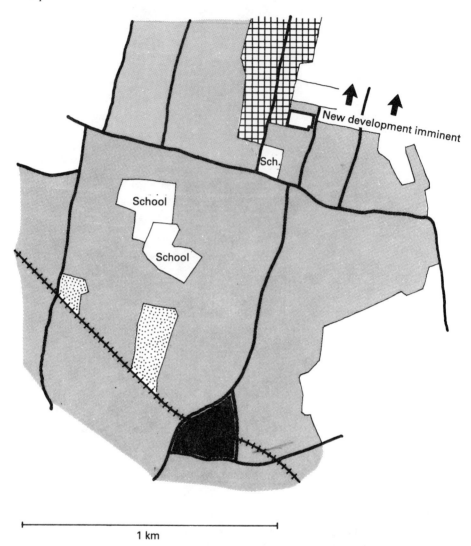

New development imminent

1 km

Fig. 14.5 Irrational opposition to development. In this rapidly growing town, the problem is to maintain a reasonable degree of compactness. In the vicinity of the appeal site development is steadily continuing towards the top of the figure. Why then, for twenty years, has the council resisted development of this appeal site? There is a small access problem, easily overcome. On no other ground can refusal be justified.

A particular difficulty arises in connection with sewage disposal. In the days of town maps, councils not only performed planning functions but were also the drainage authorities. They could therefore fairly readily match the allocation and release of land for building with the extension of their sewage works or the construction of new sewage works. Now, however, there are Water Boards which do not perform planning functions; they may make representations about

500 m

Fig. 14.6 More irrational 'white land' allocation. An island of white has unaccountably been left in the middle of a small town and an application to build houses on part of it has been made. This was successful on appeal, but why should the appellants have needed to fight an appeal? There was no rational objection to their proposal.

planning applications which affect their functions, but cannot secure that these representations are heeded. Moreover, the inadequacy or otherwise of sewage works seems to be a very indefinite thing. Authorities responsible for sewage disposal understandably act prudently and conservatively. It has not been unknown for them to suggest that their works were on the point of being unable to cope with further loading when in fact they still have a good deal of capacity in reserve.

Figure 14.7 illustrates the difficult and unsatisfactory nature of the situation. Here there was a large village or small town, it is difficult to be sure which, which had grown rather rapidly and in rather disorderly fashion over the last fifteen years. It may well be that the pre-1974 district council had more dele-gated development control powers than it ought to have been given and exer-cised them unwisely. The application to build forty houses was far from unreasonable. The land was topographically entirely suitable, its location in relation to the centre and in relation to other housing was quite suitable. It was refused planning permission on a variety of grounds, most of them specious.

As has earlier been suggested several times, being rather near an area of special landscape value does not necessarily do anything to disqualify a piece of land from having houses built on it. That was the principal reason for refusal in this case, together with an extremely vaguely stated policy of 'growth restraint' which, if it had ever been seriously pursued, had evidently not been pursued for some time, judging by the amount of development which had recently been permitted. The Water Board, however, said that the proposed

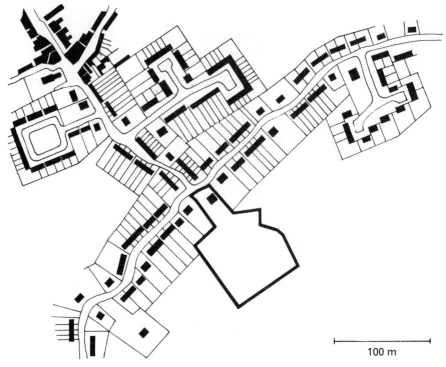

100 m

Fig. 14.7 Spoiling the view? The main ground for refusing this application for housing was that it would in some way damage an area of high landscape value a mile or more away from the bottom of the figure. Why other recently permitted development should not be thought to have done this is mysterious, as is what damage could in fact be done. There was also a question of overstraining sewerage facilities but this was inconclusive. In the end, what was fatal to the appeal was the very bad road access.

development would overstrain the sewage works, which could not (or would not?) be extended for some years. The growth restraint argument had no merit. The nearness to land of outstanding landscape value had no merit. The appeal was determined by written representations, so that it was not possible for the Water Board's objections to be reliably evaluated. Their representations were meagre and unconvincing. The appeal might therefore well have been won and, if the Water Board's objection was really justified, this might have caused a good deal of harm because of the escape of untreated sewage or expenditure on the extension of the sewage works at the expense of more necessary work elsewhere. It is surprising that the council did not opt for the appeal to be dealt with by way of an inquiry and/or that the Water Board did not take more trouble with their representations. Perhaps, in fact, these failures and omissions indicate that the objection was not a very serious one. However, the appeal failed because the road access to the site was perfectly dreadful. It was so bad that it could not have been made tolerable without massive public expenditure. So the council and the Water Board were lucky, luckier than they deserved to be. The council made no particular effort to demonstrate the inadequacy of the road access.

Density and house types

For a brief but more thorough explanation of the nature of housing density, its measurement and control, the reader is referred to Chapter 2 of *Town Planning Made Plain*. Once more the great difficulty is that councils are often confused about what they want to try to do, why they want to do it and how it can be done. In the very simplest terms, the more land there is around a house the less likely are its occupants to interfere with the privacy and comfort of their neighbours or to be interfered with by them. Vertical barriers such as walls can mitigate some but not all of the bad effects of houses being too close together. It ought to be possible for everyone who wants it to have a garden of fair size in which to grow flowers or food or for his small children to play in safely under close watch. On the other hand, no one ought to have to have a garden bigger than he wants. The bigger the house plots the lower the density and the lower the density the more a town is spread and the poorer the levels of accessibility for its residents. There is therefore a powerful argument for keeping house densities as high as is compatible with the other desiderata just mentioned. (This is, in fact, too crude a statement; beyond a certain point, high density may operate adversely in terms of accessibility because the amount of road space available is insufficient to carry the traffic and the gain of spatial compactness is offset by traffic congestion.)

From 1945 onwards the better planning authorities did their best to adopt and work out housing density policies which would be consistent with the aims just outlined. Decade by decade the task was made more difficult for them. To cut a long and miserable story short, the situation has now been reached in which government policy is to encourage 'full use' of housing land and to regard the amount and standard of building accommodation and the amount of private land in the form of garden as a matter for competing private builders to deal with by meeting the expressed demands of their customers. By any standards this is false thinking and bad policy. By and large it pays builders to build as densely as they are allowed (up to certain very high limits). The 'customers' do not and have never had the sort of choice that cigarette smokers, chocolate eaters and vegetarians are used to. They are offered the least that the builder thinks he can get away with at the highest price that he thinks he can charge. The housing need of many people is not at all the same as their ability to pay. Many large, low income families have a great need for a large house and for a large garden in which children can disport themselves and food can be grown. They are about the last kind of family to get such a home.

There is another aspect equally important from a different point of view. In 'green field' development the council can specify the density it will permit and by doing this can make reasonably accurate calculations about the provision of roads, open space, shopping and schools that will be needed to cater for the new population. But in areas of existing housing it is likely to be defeated by successive waves of applications for piecemeal development at substantially higher densities than those existing. Many councils have only themselves to blame for not laying down in detail what density they will permit, but even those which do are liable to be defeated by, on the one hand, anticipated redevelopment not taking place for one reason or another or, on the other hand, by losing appeals against refusals for permission on the ground of excessive density because of ignorance on the part of inspectors or DoE administrators. This is a very complicated matter, likely to lead to difficulties and partial defeats even with everybody trying to do an intelligent best. In the absence of that desirable state of affairs frequent defeats are certain.

To give a simple example of what is being talked about, imagine, as an extreme case, an area of 50 ha developed at an average density of 10 dwellings per ha and an average occupancy rate of 3 persons per dwelling. That gives a total of 1500 people. Gradually, redevelopment takes place until there is a total of 1500 dwellings occupied by 4500 people. The demands for road space, school spaces, open space and shopping facilities produced by those extra 3000 people are likely to make complete nonsense of any planning proposals prepared on the assumption that only 1500 people would need to be catered for.

The point is so obvious that one would think that any government of whatever political complexion would understand and act in accordance with it, but none seems to and nor do most councils; Westminster is not deafened by the cries of indignant councillors protesting against stupid DoE housing density policy.

As against this, there is of course much zealous preservation of areas of housing of marked quality, especially in conservation areas, both on the part of councils and the DoE. But it is hard to find any clear indication of consistency of policy even in this regard. Earlier I put what might be regarded as an 'egalitarian' case for varied housing densities, including some low density housing. It is equally possible to put a case from a completely different point of view. Are there to be no areas of low density housing in which people can live in the reasonable expectation that the very considerable benefits of low density will continue to be enjoyed? After all, if they bought recently they will have paid enormous sums for these advantages. Yet it sometimes seems as if anybody in such an area who has a bigger garden than he wants will have a good chance of getting permission to build a house on the unwanted part. At a point well below the extreme of the case postulated a little earlier, the whole character and 'ambience' of an area is changed if the number of houses in it is greatly increased. An environment in which vegetation used to predominate becomes one in which buildings predominate, lightly trafficked roads become heavily trafficked roads, rubbish, previously hardly ever seen, becomes all too visible and so on. Of course there are a good many such areas in which the arguments in favour of redevelopment and higher density are irresistible, but this ought to be done as the result of a deliberate, well-considered policy, not by a series of unhappy accidents.

There are some areas of housing where there can be no definite privacy objection to doubling or trebling the numbers of houses, simply a general objection to having more people in an area than roads and public facilities and services can reasonably deal with. This is most especially so in the all too numerous areas of low density housing which are neither in nor spatially related to a town or village and for which the very best policy would be demolition, not sub-division! Figures 14.8 and 14.9 illustrate some points about density increase. Most of the arguments which have been rehearsed in the last few pages of course apply equally to conversion of single family houses into two or more flats, but this leads us, necessarily, to a brief discussion of house types.

House types

There is still a little confusion in some quarters about the definitions of different types of dwellings, so it may be helpful to say that my understanding, shared I think by most people, is that a house is a dwelling which has its own inde-pendent access to the ground, indeed some of its accommodation at ground level, and which though it may be joined to other dwellings on one or both sides has no other dwelling below it and only occasionally (in the quite rare case of two-storey houses with a storey of flats above them) has another dwelling immediately above it. Houses nearly always have *some* outdoor space used and enjoyed exclusively by their inhabitants. Flats, on the contrary, do not necess-arily have any direct access to the ground, may have other dwellings above and below them as well as one each side and do not necessarily or even usually have any outdoor space exclusively enjoyed by the residents of a particular flat.

'Maisonette' has two distinct and confusing meanings. One kind of maison-

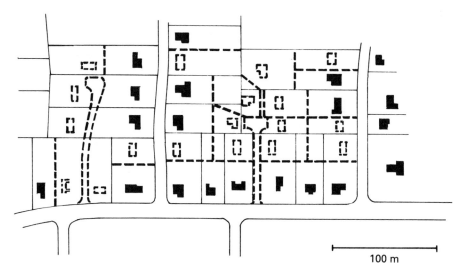

Fig. 14.8 Planned increase of density. If a plan like this exists, development can be allowed to take place bit by bit in accordance with it, without any harm.

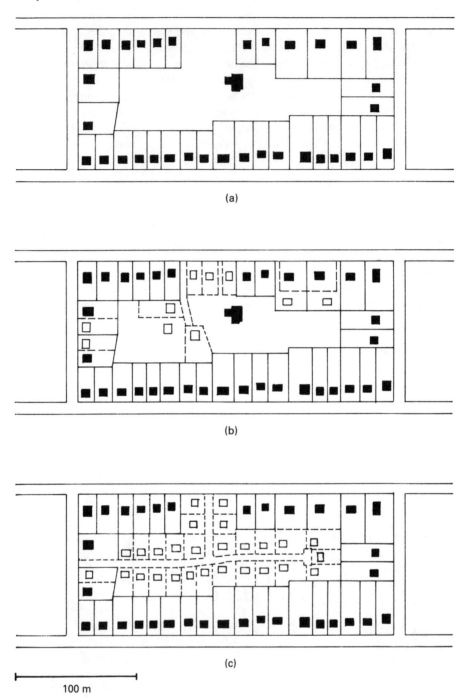

Fig. 14.9 Planned and unplanned increases of density: (a) The site as existing; (b) Wasteful, unplanned piecemeal development; (c) Economical planned development.

ette is simply a flat which has accommodation on two floors rather than one, while the other kind of maisonette is simply a pair of semi-detached houses divided into four dwellings instead of two, completely different from the first because each dwelling is on one floor only.

A detached house is a house which is not joined to other dwellings on any of its four sides; a semi-detached house is one which is joined to another dwelling on one of its sides; and a terrace house is a house which, except in the case of the end houses of a terrace, is joined to another dwelling on two sides.

Density, rather confusingly, may be measured in one of the following ways.

Dwellings per hectare is a good, straightforward direct measure of density if the dwellings are houses, but may not mean very much if they are in the form of twenty-storey blocks of flats.

Habitable rooms per hectare is another good and direct measure, better in some ways than dwellings per hectare, both because it takes account of different sizes of dwellings (twenty-five small bungalows per hectare is very different from twenty-five mansions per hectare) and because it relates better, if the calculation is made sensibly and cautiously, to persons per hectare than does dwellings per hectare. Unfortunately it has always had one rather serious disadvantage, namely that the number of habitable rooms per hectare can be varied substantially without getting planning permission by either inserting partitions to increase the number of rooms or by removing them to decrease the number of rooms. Further, with the general use of central heating and the increased use of 'open plan' house designs, the concept of the habitable room has become rather hazy.

Persons per hectare is an important measure. Dwellings per hectare and habitable rooms per hectare, are measures of building intensity, though very rough ones, and so rather vaguely related to 'amenity'. Persons per hectare is much more definite; it gives the essential information needed to work out needs for provision of road space, parking, schools, open spaces, etc. It has one great disadvantage; it is a prophecy, not a fact. Short of a breach of overcrowding law there is no control at all over how many or how few people occupy a given dwelling. For all that it is far from impossible for reliable prophecies to be made by informed people using sensible methods.

Habitable floor space per hectare (though rarely used), is, in my opinion, the best method of measuring and prescribing residential density, in combination with dwellings per hectare. It gets over the difficulty of changes caused by insertion or removal of partitions and so provides a more reliable index from which to calculate probable population density. If the measurement and prescription include dwellings per hectare, then not only do predictions of population density become much more accurate, but the prescribed density, as a 'builders' brief', is sensible, informative and usable. Habitable floor space may roughly be defined as all the floor space in a dwelling except for that taken up by hallways, passages, bathrooms and lavatories and also in some cases by kitchens too small to be used for anything except cooking and washing up. Bed spaces per hectare, sometimes used as a measure, is useless. One family's living room is another's bedroom.

Gross density and net density also cause some confusion. Gross density can pretty well be ignored for development control purposes. It is simply the total number of people living or expected to live in an area divided by the total area in which they live, including schools, open space, shops, etc. Net residential density, however, is simply the amount of accommodation or number of persons divided by the amount of land occupied by buildings, gardens and roads.

Density, and the ways in which it may be measured and the uses to which the measurements may be put, is a minefield for the uninitiated. More than with almost any other aspect of town planning appeals it is necessary, in preparing evidence, to make sure that one is saying exactly what one means and to say it with the utmost clarity, and, under cross-examination, to insist that questions are worded with sufficient clarity and precision for an accurate and reliable answer to be given. Comparatively few advocates have any clear idea of what they are talking about in relation to housing density; if they are allowed to blunder along in imprecision they may do far more harm to your case than they deserve to be able to do. Once more I have to draw attention to *Town Planning Made Plain*, in which in various places housing density is explained as clearly as I can, especially on pages 12 to 19 inclusive.

Very obviously, some types of dwellings suit many different kinds of families (the two-storey, three-bedroom semi with a sizeable garden provides reasonable satisfaction and comfort for a very large number). Some types suit a small proportion of families extremely well but do not suit the rest at all (flats in tall blocks are a good example of this, and they have been built in numbers vastly exceeding the families suited by them). Large houses with large gardens suit large families but are usually only available for the well-to-do. Small houses with large gardens suit quite a lot of families. They are so hard to find for sale that one suspects that demand greatly exceeds supply.

Pretty obviously, an enlightened and humane planning policy would do its best to ensure a mix of dwellings as well matched as possible to the inevitably varying demand for them. As mentioned earlier, good planning authorities used to try to do this, but seem to have abandoned or to have been induced to abandon the attempt. In consequence there is a mis-match between housing demand and housing supply, dissatisfaction with which finds expression in planning appeals. There are, quite evidently, extensive housing areas in which there are far more flats than there is a real demand for flats. This means that quite a lot of families who would rather have a house and garden are forced to live in a flat, though this wish can hardly find expression in planning appeals. What does find expression there is a result of the equally common almost complete lack of flats in many areas. This produces a considerable number of families who have no wish at all for a house and garden but have to accept one, with consequent dissatisfaction to themselves and often with detriment to the appearance of the locality because of neglect of the garden. However, in this case, strong attempts are often made to make supply catch up with demand by making applications to convert houses to flats. Some of these are resisted.

There can seldom be a case for refusing permission for the conversion of an ordinary three-bedroom, five-habitable-room house into two flats. Physically, the conversion is easy; the effect on neighbours is hardly likely to be appreciable. Because of the need to produce an extra bathroom, lavatory and kitchen some habitable space will be lost, and it may well be that the only town planning effect of the conversion will be that four people live where only two lived before. It may also be that two cars live where only one lived before. In an ordinary area of suburban semis, it is not likely that this will have any harmful traffic effect. Nevertheless the immediate density is doubled, in terms of population, with each such conversion; multiply that a few hundred times over fifty hectares and the dire results about overstraining facilities and services mentioned earlier would become apparent. It is often in rather vague recognition of these facts that applications for flat conversions are refused, but without the specific kind of density policy needed to justify refusal.

It may be worth mentioning the question of room sizes. Some councils have refused applications for housing on the ground that the room sizes proposed were not large enough. It was usually said that they did not comply with 'Parker-Morris standards'. In paragraph 14 of Annex A of circular 22 of 1980 the DoE come down rather heavily against this. They bring in the 'customer negotiation' argument. Once more, in the absence of a strong, rational, tightly operated density and associated planning control policy, there is little one can say. If people are willing to buy houses with very small rooms, who are the council to forbid it? A 'common-sense' argument in simplistic supply and demand terms; but erroneous if one thinks of housing as social capital for which government at its various levels has responsibility, rather than as goods which can be sold like a pound of plums.

Layout

By layout one means the way in which, in a housing area, the buildings, open areas, plot boundaries, roads and footpaths are arranged in relation to each other. The valid criteria in assessing the merits of a layout are the variety of house types, the convenience and variety of plot shapes, privacy and the levels of safety, freedom from traffic congestion, and appearance which are achieved. Obviously, the whole range of these criteria does not apply to a very small area of housing. To these should be added the question of economy. This may, surprisingly, not be a matter of much concern to a developer. Many developers and their advisers seem little aware of the money they spend on uneconomical layouts in a way which does not produce commensurate benefits. This is not a matter about which councils worry, or perhaps should worry. However, it is a matter for public concern if roads which eventually will have to be maintained by the public are unnecessarily long or wide, and if the amount or arrangement of incidental open space, which will also have to be publicly maintained, is inappropriate.

Extensive areas of new housing really ought to pose no problems. Many councils sensibly and justifiably point out to developers that they will save time, trouble and money by employing a competent designer rather than an incompetent one whose efforts are likely to be refused planning permission and to be rejected on appeal, but all areas of housing of peculiar shape or closely intertwined with existing development are likely to pose substantial problems, especially those relating to privacy and access.

Access

As regards access there is no better guide than *Roads in Urban Areas* as, subsequently to its first publication, amended and metricised. The essentials to bear in mind in the access aspect of a housing layout are that, though the carriageways of roads should not be wider than is necessary for them to carry without obstruction the traffic they are likely to need to carry, at the very least no carriageway should be too narrow to allow two large vehicles to pass each other. Straight lengths should not be so long as to encourage excessive speed (physical impediments are better than any legal restrictions). Under no circumstances whatever is a direct crossroads permissible. Adequate sight lines must be arranged at every road junction. Accesses to the existing road system must be so arranged that the traffic likely to be thrown on them will not produce traffic flows greater than those deemed acceptable in *Roads in Urban Areas*.

This is not the place to go into a mass of technical detail. In general it is unwise for councils to permit accesses which would violate any of the principles just

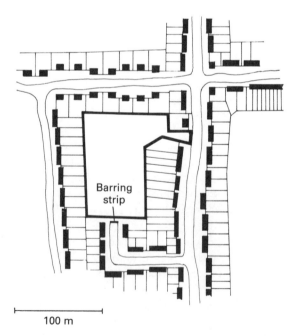

100 m

Fig. 14.10 A 'barring' strip threatens to frustrate development. The alternative access is too narrow to be ideal but its use is preferable to losing the land for housing purposes.

suggested. Equally, however, they should not seek standards which are unnecessary and may be unattainable. Figures 14.10 and 14.11 are examples where, in different ways, councils tried to do this. In the case of Fig. 14.10 an adjoining developer used the wholly disreputable device of the 'barring strip', i.e. stopping a road just short of an ownership boundary in order to hold an adjoining owner to ransom, to frustrate what would have been a natural and appropriate housing layout. What the council should have done was to have sought and used compulsory powers to thwart him. I do not know whether in fact it would have been feasible for the council to have acquired the barring strip itself – i.e. a bit of land about seven metres by two metres – but it would have cost them very little on any rational valuation basis. Failing that, however, the alternative access was quite acceptable. Instead, they supported villainy by refusing planning permission on the grounds of bad layout. Fortunately they lost on appeal.

In the case of Fig. 14.11, already referred to with indignation in Chapter 11, the council, if they thought the matter through at all, were seeking to impose standards far above the norm. Unfortunately, because of a bad inspector, they succeeded.

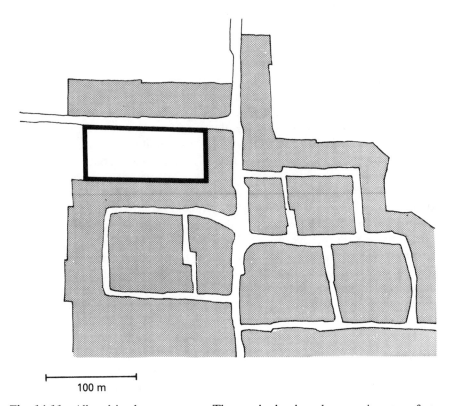

100 m

Fig. 14.11 Alleged inadequate access. The nearby local road system is not perfect for modern traffic purposes but the proposed development could not conceivably overstrain the capacities of the various junctions within it which are the crucial points where congestion might occur.

In the case of many applications for individual houses or small groups of houses, however, the impossibility of providing adequate and safe road access is completely damning. Even if a site is on all other grounds entirely suitable, very bad access is by itself a sufficient reason for refusal. In the past few years I have been surprised by the large number of sites for single houses or small groups of houses which I have seen which, even though they may have been refused permission by the council on entirely different grounds, had unacceptably bad access. I think the explanation is that most of the land indisputably suitable for housing in terms of location in this country has been used up and that much of what remains is at least temporarily disqualified by bad access.

If urban and village development is to remain compact, something will have to be done about this. It would be perfectly rational and valid in some cases to argue that there is a great deal of existing development fronting a road and that conditions are already highly unsatisfactory for existing residents, so that a new application should serve as the impetus to force radical improvement of the road. It is difficult to think that such an argument would actually succeed at a particular appeal, but, cumulatively applied over some years, success might well be achieved by persuading the council, rather than an inspector, of its force.

Parking

Changing circumstances and habits have not been sufficiently appreciated and incorporated in the development control practice of many councils. It used to be assumed that every car needed a garage, while until about 1960 vehicles parked on the road at night had to be illuminated by sidelights and rear lights, with a consequent drain on batteries which they could hardly survive. Moreover, car ownership was quite low in areas of terrace housing. So most long-term parking in residential areas was in garages, or at least off the road, blocks of garages, at the rate of about one garage to four houses, being provided in local authority housing estates. There was no problem in most areas.

With freedom to park overnight without lights, car bodywork becoming, or assumed by owners to have become more resistant to weather, car ownership becoming higher in areas of terrace housing, more new terrace housing being built and carriageways of roads becoming generally rather narrower, this has changed. It is now quite common to find residential roads where there are no garages, the house plots are far too narrow to provide enough kerb space for one parked car plus manoeuvring distance per house and the carriageway is not wide enough to accommodate two lines of parked vehicles and two vehicles moving in opposite directions. This is a nuisance; it is customarily somewhat ameliorated by the fact that, often, car ownership does not amount to one car per house and by cars being parked illegally but fairly harmlessly, with their nearside wheels on the footpath.

There is not much that can be done about it in most existing residential areas. In new housing areas councils often prescribe that the layout shall provide for two off-street parking spaces per house. This will probably ensure that vehicles moving along the street in opposite directions can pass each other, but vehicles may often have difficulty getting into and, much worse, out of the off-street parking spaces because of vehicles parked in their way on the street; nevertheless, a tolerable solution. What is useless and indeed harmful, is to refuse permission for one or two houses sought to be nudged into an existing layout, because it is not physically possible for two off-street parking spaces per house to be provided. To do this, in the absence of a comprehensive redevelopment plan does no good (a drop in the ocean) and may prevent creation of a splendid house for a family (possibly a non-car-owning family, though that cannot be ensured).

'Infilling', 'rounding off' and 'back land'

These are expressions which confuse and mislead and which need some analysis.

Infilling is generally taken to mean development of lengths of frontage left vacant in a row of existing houses, the vacant gaps being short in relation to the total length of development. That development of such gaps would constitute infilling and therefore be permissible, even though in that particular location a larger amount of development would not be, is often used as an argument at appeals. I think it is usually a bad argument. If development is wrongly placed then only harm can result from adding to it, however small the addition and the harm. On the other hand, although two wrongs do not make a right, the infilling argument may sometimes produce the right result for the wrong reasons in cases where some dogmatic and unjustified restraint has been placed upon the reasonable growth and renewal of a village. In such cases it is the unreasonableness of the policy which should lead to success rather than the infilling argument.

Some councils have fairly elaborate definitions of what is acceptable infilling and what is not, in terms of a maximum acceptable gap in development to be regarded as infilling, or the proportion of open frontage compared with developed frontage. I do not think these are useful. Development is either reasonable or not reasonable, and devices like this tend simply to discourage careful and sensible analysis, including items such as the effects of varying levels upon the appearance of a proposed development.

Rounding off is rather different. Here, one is apt to be talking of ten or a dozen houses rather than one or two houses. In such cases there may well be a good argument for completion on the grounds that development nearby, in its existing state, is visually incomplete and its appearance would be improved by the rounding off. It may also be argued, rather more remotely but quite validly, that costly roads and services have been provided which are not being fully used. Better a dozen houses which use an existing road, existing sewers and water mains, etc., than place them elsewhere with the need to build a new road, etc.

Back land is something else again. Literally all land behind existing road frontage is back land and so if no back land were developed, all development would be ribbon development. The somewhat pejorative meaning attached to back land, therefore, can only properly be attached in rather special cases. Unfortunately, as with green belts, though to a far less extent, the allegation that a proposed development would be back land development is very often thrown around by councils as a sort of bogey term. Real back land development, in the genuinely pejorative sense, is that shown in Fig. 14.9(b), where accesses are thrust between existing houses in a low density area in an uncoordinated way. In cases such as this there is real loss of useful building land. The original houses may date back to the nineteenth century and be near the end of their lives; the gardens may be much longer than most people want and, surprisingly, the location may be quite near a town centre. In these circumstances, redevelopment at a substantially higher density is well justified. But of course it needs to be coordinated development and every bit of uncoordinated back land development makes this progressively harder and harder to achieve.

The worst kind of development of this type is what is known as tandem development, where a new house is built behind an existing house and the driveway of the existing house is continued past it, so that it is shared as an access by the new house. There is then often a combination of inadequate privacy for the two houses to be created, inadequate access and frustration of any chance of proper redevelopment of the road block as a whole. Several times, in determining appeals, I have sought to console unsuccessful appellants by indicating that they had been saved from producing two unsatisfactory houses where one satisfactory house now stands.

Councils do not exactly fall over themselves to produce the street block redevelopment plans needed, though they ought to be keen to do so. But where there is a genuine case for splitting up existing house sites, there is no need to wait for such plans. An application accompanied by an indication of how the proposed sub-division would fit in with an ultimate coordinated replanning (as might have been done in the cases shown in Figs. 14.8 and 14.9) ought to bring planning permission provided that what is proposed does not blatantly favour the present applicant at the expense of future applicants. Figure 14.12 is a very odd special case. Permission was refused on the grounds that the proposal might prejudice proper redevelopment of a wider area. But there was no prospect of such redevelopment.

Where a layout has been carefully prepared so as to give the benefit of particular views to houses within it, and when, particularly, such houses have been bought in the knowledge of the existence of that layout, it may be altogether unreasonable to give permission for infilling which would spoil the whole conception. Figure 14.13 exemplifies this well. The East Anglian appellant who lost this appeal expressed himself as much aggrieved, but he deserved to lose, and, if he had won, his neighbours would have had much more reason to be aggrieved. Figure 14.14 is apparently similar, but in this case the appeal was lost because the apparent village was not really a village at all, but a piece of bogus sporadic rural development whose inhabitants deserved no special consideration. The reason for dismissal of the appeal was that the proposed development would spoil a fine view for users of the road and that there was no reason to have further development there anyway.

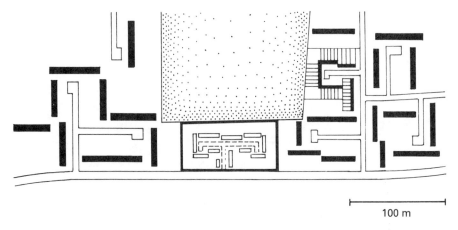

Fig. 14.12 A proposal allegedly prejudicial to satisfactory comprehensive redevelopment. But the existing development to the left is massive and has a probable further life of a century or more. That to the right is housing with a similar expectation of life. At the top is a famous football ground.

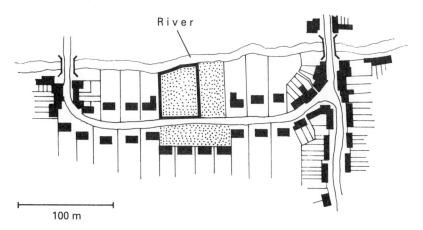

Fig. 14.13 Proposed development which would certainly ruin a view. A carefully planned layout provides a river view from many houses.

Privacy

This is a subject in respect of which I believe there is great need for specific and rationally defensible standards to be worked out. As between neighbouring houses, privacy cuts both ways. One wants to be protected from unwelcome sights, sounds, smells, etc, produced by neighbours, yet feel able to live freely without fearing that one may oneself be producing sights, sounds, smells, etc., which will be unwelcome to neighbours. This is, of course, very subjective; What bothers one person may not bother another at all. The best that a public

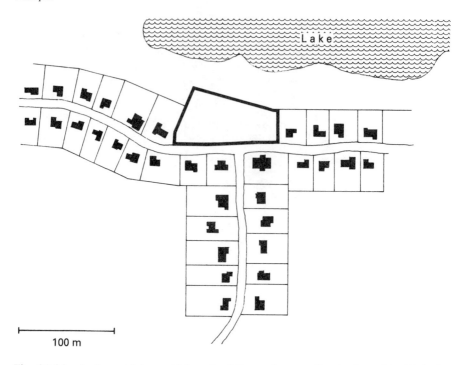

Fig. 14.14 A view which would be ruined for road users. On the face of it this looks like reasonable infilling, but the housing is without merit and ought not to be there, and there is a fine view to the lake and beyond from the road.

body exercising development control can hope to do is to satisfy persons of normal sensibilities; it cannot hope to cater for the exceptionally sensitive. It is therefore necessary to think out carefully and express as precisely as possible, the physical conditions which are thought to meet that requirement. Once more I must refer the reader to *Town Planning Made Plain*, especially pages 15 to 19 inclusive. Reference is made there to the Essex County Council's *A Design Guide for Residential Areas* which probably comes as close as anything yet produced to a satisfactory privacy code, though, as I make clear, I do not think it comes nearly close enough. It seems fairly clear that a distance of the order of a cricket pitch, 70 ft, 21 metres or whatever mode of expression evokes the most vivid image, is the minimum distance from which English people of average sensibility are happy to be scrutinised, i.e. from the windows of houses opposite or from the common back garden fence. Note that this excludes scrutiny from the street, which is passing scrutiny, not scrutiny at length, and therefore can readily be tolerated from a shorter distance.

Smaller distances than this can be tolerated, subject to certain safeguards: in front and behind clerestory windows (that is, windows set with their sills above eye-level rather than at the ordinary height) obviously diminish scrutiny and give a feeling of privacy to the potential scrutinee. They ought to be provided where windows have to be placed at less than the critical distance and face habitable windows of other houses. Windows at the side, which ought to be avoided where possible, and which are usually very much closer than the critical distance, also need to be clerestory windows; if this is impracticable, obscured glazing should be used. Where back gardens have to be appreciably shorter than the critical length the difficulty can be partially rectified by the erection of a fence or wall extending to above standing eye-level. This obviates overlooking from the garden behind, but of course does little or nothing to cut down noise from the backing garden. Figure 14.15 illustrates some of these points.

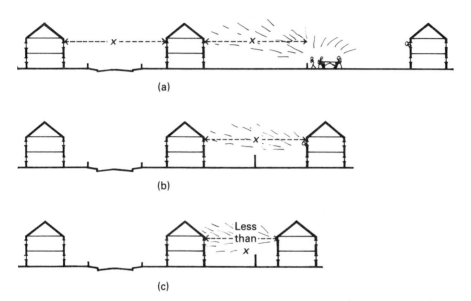

Fig. 14.15   Privacy. (a) The 'x' distance (about 21 m, 70 ft) maintained at front, window to window, and at back, back fence to window. Satisfactory. (b) 'x' maintained window to window, but not from fence to window; high fence needed. (c) Reduction below 'x' of window to window distance; clerestory windows needed.

Evidently, the higher a building that overlooks one's house, the greater the number of overlooking windows and the greater the feeling of being overlooked. Account needs to be taken of this.

Near where I recently lived there is a fifteen-storey tower block of flats directly looking towards the house from about 100 metres, but one is quite unaware of being overlooked. If it were a *long* block of the same height the feeling would be very different. Privacy requirements cannot be expressed adequately in a mechanical code. Having mentioned my own house it is interesting to reflect that the houses behind it are appreciably closer than the critical distance, and although I was not personally aware of being tiresomely overlooked from them, I did feel constrained in looking out towards them in case I gave their occupants a sense of being spied upon.

Numerous planning appeals turn, or ought to turn, upon whether proposed development will impose unreasonable loss of privacy upon neighbours. I think that, in most cases, testing the proposal in the light of the foregoing paragraphs will give a reasonably clear answer as to whether the proposal is acceptable or not. However, there are exceptions. They arise especially often with house extensions projecting either in front of or, much more often, behind existing houses. In very few cases in ordinary housing areas do these extensions actually diminish the daylight received by neighbours below a fully acceptable level, but they may very appreciably reduce the amount of sunlight received, not only in the house but in the garden and they may severely reduce the extent of outlook from windows.

This is a different matter from 'buying the view'. People can reasonably expect, in ordinary houses, not to have to look at a blank wall a few feet away which substantially reduces the amount of sky visible, even though there is plenty of sky left to provide the necessary daylight. A good deal depends upon orientation. (See Fig. 14.16.) If part of the northern side of one's garden is adjoined by the wall of a house extension it might often be something of an advantage, since it will cut out no sunlight but may cut out cold winds. On the southern side the position would be quite different, and so it would be on the eastern and western sides, where sunlight will be coming from a low angle and quite a low obstruction will exclude much more sunlight than it would if it were on the southern side.

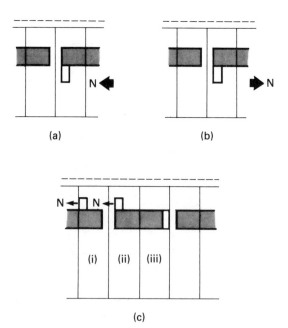

Fig. 14.16 House extensions. (a) Loss of sunlight to neighbour on left. (b) No loss to neighbour. (c) Some orientations, (i) and (ii), impose loss of sun on neighbour's front garden but actually improve privacy. In all cases the impact of two-storey extensions is much greater than with a single storey. Any side windows near boundaries should be clerestory, especially in the case of (c) (iii).

146

Apart from all these fairly definite factors, difficult though it may be to assess them accurately enough to be able to say with confidence whether they are sufficiently detrimental to neighbours to be fatal to the proposal, there is the unquantifiable matter of the development having what is frequently called by inspectors an 'overbearing' effect. This can be very real. I lived for a month in a house in Montevideo immediately adjoining the rear boundary of the modest garden of which was a fifteen-storey office block. The relevant elevation was blank, there was no serious diminution of light or sunshine or, of course, loss of privacy, but it was certainly overbearing.

In dealing with matters such as this, two tests may be useful and incorporated in the evidence of either side at appeal. The first may be expressed as 'Would I as an ordinary person of normal but not excessive sensibility, mind this?' The answer to that question, amplified by sensible if unquantifiable reasons, may well provide a convincing answer. The second is to ask: 'If this proposal were put forward as part of an original layout and one were considering whether that layout should be given planning permission, would one regard it as acceptable?' That too may give a useful answer, though there has to be some modification. If the existing layout is peculiar and unsatisfactory it may be necessary to be more tolerant about modifications than one would otherwise be.

No such tolerance was needed in the case shown in Fig. 14.17, where the

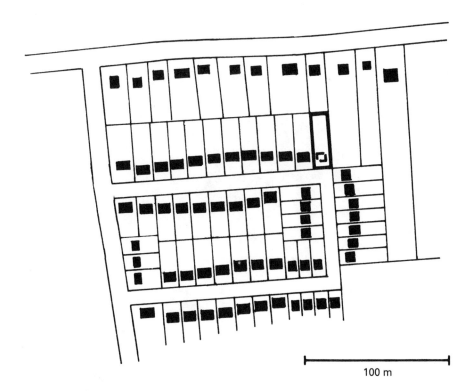

100 m

Fig. 14.17 Refusal of permission for completion of layout

147

'infilling' which had been refused was totally consistent with a satisfactory original layout and was probably originally drawn in on that layout, only to be deleted when the land concerned could not be acquired.

The question of appearance is important in relation to infilling, rounding off and house extensions. 'A cramped appearance' is an expression often used by inspectors in decision letters, and it is a good one. Many proposals for such development may not be disqualified on any of the grounds discussed in the last few paragraphs but inevitably give the effect of being uncomfortably squeezed in. In these cases too the test of whether the proposal would have been acceptable as part of an original layout may be useful. (See Fig. 14.18.)

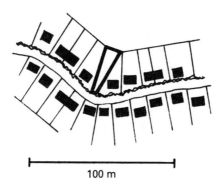

100 m

Fig. 14.18 'Cramped' development; a house here would look very uncomfortable however well designed.

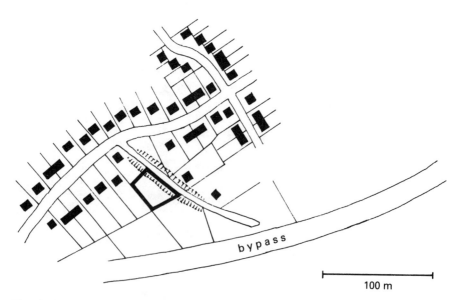

bypass

100 m

Fig. 14.19 This application for a house was refused unreasonably on the grounds that the site was not allocated for development; it ought to have been refused because of the quite inadequate road access, likely to become blocked frequently.

Finally, a curious example of a council doing the right thing for the wrong reason. (See Fig. 14.19.) The extraordinary reason given for refusal was that the appeal site was not in an area allocated for development. The area was entirely suitable for development, but the very narrow access road, in a deep cutting, was quite inadequate.

15

Business

The question 'Is it development?' often arises in relation to changes of use to or within a business use. A large proportion of business uses are not in fact listed in the Use Classes Order but are *sui generis* – uses on their own. A change of any business use from or to one of these will, therefore, provided it is a *material* change of use, need planning permission. (Permission is never needed for a change that is not material: it is not development.)

Difficulties arise in 3(3) of the order from the words 'A use which is ordinarily incidental to and included in any use specified in the Schedule to this Order (i.e. the list of use classes) is not excluded from that use as an incident thereto merely by reason of its specification in the said Schedule as a separate use'. There can be great argument about whether something is 'ordinarily incidental to'. What does 'ordinarily' means and how substantial can something be and yet remain 'incidental to' something else?

Confusion is caused by the inclusion in the definition of 'shop' in 2(2) of the words ' . . . or for any other purpose appropriate to a shopping area'. One must presumably conclude that uses similar to (*not* incidental to) a shop, and certainly appropriate to a shopping area are nevertheless excluded from this helpful generality if they are specifically defined as something else elsewhere in the order. Examples are banks, which are included in the definition of 'office', and launderettes, betting offices, restaurants, and pubs. One would think that since post offices (excluding post offices mainly used as sorting offices) are included in the definition of 'shop', presumably as buildings 'used for the carrying on of any retail trade or retail business wherein the primary purpose is the selling of goods by retail' a bank would similarly qualify. Also, it is hard to know what goods a building used 'for the reception of goods to be washed, cleaned or repaired' (included in the definition of 'shop') sells by retail. These are defects which need to be remedied.

One must not forget that not even all shops, proper, are given exemption from the need to obtain planning permission for changes of use within the shop class. Change from an ordinary shop to a shop for the sale of hot food, tripe, pet animals or birds, cats' meat or motor vehicles needs permission (though not a change from one of these back to an ordinary shop).

In order to fight planning appeals in this strange area of confusion it is useful to try to keep in mind the basic idea behind the Use Classes Order. This, I think, was to list a range of 'high street' activities within which the interplay of demand and supply should be allowed to determine provision of facilities and services without the need for innumerable applications for planning permission (or the risk of over-zealous Enforcement Notices) in respect of quite minor changes. Perhaps, also, it was to prevent councils trying to act in the role of 'public estate agents', trying to determine that there should be so many grocers, so many drapers, so many butchers, etc., in a particular shopping area: a role for which councils are unsuited for several reasons. This flexibility, however, obviously had to be limited at least a little to avoid the springing up of 'unneighbourly uses' or worse, concentrations of unneighbourly uses likely to damage the usefulness and prosperity of a shopping area. Hence (though there may have been confusion of thought in this) selection of some kinds of 'nasty' shops which had to have planning permission even if an 'ordinary' shop were already there and, in the 1960s, the inclusion in the 'nasty' list of shops for the sale of motor vehicles. At that time some shopping centres were becoming swamped by huge frontages of glittering showroom windows, enclosing glittering motor cars, to the evident detriment of the compactness of shopping areas and diminution of the supply of ordinary shops. There was no doubt about the reasonableness of that particular provision. The *Encyclopedia of Planning Law and Practice*, pp. 35234–8, gives much useful information about the order.

Apart from confusion, many applications within shopping areas are turned down for very flimsy reasons. What should councils really be trying to do in controlling business uses? I suggest that:

1. They should be concerned to secure the establishment and continuance of business areas of appropriate size in appropriate locations, a hierarchy of service centres, to ensure that everyone has every service as close to him as is economically practicable in terms of the minimum catchment populations needed if various facilities and services are to operate successfully.
2. The number of such centres should be as small as is consistent with the above requirements, since every business has *some* adverse effects on the amenities of adjoining dwellings.
3. Adequate road access to each centre needs to be constructed with the greatest possible speed in accordance with a detailed, rational road plan, and sufficient parking provided. The intensity of the development permitted should be related to road, pedestrian and parking capacities.
4. Every centre should be converted as fully and rapidly as possible to a pedestrian precinct.
5. Each centre should be as compact as possible in order to minimise its 'perimeter of nuisance'.
6. Within each centre, similar and compatible uses should be juxtaposed and

incompatible uses segregated. Uses likely to be tiresome to nearby residents should be separated from housing as much as is practicable, i.e. in simple terms, put in the middle of the area rather than at or near its edges.

7. Development control is about land and its use, not about morality or people's behaviour or the encouragement of socially desirable uses and the discouragement of 'undesirable' uses. Nor is it about either the encouragement or discouragement of competition.

8. People who *live* within a business centre cannot expect as high a standard of privacy or freedom from noise as those who live elsewhere.

That seems to me to be a set of assumptions which can appropriately underlie and be used to support the detailed arguments advanced on either side at a planning appeal. Unfortunately, too many appeals are fought on details alone, without reference to underlying assumptions.

Many of the bigger central area redevelopment schemes carried out have been 'partnership' efforts between councils and developers and have not been the subject of refusals of planning permission; it is in relation to these major developments that considerations of appropriate intensity of development in terms of the adequacy of the road system and parking provision and the creation of pedestrian precincts are most likely to arise. The 'hierarchy of service centres' aspect should of course have been dealt with long before by county, town and supplementary town maps and, later, by structure and local plans, but many centres have not been planned with these considerations in mind, or, even if they have been in mind, not dealt with in sufficient detail. The creation of a minor group of shops, or, because of the lack of any such planned groups, a 'spot' business use such as an isolated shop or pub becomes the subject of appeal when the issue should have been put beyond dispute by allocation in a plan.

The importance to a council of having sensible detailed plans, of whatever status, available to back their arguments at appeals must be stressed. Two examples (see Figs. 15.1 and 15.2), show how in the one case the availability of such a plan led to a council winning an appeal which otherwise it might very easily have lost, and in the other case how, in the absence of a plan, the council could hardly hope to win. In that case, perhaps, a plan might not have led them to victory but instead might have demonstrated to them that they had no case and might have induced them to give planning permission and not waste money on an appeal. Propositions 5, 6, 7 and 8 in the above list are all likely to be debated very frequently at appeals, either directly or by implication.

Before proceeding further, one should dispose of the issue of 'regional' or 'out of town' shopping centres, sometimes associated with the term 'hypermarket'. How can there be a case for such a development unless it is to form the nucleus of the town centre of a new town? The crucial thing about retail services is that they should be as close to their customers as possible; putting a shopping centre on a 'green field' site puts it as far as possible from its customers. What trade can it hope to draw, except at the expense of existing town centres? And if existing town centres in the locality are inadequate in some way, why not enlarge or otherwise improve them rather than allow what can only be an

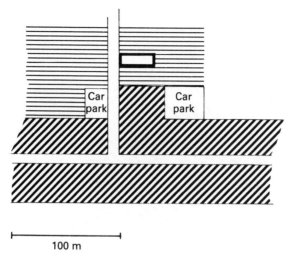

100 m

Fig. 15.1 Central area 'zoning' justifies a refusal for a shop in an office zone.

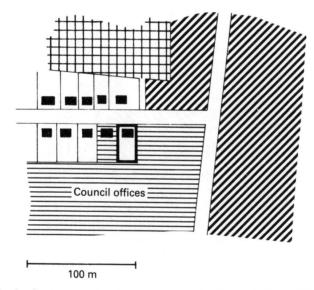

100 m

Fig. 15.2 Lack of a town centre plan renders a refusal meaningless. Why should this house not be converted to offices?

absurd and damaging piece of anti-planning?

A particular problem is central area 'creep'. (See Figs 15.3 and 15.4.) Town centres for which there is no clear, definite plan often have indefinite edges, and uses appropriate to a town centre often then 'bleed' outwards from them. Even good town centre plans often leave, untouched, draggles of shopping and similar uses outside the ring road that surrounds the centre, in the hope that these will

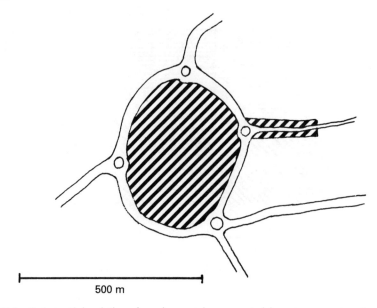

500 m

Fig. 15.3 Substantial existing shopping not incorporated in a town centre plan, i.e. left outside the inner ring road

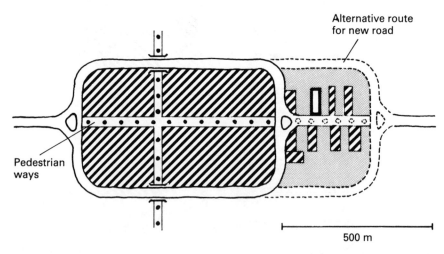

Alternative route for new road

Pedestrian ways

500 m

Fig. 15.4 Similar to Fig. 15.3, but easily remedied in this case by changing the route of the inner ring road

go away, or because of reluctance to pay the compensation involved in extinguishing them. But these fringes must, logically, either be brought within the planned town centre or eliminated. Few places are more undesirable, by attracting excessive parking and traffic and encouraging cumulative urban blight, than are these classic 'areas of transition and decay' of urban geographers.

It may be possible, though it will certainly be difficult, to win an appeal against refusal of permission for a shop or other business proposal in such areas by demonstrating that the best practicable central area plan could and should conveniently and economically have embraced the appeal site (see Fig. 15.4).

The interests of people who live in or near a business area obviously need to be protected, but reason and experience show that there is a limit to the extent to which protection is practicable and also that a balance needs to be struck. It is in many ways advantageous to live near shops (I wrote that sentence only three minutes ago and am now opening a packet of cigarettes which I have meanwhile bought at the local shopping centre). With that advantage, almost inevitably, except when very good and detailed planning has actually been carried out, go disadvantages: excessive movement and parking of vehicles, noise, rubbish. One has to choose, if one has a choice, and one is entitled to anticipate that the local council will not allow a shopping centre to bleed outwards to the further disadvantage of nearby residents.

The case of people who live actually within a business area, not just close to it, is rather different. The needs of the business area have to come first, or it will be of little use as a business area. If they did not and it therefore declined, it would almost certainly become even less attractive than before to people living within it. A further distinction needs to be made between residential buildings which have ground floor residential accommodation and those which are simply flats over shops or other business uses.

In the former case, if a plan has made appropriate land use allocations, the owners will probably make a fortune before long by conversion of the premises to business use and any tenants will be rehoused; rationally, the current residential use should be ignored for town planning purposes. But if so much land has been allocated for business purposes that there is little prospect of conversion to business use of residential buildings within the area, an error has been made which can only be put right by amending the plan, not just by means of appeal decisions, though, as noted earlier, appellants may assist and hasten the process by putting forward proposals as part of their case.

Nevertheless, there are exceptions to the above. Figure 15.5 shows one. Here, in a south coast resort, owners of a row of apartment houses very understandably joined the council in objecting to the conversion of one of a row of shops on the opposite side of the street to an indoor games centre and won at appeal. In this case, I think, the apartment houses were a sufficiently large element for a potentially very tiresome business use to be prevented from coming close to them. There were parts of the central area where that objection would not have applied.

Dwellings above business premises in a business area are, I think, in quite a different situation. In their case, the interests of the business area must clearly prevail: the dwellings are the intruders, not the business. They are inherently unsatisfactory dwellings. They may be suitable for students or others who find it attractive to live very close to the glittering lights, but for most people for most of the time they are not much use. They will be noisier, messier, subject to unwanted bright lights late at night, will very likely have awkward access and

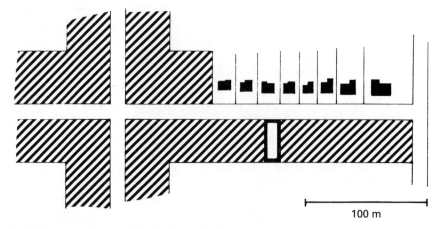

Fig. 15.5 An unreasonable site for an indoor games centre

will not have their own outdoor space or exclusive parking area. Most people are unlikely to want to live in such dwellings for long if they can afford not to.

Yet residential use over business premises is fiercely defended by many structure plans. Platitudinous rubbish is talked about 'maintaining housing stock' and encouraging 'liveliness' in town centres by retaining residential accommodation within them. In fact the more residential accommodation there is in the town centre the more people there are who are likely to be uncomfortably housed and the more the centre is likely to be handicapped in carrying out its proper functions.

It is quite difficult to win an appeal against a refusal of planning permission for the conversion of residential accommodation over business premises to business premises. The wording of approved structure plans is likely to be difficult for even the most enlightened inspector to get around. It is particularly difficult for him to do so if several of his colleagues have disallowed similar appeals in the vicinity comparatively recently. What he can surely do and ought to do is to draw attention to the inappropriateness of the policy and, often, to the extent to which it has evidently not been applied.

In practical terms, it is very difficult indeed for a council actually to prevent the use of previously residential accommodation over business premises for business purposes. Put up residential looking blinds in the windows and storage can be carried on to almost any extent and almost indefinitely without the council finding out. Office use may be trickier to carry on unobserved, but a really agile operator might be able to make a good case at an appeal against an Enforcement Notice by saying that it was merely ancillary to residential use. If a flat is furnished in a way appropriate to a flat, even if there are also one or two typewriters and filing cabinets there, how can a council demonstrate that it is not primarily used for residential purposes even if no one actually sleeps there? I am not suggesting that one ought to deceive councils habitually, but just as silly questions call for silly answers, silly policies will almost inevitably produce slightly devious behaviour.

Isolated business uses in residential areas cause special problems. On the whole they are to be deplored, because the 'perimeter of nuisance' around such a use is likely to be nearly as large as that caused by a small centre. In other words, a *group* of six shops is likely to cause less disturbance than the total disturbance caused by six widely separated shops. For this reason, the old sentimental love for 'the corner shop' is misplaced: they should be grouped. With changing retail patterns, this must not be taken too literally; one large multi-purpose shop may easily combine all the functions of half a dozen little shops. Nevertheless, the principle holds. Moreover, one permitted isolated business use may bring embarrassing consequences in its train. A recently built pub is surrounded by houses. One feels sure it should not have been allowed but it was, and perhaps has done no great harm. Perhaps also the reason that it has done no great harm was that it is ill-sited and therefore does not attract very much trade or cause very much disturbance. Now, however, the owners, having realised that it is not a very successful pub, attempt to sell it, and application is made to use it as a betting shop. Why on earth should a betting shop be permitted all on its own in the midst of housing? Is the surrounding population unusually addicted to gambling? More likely this is a sheer gamble in another sense.

By contrast, Fig. 15.6 shows that several pubs were foolishly permitted on

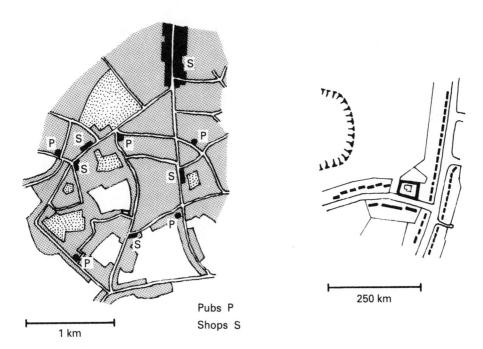

Pubs P

Shops S

1 km

250 km

Fig. 15.6 Making the best of a bad job. The pubs should have been placed with the minor shopping groups, but as this was not done the proposed new pub logically completes a pattern (*left*). The site is a good one for avoiding interference with the privacy of neighbours (*right*).

157

isolated sites instead of within or adjacent to the local shopping centres. Nothing can now be done about that, but there is a clear case for a further pub to be built on the appeal site in order to complete a rational accessibility pattern, and the siting details are in its favour. It is accessible, but not cheek by jowl with any housing. This is a very important consideration in respect not only of isolated business uses such as this, but also in relation to any minor group of shops. The general location ought to be determined in accordance with an accessibility pattern, but having regard also to such matters as avoiding a site very close to adjacent houses. It is a sound saying that everyone wants a pub just up the road, but no one wants one next door.

Conversion of quite ordinary kinds of shops to special kinds of shops such as hot food shops, pet shops and to 'shop-like' uses such as betting offices, pubs, estate agents' offices and filling stations poses considerable problems. On the one hand there is a perfectly good argument that hot food shops and pet shops can only be objectionable in a shopping area because of smell and that other legislation is available to deal with that, therefore planning powers should not be invoked to deal with matters which can be dealt with by other legislation. That I think is a good argument in relation to pet shops and not quite so good in relation to hot food shops. As a matter of common experience, these stay open late, attract a considerable number of customers after pubs have closed and produce a good deal of rubbish: chip wrappings, plastic containers and so on, thrown into the nearby streets.

It is sometimes argued that just as smell can be controlled by other powers, the gathering of crowds can be controlled by other powers, namely the police. That is true, but the time factor here needs to be taken into account. Noisy crowds may have been present for quite a long time before they attract the notice of the police, and the process of dispersing them may in itself be rather disturbing. No argument can legitimately be taken too far and the 'other powers' argument is here, I think, decidedly taken too far. The proper solution for many of the uses being discussed is to embed them in the hearts of business centres where nearby housing will be insulated from them by less tiresome business uses.

Considerations such as those just mentioned can often, rationally and convincingly, be brought forward by both sides at an appeal. Unfortuately, irrelevant and irrational arguments of the 'snob' or 'morals' kind are too often intruded. I wish that inspectors would more frequently indicate, clearly and forcibly, that they are not interested in such arguments.

Councils might avoid a good deal of difficulty if they were more willing to consider sympathetically applications for such uses on sites where they are clearly appropriate. Figure 15.7 illustrates this well. What better site could be found for such a use? It is central and accessible, yet very well insulated from housing, but it was only permitted on appeal.

I think that banks and estate agents' offices can usually acceptably be incorporated within shopping frontages. Motor car salesrooms, already briefly discussed, are a different matter. They need to be set aside from shopping frontages. Filling stations are also a different matter. Those within urban areas are

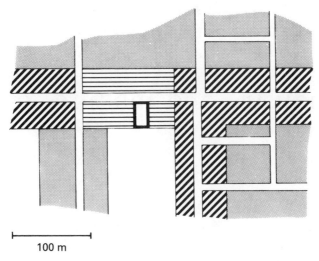

100 m

Fig. 15.7 A good site for an amusement centre. The council objected to it, but it is hard to think of anywhere where it would cause so little disturbance. Warehouses adjoin.

very appropriately associated with business centres, in order to minimise the perimeter of nuisance, but they need to be on the edges of such centres in order not to reduce the compactness of the centre. Like pubs, they also need to be tactfully insulated from adjacent houses.

Many business uses close to housing can be made less tiresome to residents if their opening hours are reasonably restricted. This applies especially to hot food shops. It is, of course, bad luck on a new hot food shop if restrictions on opening hours are applied to it which have not been applied to its competitors in the vicinity. Unhappily there is no definite answer to that problem.

16

Industry and mixtures of uses

The definition of 'industrial building' in 2(2) of the Use Classes Order, is of special importance, together with the associated definitions of 'light industrial building', 'general industrial building' and 'special industrial building':

"'industrial building" means a building (other than a building in or adjacent to and belonging to a quarry or mine and other than a shop) used for the carrying on of any process for or incidental to any of the following purposes, namely:

    (a) the making of any article or of part of any article or

    (b) the altering, repairing, ornamenting, finishing, cleaning, washing, packing or canning, or adapting for sale, or breaking up or demolition of any article, or

    (c) without prejudice to the foregoing paragraphs, the getting, dressing or treatment of minerals,

being a process carried on in the course of trade or business other than agriculture, and for the purposes of this definition the expression "article" means an article of any description, including a ship or vessel;

"light industrial building" means an industrial building (not being a special industrial building) in which the processes carried on or the machinery installed are such as could be carried on or installed in any residential area without detriment to the amenity of that area by reason of noise, vibration, smell, fumes, smoke, soot, ash, dust or grit;

"general industrial building" means an industrial building other than a light industrial building or a special industrial building;

"Special industrial building" means an industrial building used for one or more of the purposes specified in Classes V, VI, VII, VIII and IX referred to in the Schedule to this order;'

The following classes in the Schedule to the Use Classes Order deal with industrial buildings. Unless a condition attached to a permission specifically states otherwise a use within one of these classes can be changed to any other use within the same class without permission.

- *Class III*. Use as a light industrial building for any purposes.
- *Class IV*. Use as a general industrial building for any purpose.
- *Classes V to IX* (inclusive). These define in considerable detail various kinds

160

of special (i.e. noxious) industry, within each of which changes can be made without obtaining planning permission, but not from one to another.

The position is a little complicated because Class III in the First Schedule to the General Development Order enables change from a light industrial building to a wholesale warehouse or repository (Class X) to be made without planning permission being obtained and vice versa. (How this came to be put in the General Development Order rather than the Use Classes Order is mysterious.)

In homely terms, light industry is industry deemed to be pretty well harmless, special industry is noxious industry, and everything else is general industry.

Nothing more will be said about special industry, for detailed expert knowledge about the numerous and varied unattractive substances and processes involved is hardly likely to be possessed by the general town planning practitioner. Fairly obviously, special industry needs to be very thoroughly spatially separated from all other uses except perhaps general industry.

General industry too, needs to be well separated from housing. There is a certain sentimental line of thought which suggests that this is not so. It is argued that some mixture of housing and industry is healthy, counteracting the evil Industrial Revolution idea that work is hell and separated from pleasurable living. I do not think there is anything at all in this argument. Industry produces noise, smell, smoke, fumes and traffic. It is of course true that, as with hot food shops, amusement centres and so on, as discussed in the previous chapter, other legislation exists and can be invoked to mitigate the unneighbourly effects of industrial activities. However, this legislation is clearly not entirely effective, for there are many places in which one knows where one is simply because of the characteristic industrial smells associated with them, and I remember one appeal case where one of the reasons for opposing the extension of a perfume factory, was the smell it caused!

There are, of course, some curious anomalies. Figure 16.1 illustrates a case in which an additional industrial building was refused planning permission on the grounds of detriment to the amenities of a row of houses opposite. Here it was decided, I think rightly, that there was a large area so predominantly industrial that its interests had to prevail over those of a small quantity of what amounted to intrusive housing.

Light industry probably causes more problems in connection with planning appeals than all other kinds of industry put together. The source of the trouble is that the concept embodied in the Use Classes Order definition is a false one. It is not only false, it is confused. Light industry has been variously thought of as 'clean industry', industry where the value of the goods produced is high per unit volume and industry that does not need heavy machinery. Traces of all these concepts are mixed together in the Use Classes Order definition and it introduces yet another conception '. . . such as could be carried on or installed in any residential area'. Whatever can this mean? At first sight one might think it meant that the activity had to be so innocuous that it could be carried on in even the most elegant, low density, stockbroker country. But that does not help

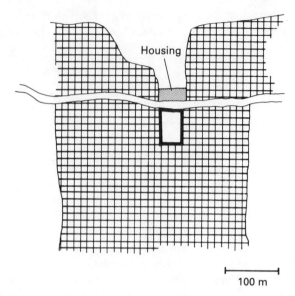

Housing

100 m

Fig. 16.1 Housing intruding into industry

at all. Innumerable things that could in fact be carried on in such areas without offence (though the residents would not think so) would be highly offensive in a high density residential area. Vibration caused by machinery which would be imperceptible if 100 metres away might be very tiresome indeed if only 15 metres away. So, to make any sense, the wording ought to be ' . . . carried on or installed in even the densest residential area'.

Next it is to be noted that the sources of detriment to amenity mentioned in the definition do not include any detriment caused by traffic. There are plenty of high density residential areas in which the street system cannot hold any additional traffic without congestion. The manoeuvring of vehicles, either adjacent to or on the site, may cause a great deal of annoyance to nearby residents, but can hardly be supposed to be part of 'the processes carried on or the machinery installed'. In considering an application for permission for light industrial purposes, a council ought therefore to consider not only the matters mentioned in the definition, but traffic considerations as well. It would hardly be a successful industrial undertaking which, however 'light', did not produce more traffic than several houses.

Development Control Policy Note No. 3 'Industrial and Commercial Development' contains the following curious statement: 'Most industrial development is expected to take place in areas allocated for the purpose in the development plans, but there are of course exceptions. As the above extract from the Use Classes Order implies, certain kinds of light industry may be acceptable elsewhere, and even, if conditions are favourable, in residential areas.' Inexcusably, 'light industry' is there used in some undefinable sense different from that of the Use Classes Order, since the Use Classes Order *defines* light industry as industry acceptable in residential areas!

It is very important for planning officers and consultants under cross-examination to insist that each time the expression 'light industry' is used in a question, it should be made absolutely clear in what sense the expression is used. I seriously doubt whether there is really such a thing as light industry as defined in the Use Classes Order. I do not think there is any industrial process which could be carried on without detriment to amenity in any residential area, however dense. But even if there are a few, it would be very dangerous to give permission to use any building for light industrial purposes without conditions being attached to specify precisely the kind of activity permitted to be carried on, hours of operation and so on. Without such limitations a change which would be capable of being considered to be within the use class might take place and have very bad consequences.

What is perhaps an even more serious problem arises from the amendment to the General Development Order, made by SI 1981 No. 245, to allow changes between light industrial use and wholesale warehouse use to be made without planning permission. There are plenty of sites where a warehouse use generates very little traffic but any increase of traffic, such as that likely to be caused by change to light industry, would be intolerable. Conversely, there are plenty of sites where some kind of light industry would be unobjectionable but where storage of smelly goods or of goods the placing or removal of which causes a great deal of noise would be highly objectionable to nearby residents.

It is my belief that things would be clearer and more satisfactory if Use Classes III, 'Use as a light industrial building for any purpose', were deleted from the Use Classes Order. All industry other than special industry would then be general industry. With this should go removal of the ability to change between industrial use and warehouse use without planning permission being obtained. As explained, sites perfectly suitable for one may be highly unsuitable for the other.

Mixed uses

These problems and others are especially acute in areas where the uses are so mixed and two or more uses are so well established that no *predominant* use can be said to exist, and the prospect of declaring and enforcing a future predominant use is too remote to seem practicable (though councils are often too faint-hearted about this). In these circumstances, the best that can be hoped for is to control development in such a way that no change is permitted that is likely to cause material detriment to any of the other uses in the vicinity. Unfortunately, in such places, prevailing conditions are likely to be already so bad that the difficulty may be for the council to assert convincingly that any particular proposal is likely to worsen them appreciably.

Figure 16.2 is a good example of this. The council behaved stupidly and the appellant behaved ignorantly. The council were foolish enough to say that the area was residential and base their determination upon this palpably false assumption. The applicant did not realise that by applying simply for 'light

163

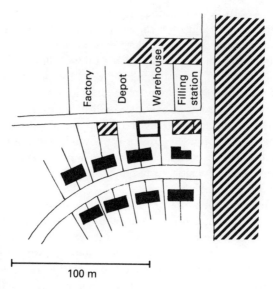

Fig. 16.2 An unplanned confusion of uses which makes good development control almost impossible.

industrial or warehouse use' he made it impossible for the council or the inspector at the subsequent appeal to give a permission safeguarded by adequate conditions limiting the use to be carried on to something specific and harmless.

Another problem to be found in areas of mixed use is the false argument that something should be allowed because 'at least it will be better than what's there now'. It is the function of town planning to bring about satisfactory conditions, not merely to be content with making the bad slightly less bad, particularly when, as is often the case in such circumstances, the change may make the eventual sorting out of uses more difficult to achieve. Figure 16.3 shows a case where the proposed development was alleged to 'be better than what's there' but would, as well as being harmful to nearby residents, have exacerbated a mixture of uses previously only incipient.

A block of lock-up garages intended for the use of nearby residents had gradually deteriorated until the garages were entirely used for the storage of the goods of shopkeepers or stall-holders in the adjacent street market. Not only were goods stored in the garages but in the concrete area between them. These goods were untidy, often smelly and attracted rats. The garages were frequently vandalised and set on fire. Then came a splendid idea. Pull down the garages and put a block of two-storey light industrial workshops there. But the proposed building would actually reduce the daylight received by houses opposite below an acceptable minimum. Their privacy would be gravely reduced by people walking along the first floor level walkway, and that of residents at the side by those using the (inevitably unsightly) external staircase giving access to the walkway. The space allocated for parking vehicles was inadequate and it is

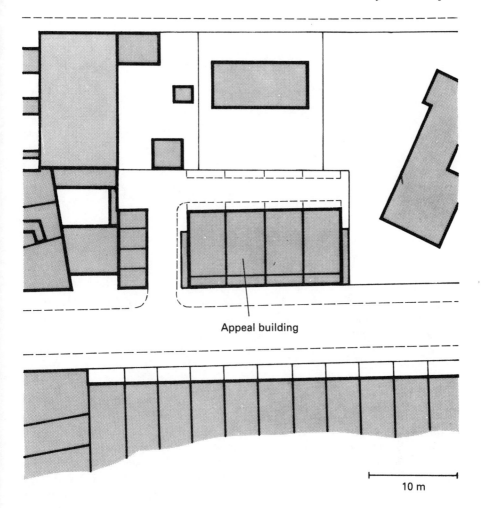

Appeal building

10 m

Fig. 16.3 An undesirable mixture of uses sought to be introduced. The proposed two-storey workshops would reduce the daylight of neighbours below a reasonable amount, would subject them to unreasonable noise, loss of privacy and general disturbance and would increase traffic and parking above the ability of the street to absorb.

certain that if the proposal were to be carried out, many would park in the street outside which at present can only just deal with existing traffic. All the other disadvantages discussed above in connection with what light industry really is and the implications of being able to change between light industry and warehouse, would exist.

165

17

The open country and village

A good deal of the material in this chapter necessarily overlaps with that in the next, 'The Urban Fringe' and also to some extent with Chapter 14, 'Housing', but in this chapter emphasis is laid upon whether development of the kind contemplated ought to be permitted at all in the kind of location proposed rather than whether it is slightly misplaced or in the wrong form.

Green belts

In Chapter 10 attention was drawn to the confusion and anomalies produced by official pronouncements about various categories of open country and to the dangers to which these give rise. The worst of these dangers relates to green belts, and we shall come to these in a little while, but first some elementary statement of principle is needed in order to provide a rational basis for contesting appeals in which green belts are involved.

The view which generally prevailed in this country before 1945 and still prevails in many countries was that undeveloped land was to be regarded as potentially developable unless some definite reason could be given for not developing it. Accordingly, pre-1947 'planning schemes' showed vastly excessive areas allocated for development, and other areas wholly or partially restricted against development, either permanently or temporarily. Land liable to flood would be permanently restricted and land lacking piped and wired services would be temporarily restricted pending the provision of such services. Other land, though *allocated* for development, was 'zoned' in such a way as to discourage development. Housing densities of one house to ten or more acres, sometimes even one house to a hundred acres, were prescribed to prevent development, not to limit it, but because development was not actually prohibited, payment of compensation was avoided.

Limited success attended this method, which was wholly discarded by the new planning system created by the 1947 Act. This assumed that no village or urban development, and, most importantly, no housing except special houses for key agricultural workers, would be allowed anywhere except in areas specifically allocated for development in a development plan. Anywhere else the onus was on the developer to demonstrate either that an error had been made in not allocating the land for development, or that there was some special, irresistible reason to allow that particular kind of development on a particular site. The picture was drawn by Sir Patrick Abercrombie of 'islands of red' (development) in 'a sea of green'(country). (See Fig. 17.1.) There was the further concept of 'white land' as 'areas in which it is intended that existing uses will for the most part remain undisturbed'. A further safeguard was that development plans were supposed to divide land for development into areas for sequential release in stages: land likely to be needed during the first five years after the coming into operation of the plan; then land likely to be needed between the sixth and twentieth years and finally land thought likely to be ultimately needed for development, but not until after twenty years. On that basis most 'white land' could be regarded as 'green', most of it not being likely to be needed for development for many years, provided reasonably accurate estimates had been made of need and demand for land for development in the course of preparing the plan.

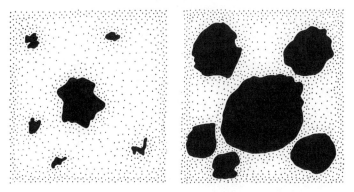

Fig. 17.1 (*Left*) Patrick Abercrombie's concept of islands of development in a sea of green compared with (*right*) 'development anywhere except where specifically prohibited'.

Unfortunately, things did not quite work out like that. Town plans were not prepared quickly enough, and, until they were prepared, developers would 'have a go' almost anywhere, hoping that, in the absence of a plan, the arguments against development would not be sufficiently well ordered and marshalled to succeed on appeal. On the other hand, where town plans were prepared reasonably quickly, they tended to allocate quite inadequate areas of land for development, especially that programmed for release during the first five years. Pressure to develop land programmed for later development and even 'white' land therefore began to build up absurdly early.

    Partly, but only partly, to counter this pressure, green belts were inserted into development plans. Areas of outstanding natural beauty, national parks and areas of special control for the purposes of the advertisement regulations were also prescribed, not so much actually to prevent the spread of development, except in the case of the green belts, as to impose special control over the quality of any development permitted. As we have seen in Chapter 10, such things have now proliferated to an extraordinary extent, and though the idea of controlling the quality of development still remains, the greatest emphasis is laid upon preventing the spread of development in areas to which such restrictions are applied. The latest device is the conservation area, in which control of quality rather than prevention of mere spread is emphasised.

Circular No. 42 of 1955 of the then Ministry of Housing and Local Government is an important policy document worth reproducing in full:

CIRCULAR No. 42/55

Dated August 3, 1955, issued by the Ministry of Housing and Local Government

GREEN BELTS

1. Following upon his statement in the House of Commons on April 26 last (copy attached), I am directed by the Minister of Housing and Local Government to draw your attention to the importance of checking the unrestricted sprawl of the built-up areas, and of safeguarding the surrounding countryside against further encroachment.

2. He is satisfied that the only really effective way to achieve this object is by the formal designation of clearly defined Green Belts around the areas concerned.

3. The Minister accordingly recommends Planning Authorities to consider establishing a Green Belt wherever this is desirable in order:
(a) to check the further growth of a large built-up area;
(b) to prevent neighbouring towns from merging into one another; or
(c) to preserve the special character of a town.

4. Wherever practicable, a Green Belt should be several miles wide, so as to ensure an appreciable rural zone all round the built-up area concerned.

5. Inside a Green Belt, approval should not be given, except in very special circumstances, for the construction of new buildings or for the change of use of existing buildings for purposes other than agriculture, sport, cemeteries, institutions standing in extensive grounds, or other uses appropriate to a rural area.

6. Apart from a strictly limited amount of 'infilling' or 'rounding off' (within boundaries to be defined in Town Maps) existing towns and villages inside a Green Belt should not be allowed to expand further. Even within the urban areas thus defined, every effort should be made to prevent any further building for industrial or commercial purposes; since this, if allowed, would lead to a demand for more labour, which in turn would create a need for the development of additional land for housing.

7. A planning Authority which wishes to establish a Green Belt in its area should, after consulting any neighbouring Planning Authority affected, submit to the Minister, as soon as possible, a Sketch Plan, indicating the approximate boundaries of the proposed Belt. Before officially submitting their plans, authorities may find it helpful to discuss them informally with this Ministry either through its regional representative or in Whitehall.

8. In due course, a detailed survey will be needed to define precisely the inner and outer boundaries of the Green Belt, as well as the boundaries of towns and villages within it. Thereafter, these particulars will have to be incorporated as amendments in the Development Plan.

9. This procedure may take some time to complete. Meanwhile, it is desirable to prevent any further deterioration in the position. The Minister, therefore, asks that,

where a Planning Authority has submitted a Sketch Plan for a Green Belt, it should forthwith apply provisionally, in the area proposed, the arrangements outlined in paragraphs 5 and 6 above. (Permission to reproduce given by HMSO.)

The thinking in this is curiously confused and does not stand up to close analysis. It is difficult to know why, within the general assumptions of the 1947 Act, a belt of open country round a large town should not be maintained simply by refusing permission for development outside areas allocated for development. Green belts have actual disadvantages; where they have been too tightly drawn around a town, a demonstrated need to relax them a little to provide room for necessary development has been regarded as defeat for green belt policy and resisted as such, instead of being more sensibly viewed as evidence of a green belt boundary having been wrongly drawn.

Exactly the same thing can be said about avoiding the merging of two settlements. Assuming this to be a good idea, which it usually will be, all that had to be done was to refuse permission for any development outside areas specifically allocated for development.

As to the maintenance of special character, no one has ever succeeded in explaining clearly what this means.

The objects of and means of securing green belts, as expressed in or deducible from official pronouncements, development plan written statements and appeal decision letters, are rather different. Shorn of tactful and soothing language, they might be said to have developed into the following:

1. Green belts are areas in which the intention that 'existing uses will for the most part remain undisturbed' is *really* intended to apply. No one is going to get permission there for anything unless it is related to agriculture or forestry. One can't actually say that, but that's what will happen, except once in a very blue moon. This will help to prevent inspectors making unfortunate recommendations to allow appeals which would be embarrassing from the point of view of policy preservation and face-saving, however technically sound they might be.

2. Green belts are areas in which growth generally is to be damped down in pursuance of vague regional planning policy related to the distribution of population and industry, even in towns surrounded by a green belt and in 'window' villages (i.e. the larger villages surrounded by a green belt but not actually included in it). In other smaller villages in a green belt, inclusion in the green belt will save the trouble of considering seriously whether or not an appeal merits being allowed.

3. Green belts are meant to look nice, so anything that can't readily be turned down on other grounds in a green belt can be turned down on the grounds that it will damage the appearance of the green belt, even if it is something as irrelevant to that as a proposal to build a shop in a village street.

4. If no other reason for turning down development in a green belt can possibly be shown to hold water (e.g. where the boundary of the green belt has manifestly been wrongly drawn to a gross extent, so as to include within it land obviously eminently suitable for development) it can still be turned

down, and face be saved, on the grounds that to permit it would be to permit 'nibbling at the green belt', that terrible cumulative results would occur if such a thing were allowed to take place: once let the water in, and there's a precedent; where would it stop?

It has to be emphasised that, almost certainly, these attitudes have been adopted in the belief that councils could not be trusted to withstand sporadic rural development consistently, nor inspectors to recommend (or worse, latterly, make) appeal decisions with appropriate consistency and severity. Figures 17.2 to 17.5 illustrate some of the absurdities that result. The first one is particularly ridiculous. In this case the application was for a nursing home for elderly people, on a site on the edge of a village. It was a large village, and had previously been a 'window village', i.e. one in which some development might be allowed, despite the village being surrounded by green belt. However, for some inscrutable reason, this policy had been changed, and the 'window' had been removed, which meant that the ordinary green belt prohibitions would be applied. As can readily be seen from Fig. 17.2 this is nonsensical. Whatever the status of the land in the development plan, here was a thoroughly good use for the site. It was sufficiently accessible for necessary staff to get there easily, was within the existing built-up area, was physically suitable for such development and had satisfactory road access. No affirmative answer could be given to the

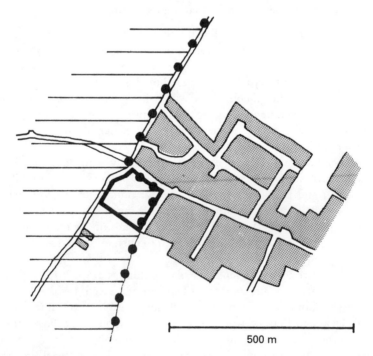

Fig. 17.2 A nursing home on the edge of a village unreasonably refused permission 'on green belt grounds'.

crucial question 'What possible harm could result from giving permission for this development?' The appeal was allowed.

The case shown in Fig. 17.3 was quite remarkable. Permission for the development of fifteen hectares or more of land for housing was refused on the grounds that it violated the green belt between two towns. But it was not between the two towns. It was in one, quite remote from the other, and screened from it by a great deal of residential and other development, much of it continuous and far from sporadic. It needed three appeals to get permission for this land. The first time the inspector recommended against it on the grounds that it did violate the green belt and the Minister agreed with him. The second time, the inspector accepted that it did not violate the green belt, but was overridden by the Minister. The third time an inspector again thought that it did not violate the green belt, and this time the Minister agreed with him. It is important to emphasise that these three appeals took place over a period of not more than four years and that during that time there was no change at all in circumstances. The appellants had to go on until they got both a sensible inspector and a sensible administrator working at the same time.

Figures 17.4 and 17.5 are examples of manifest errors in drawing the bound-

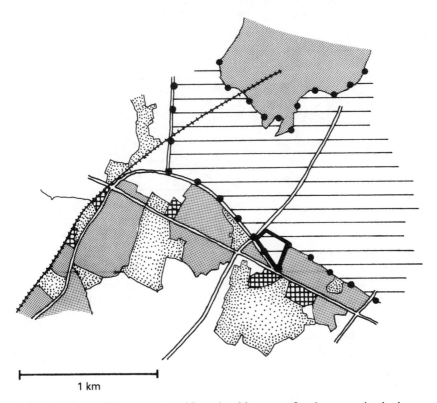

1 km

Fig. 17.3 Urban infilling unreasonably resisted because of an inappropriately drawn green belt boundary.

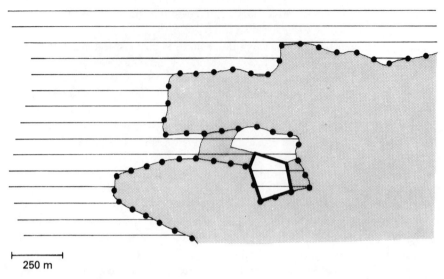

250 m

Fig. 17.4 It is difficult to think that the boundary of the green belt here was drawn for any reason except to limit compensation if the appeal site and adjacent land needed to be compulsorily acquired for schools or open space.

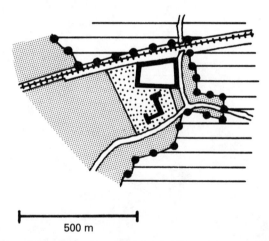

500 m

Fig. 17.5 A strange little piece of 'orphan' land. The real reasons for the mysteriously successful resistance to its use for housing remain obscure.

aries of green belts which the councils concerned ought to have put right for themselves without the need for developers to go to appeal. They did not, and both appeals were dismissed on the view of the Minister that they constituted 'nibbling at the green belt'.

The especially irritating paradox of green belts is that although the intellectual level of green belt policy is moronic and its application indefensible, it has nevertheless probably been the most successful of all British planning policies, continuously for nearly forty years. The mere use of the words 'green belt' has caused proposals for development to wither like salted slugs and Britain has probably been more successful than any other country in the world of comparable population density in keeping large areas of countryside open and unspoiled. The verdict of history may well be that the prevention of fairly numerous desirable developments because of over-rigid and irrational green belt policy was a small price to pay for the benefits, especially as severe limitation on planning permission has undoubtedly stimulated a great deal of admirable rehabilitation, improvement and minor redevelopment of buildings within villages. Unhappily, the days of success may be coming to an end. Since the General Election of 1983, governmental regard and support for town planning has seemed more in doubt than at any time since the Second World War. Builders, always restive, always urging release of more land for housing, are gaining political support and it is to be feared that the past irrationality and excesses of green belt policy may produce excessive backlash. If only every town and village had early had a definite plan showing limits for its development, and any development outside those limits had had to be treated as a substantial departure from the development plan about which the DoE had to be informed if permission was contemplated, things would surely have gone better.

One can only hope that reason will prevail, and one way to help make it prevail is for both consultants and planning officers, in dealing with green belt or similarly described land, to try to talk in terms of real merit rather than to fling conventional wisdom clichés back and forth at each other.

Over the years, the odd circumstances described above have inevitably produced a certain complacency in councils and their officers: no need to try very hard when you know you can't lose. Some councils now worship and rely on the magic words 'green belt' so much that, in rural areas which they can't get included in a green belt because the DoE will not agree, they say that they are 'applying green belt policies'. In one strange way, of course, this is quite sound, because any sensible rural planning policy would be very restrictive and should be applied all over rural Britain. Other councils go even further and include in grounds of refusal a statement that the site is 'near' a green belt, or area of outstanding natural beauty, etc. Yet others assert that a site is in a green belt, but if one succeeds in plotting a vaguely drawn green belt boundary from a structure plan diagram or written description onto an ordnance map, it can be seen that the site is not in fact in a green belt. If the day came when councils had to do better than that to win appeals it would be a good thing, and they ought to start practising now. The great majority of non-agricultural applications for planning permission in rural areas merit refusal, but it is important for the future that they should be refused for sensible reasons.

The arguments for refusing planning permission for nearly all housing outside towns and villages are quite definite and strong. The DoE's Development Control Policy Note No. 4, *Development in Rural Areas*, puts it quite well in paragraph 2:

The fact that a single house on a particular site would not be very noticeable, is not by itself a good argument for permission. It could be repeated too often. If people were free

173

to build houses wherever they wished in rural areas, they would soon be dotted all over the countryside and strung out along the roads. The face of the countryside as we know it today would be changed, a lot of farm land would be lost, and the cost of extending water, drainage and other services over long distances, would be immense.

To this should be added the need for impracticably costly improvements of minor roads caused by the much greater rural road traffic which would be produced, the sheer economic waste of the vast increase in mileage covered by vehicles, and the impracticability of locating schools and shops so that a considerable proportion of their users could reach them on foot if they wished.

A vitally important item in successful country planning, the appropriate policies for which have been both neglected and confused, is village size. Once more a brief historical retrospect is necessary. Except for a few very special kinds, villages used simply to be the dwelling-places of people who worked in the agricultural industry and of those who provided services for them: teachers, blacksmiths, parsons and the like, and their 'bosses', the squire and the large landowner.

Subject to the vagaries of geology, geography and ownership, a remarkably consistent spatial pattern and hierarchy of settlements became established. At the upper end of the hierarchy: big towns, medium-sized towns and small towns; with below them the rural hierarchy: large villages, ordinary villages and small villages or hamlets with, finally, below that, the isolated cottages of specialised farm workers who, because of the nature of their jobs, needed to live 'on the farm' instead of 'in the village'. In many areas the farmhouses themselves, the 'farm headquarters', were outside villages.

After the Second World War, planning policy, illuminated by the admirable Scott Report, sought the maintenance and strengthening of this pattern and hierarchy, and achieved considerable success. The general assumption was that only as much development would be permitted in villages as was necessary to house the agricultural work-force and those who served it, and that outside villages the only houses to be permitted would be new farm houses if a new farm was created or was to be created by severance and this severance could be justified on agricultural grounds. There would also occasionally be permitted new houses for key farm workers who could not reasonably, on grounds of maintaining security or extraordinary and irregular hours of work, be expected to live in a nearby village. Both farmhouses and these special houses would have agricultural conditions attached to planning permissions given for them, that is, conditions to limit occupation of the houses to those who worked in agriculture and their families. Adventitious rural dwellers, that is, those who neither work in agriculture nor serve the agricultural industry in some way, were regarded as undesirable intruders. They could not be prevented from buying or renting rural houses, except for those which had an agricultural condition attached, but they were certainly not going to be allowed for in the amount of land released for village housing.

Isolated houses in the country, of which many had sprung up between the wars, were also regarded as undesirable, and though the development plans did not, I think, ever actually say that none would be allowed anywhere, to get planning permission for a 'non-agricultural' house away from a village, was and remains very rare. This made sense and worked for a long time. Of course there were errors and lapses; driving across England one sometimes comes across groups of houses obviously built since 1947, of which one can only ask, 'How on earth did they get permission?' One suspects that a good many were allowed on appeal in order, at least indirectly, to help achieve the Macmillan 300 000 houses a year pledge, and it is also apparent that in a few counties, for it was the county councils that mostly dealt with such matters until 1974, control was lax.

Matters are now very greatly changed. Agricultural productivity goes up and up, but the amount of labour on the land which is needed to achieve it goes down and down. The motor car, instead of being a middle and upper class luxury is very widely owned and used. Largely because of government encouragement and greatly to the delight of builders, urban housing densities have greatly increased, except in a few fiercely, but not always rationally defended enclaves. People, probably quite a lot of them, who want a small house with a large garden at a moderate price can therefore no longer find one easily in a town and either have to give up or seek one in a village. Many such are retired couples.

Rurally located industry, the products of which are not necessarily related at all to agriculture, crops up in all kinds of surprising places: in large houses no longer practicable for use as such, in disused mills, in disused barns. They create local employment, they may be visually a little obtrusive, but it is hard to see what harm they do or might do. Professional people even run practices from houses in villages.

Many villages, even quite compact ones, have gaps in their frontages or in the groups of buildings set back from the village street which, in visual terms, ought to be filled in with dwellings. On the other hand, (see Fig. 17.6) there are many villages of such loose texture that if all sites which might reasonably be regarded as constituting rounding off or infilling were developed, the result would be to produce a sizeable town in place of the existing quite small village – a town lacking the roads, schools, shops, libraries, etc., needed for a town.

Filling in a gap within a village ought usually to be regarded as virtuous. There are exceptions to this. Occasionally a gap reveals a superb view, framed by the development on each side, and to fill such a gap would clearly be to the detriment rather than to the advantage of the village scene. This situation arises in various forms. Figure 17.7 is an interesting example. In this long village, development on the upper side of the street is pretty well continuous and from it there are pleasant views into the valley of the small river below. On the lower side of the street, however, development is discontinuous and such as there is has, for not very obvious reasons, unless it was deliberately to preserve the views from above, been tucked into hollows where it is inconspicuous. In this case the appeal was dismissed, partly because it was on a much more prominent site than other development on the lower side of the street. In any event the access was so dangerous that it would probably have been lost on that account alone.

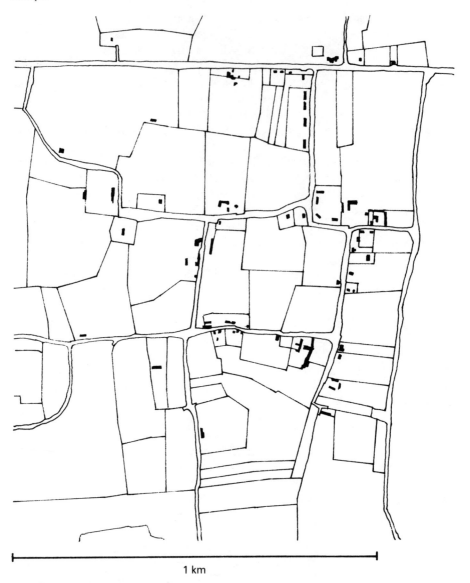

1 km

Fig. 17.6 A loose-textured village. There is enough land within its envelope to contain a town.

Figure 17.8, on the other hand, shows an appeal which was allowed. The council's expressed desire to leave gaps in the village street was difficult to support, since the land was flat and the gaps were just gaps. One suspects that what the council were really after was to protect, undeservedly, the openness and seclusion of existing residents.

It is generally, if not universally, held among town planners that a sharp

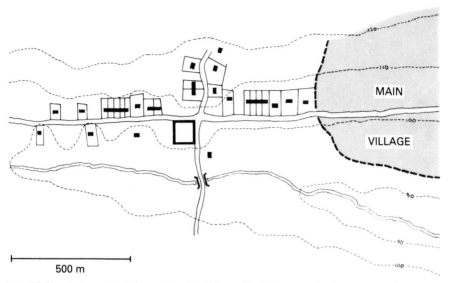

Fig. 17.7 A riverside village. Tactful siting of buildings on the lower side of the road preserves a pleasant open effect. The appeal site is not tactfully sited.

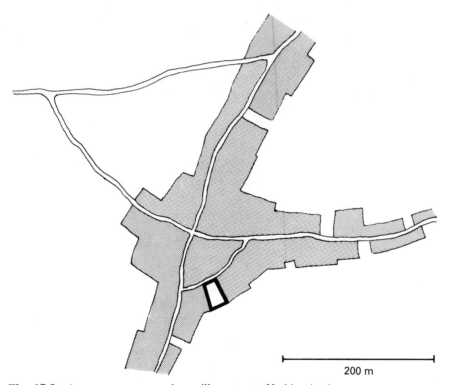

Fig. 17.8 An unnecessary gap in a village street. Nothing in the structure or topography of this village suggests that maintaining the gaps in its built-up frontages was a good idea.

transition from town or village to country is to be desired, that ideally one should as it were be able to stand with one foot in the town and the other in the country; but there is at least one council in England which thinks otherwise. It thinks that town or village should 'merge gradually' with countryside and seeks to bring this about by its development control policy. It is conceivable that particular patterns of development or countryside might sometimes justify such a policy, yet it is so much in conflict with the norm that to be upheld it should require very specific and detailed justification. The council concerned, however, is not in the habit of saying more than that they think it is a good thing. It is not therefore surprising if they are not upheld on appeal.

Very strong and definite policy is needed. At the very least it is necessary to draw tight 'village envelopes' within which councils are prepared to permit or favourably consider development – something which the better councils had already done by 1950. But even by 1968, in some areas little progress had been made. In other areas progress made previously has been abandoned. In some areas rural planning policy seems to be as crude as the following, though expressed in more dignified terms. Villages in the area are divided into three categories:

1. We'll allow a bit of development in these.
2. We *might* allow a very little development in these.
3. We'll fight *any* development in these, even building two houses on the site of a derelict abandoned large house.

These categories are usually drawn up with regard to the existing size and status of a village and/or its location in or near a green belt or other restrictive structure plan category. They seldom make very much sense, inasmuch as it is hard to see, even for anyone as enthusiastic about strong, tight village planning as I am, what actual benefit to anyone such very restrictive policies would confer. They are not only strict, but confused. The real general considerations which ought to govern development control in villages are, I think:

1. Will the development maintain the compactness of the village or unreasonably disperse it, to the detriment of the landscape?
2. Will it help to maintain or make practicable the provision of a local school, shop, sewage works, etc.?
3. Will it overstrain the road system as existing or as definitely proposed to be improved?

I do not think it would be difficult to draw up plans which took account of these factors, and it is reasonable to suggest that a policy which then readily permitted development within the envelope, subject of course to satisfactory siting, access and external appearance, but which absolutely opposed development elsewhere except for agricultural and similar purposes, would be likely to be effective and simple to operate until such time as any further shifts in the socio-economic scene suggested some deliberate change of policy.

These suggestions do of course demand an answer to the question of how large a catchment population is needed to support a shop and a school. That is for the local authorities to find out and act upon.

There are certainly many more villages and hamlets in Britain than can possibly support a shop, a school and a sewage works. What about those which cannot? I think that ruthless logic might dictate that no development whatever, even replacement of buildings which burned or fell down, should be permitted in such places; such a policy would mean that a greater proportion of the rural population would gradually become concentrated into places where accessibility to services and facilities was good and that improvement of the rural road system could be concentrated upon lengths of it sufficiently short for improvement to be feasible within the foreseeable future. But many of these little places are lovely, and if that policy were rigorously applied, they would die miserably and slowly. I doubt whether it can be justifiable to say of any place substantial enough to be called a 'place', i.e. something that is not just a row of houses, that there shall never be any new building or replacement building to maintain or complete its visual quality as a place. (See Fig. 17.9 for the distinction between a mere row of houses and a place), even though the quantity of building is similar. But I believe that a fully rigorous policy should be applied to mere rows of houses (misplaced development), otherwise how can they ever be made to disappear? Eternal replenishment of the undesirable makes no sense.

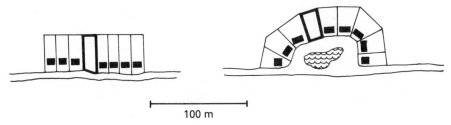

100 m

Fig. 17.9 The difference between a mere 'row' (*left*) and a 'place' (*right*) may make the difference between justifiable refusal or permission for infilling where, prima facie, there should be no more houses.

The people who live in a very small place now mostly do so because of its attractiveness, and must be presumed to realise that in doing so they will forfeit the benefits of shops, schools and main sewerage. Nevertheless it might be a very good idea for local authorities to attach a warning to this effect to any permissions given.

Great caution is needed in giving permission for development for purely visual reasons. Intending developers are not slow to claim that a building will 'complete a group' or 'constitute infilling'. Figure 17.10 shows an example. The appeal site in fact has neither functional nor visual connection with the houses to the right or the barn and farmhouse to the left. In general it is wise not to take farmhouses or agricultural buildings into account when considering whether filling the gap between them and nearby housing will 'complete' a group. In fact a large proportion of village streets show a distinct gap between the village street, consisting mainly of houses, and the nearest farmhouses,

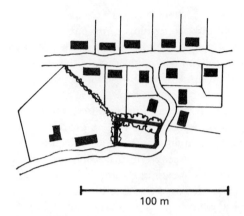

100 m

Fig. 17.10 A misleading infilling case. On the left, the farmhouse and barn seem to be almost part of the building group to the right, but they are visually separate, though they help to frame the scene. The proposed house would upset the whole scene.

though the latter, by closing a vista, may make their own different visual contribution to the village scene. One should not be dogmatic about such matters. They are often very subtle.

Figure 17.11 shows another illustration of a case in which it would not be difficult to fall into an infill fallacy. The gap between the buildings on the left and the buildings on the right seems small. Buildings set back behind the group to the left seem to suggest a certain continuity. But on the ground, this is quite misleading. The buildings to the left are old 'village street' buildings with a vista effectively terminated by the bend in the road and the trees. The buildings to

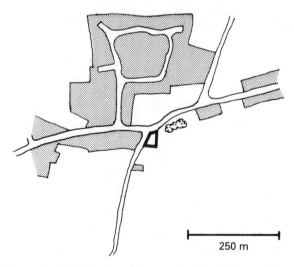

250 m

Fig. 17.11 More misleading infilling. The proposed house, judged from the map, might be thought to be reasonably placed, but in fact it would be quite intrusive.

the right are really a tiny hamlet. The set-back buildings are a recent 'accident' and should be disregarded. The appeal should have been, and was, dismissed.

Planning Bulletin No. 8 *Settlement in the Countryside*, has probably done some harm among the less sophisticated planning authorities by suggesting a needlessly elaborate process of search, analysis and selection of sites for village development. Those who have followed it too literally have got themselves into difficulties. Figure 17.12 is an example where the council concerned made a meticulous study in accordance with the suggestions of *Settlements in the Countryside*, and published it. They were then terrified that they might lose the appeal for housing on the site shown because it had been included in their study as a possible site for development. There is no point in putting on a map huge areas which might possibly be considered for development when in this case such a tiny village could not possibly merit the addition of more than half a dozen houses. Fortunately the council's fears were groundless and the appeal was dismissed.

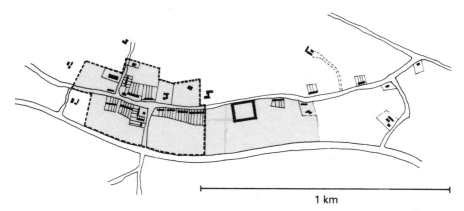

1 km

Fig. 17.12 A 'village study' which might have had bad results. The study suggested the whole of the shaded area as land on which housing development might be considered, but the broken-edged area alone is more than enough land for any expansion of this quite small village.

Of much development in villages of loose texture, in areas of 'accidental' development near villages and even more, of course, in the open countryside, it can truly be said:

All over the country there are literally thousands of sites which by stretching the meanings of the words could be regarded as infilling or rounding off. Resistance to the development of such sites is consistently carried out by most councils. If such resistance ceased to be effective and any considerable proportion was developed, the balance of development in many areas would be severely disturbed and unnecessary and costly strains would be imposed on public services and on facilities of all kinds, including schools, public open spaces and shops, and the capability of many roads to deal with the traffic they had to carry would be impaired.

One might expect that, forty years after the institution of fairly rigorous rural development control, its essentials would be common knowledge and accepted, at least among people who carry out development for a living; but the applicant who responded to a refusal of planning permission for a house in open country with 'What do you mean, "sporadic"?. There are only four other houses within half a mile', was evidently sincere, judging from his tone of voice, and is still not a rare kind of animal. However, the builder who put in the application shown in Fig. 17.13 may not repeat his inane and public-money-wasting performance, since the application shown was submitted just before the imposition of fees for planning applications.

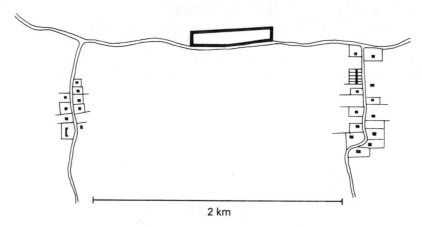

2 km

Fig. 17.13 A proposed rural ribbon of houses. There can seldom have been a less well justified appeal against refusal. The two existing hamlets shown are themselves remote, in deep countryside.

There are some very curious special cases which come to appeal. The extraordinary settlement shown in Fig. 17.14 came about as the result of several tiny hamlets becoming linked by sporadic development before planning control became effective. Here the local authority has latterly performed well. There is too much development for a 'killing off' process to be justifiable, yet a very strong distinction has to be made between sites regarded as legitimate infill and others, otherwise there would soon be virtually a linear town, wholly lacking in necessary urban services.

What can really only be called 'bogus villages' are another matter. In the more prosperous parts of England these are regrettably common. They are simply areas, sometimes quite large areas, of low density housing, lacking any nucleus of facilities or services. Building them constituted a greedy theft of countryside. Applications to increase the number of houses in them by dividing some of their enormous gardens into two and putting a new house on the severed half are quite common, and should in my view be totally resisted. By contrast, Fig. 17.15 shows an example of an unsuccessful and unmerited refusal of permission for a house on the edge of a village.

Isolated country houses. Many of the things said about other kinds of rural development apply to these but there are some special considerations. In many

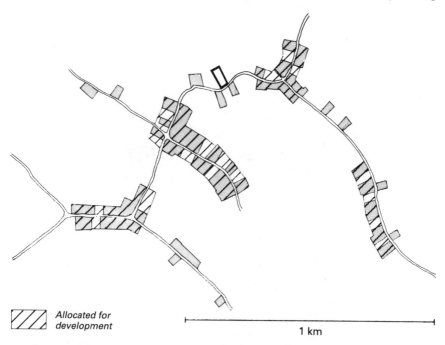

///// Allocated for
///// development

|————————————————————————————|
1 km

Fig. 17.14 Scattered rural development. As explained in the text, the council have done the best they could in a very difficult situation.

parts of the country it would be possible to find here and there sites for isolated houses which:

1. Would enable a house to be built so as to be invisible from anywhere outside the site.
2. Would be able to dispose of their own sewage within the site.
3. Had no agricultural value.
4. Could have safe vehicular access to a road.
5. Would have no appreciable adverse ecological effect.

Surely there could be no reasonable grounds for refusing such applications? Oh yes, there could and are! The appropriate replies to applicants who think otherwise are:

1. You will have visitors: postman, doctor, ambulance, friends, police. This will put a little more strain on the no doubt narrow and winding local road system, and increase the cost to the taxpayer because of greater mileages covered by the public services involved.
2. However unobtrusive you are, you will create *some* ecological disturbance, and it is important to keep some parts of the country free of human beings if they don't actually have to be there.
3. There are many more sites with the advantages you list than you think there are. If you get permission, there is no reason to refuse permission for a house

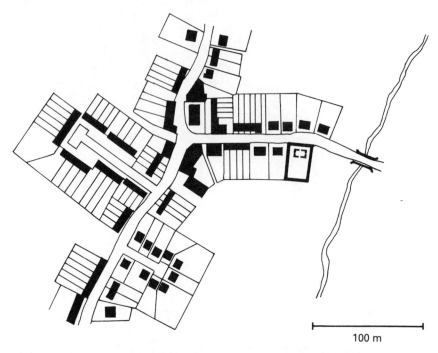

Fig. 17.15 A village house. In this remarkable case the council refused permission for a house on the grounds that the village was a green belt village in which it was not intended to allow any development. Nevertheless, quite recently, substantial development, some of which is shown above, had been permitted. The appeal site, previously occupied by a house which had fallen down, is opposite existing development and close to a small river which forms a firm and definite boundary for development.

on each of the equally good other sites and then the disadvantages mentioned above will be multiplied until they become really serious. It is neither practicable nor equitable to give permission for one such house and then to refuse permission for others equally suitably sited. It is necessary to stop the first one, or the water will flow in. Even a casual glance at Australia or the United States demonstrates this.

4. There are already, in many parts of the country, many isolated country houses, built before effective planning control. Go and buy one of those.

Such an applicant or potential applicant may adopt the last suggestion, or he may try something different. He may try to get permission to convert an existing building to a dwelling on the grounds that it is a fine old barn of great architectural merit and interest, not now needed as a barn and gradually deteriorating. Shorn of decoration, what he says is: 'I will rescue this gem if you give me permission to turn it into a house.' This is indeed genuinely a different matter. Councils should not let themselves get too enthusiastic about this kind of thing until they have considered the pros and cons, but there are cases where such conversions can reasonably be allowed. There is no kind of cost-benefit analysis that is subtle enough to determine where the balance of advantage lies in some cases. Rationally considered, there is a kind of tension and opposition. At one end of the scale the building concerned may be a gem and within, or almost within, a village envelope; then there is clearly no problem. At the other end of the scale, if its merit is very slight and it is miles from anywhere and the access is poor, there is again no problem; refuse permission. It is at points near the middle of the scale that the decision becomes difficult: 'It's quite nice, but nothing special and 300 metres outside the village.'

Some councils follow a very odd policy in green belts and other areas to which special restrictions apply, by resisting house extensions. A house built within the last twenty years or so is almost certainly going to be there for another century unless planning policy becomes so enlightened and strong that the sweeping away of all ill-sited development becomes a practical possibility. We are currently a very long way away from that. But quite a lot of councils resist enlargements of rural houses on illogical grounds. They are sometimes so illogical that it is difficult to describe them clearly, but often the argument seems to be that there needs to be a wide variety in the sizes of rural houses and that as many houses as possible, i.e. small houses, should be available for low income rural dwellers; but it seems a very odd way to proceed and quite unlikely to have much effect. Usually, I think, appeals against refusals of house extensions on these grounds ought to be successful on the grounds that such extensions will not make any difference to legitimate planning aims. Few house enlargements are likely to increase the number of occupants by more than two or three, and if enlargement is not allowed the number may well increase anyway by virtue of births and the house be occupied less comfortably. At the most, traffic is likely to be increased by one car. It is hard to think that such a policy will really displace the well-to-do and replace them with the poor. Councils who pursue this sort of policy are straining at gnats, but often swallow camels all too readily.

Finally, two other topics need to be dealt with separately. The imposition of 'agricultural' conditions is, as described earlier, a common, sensible and justifiable precaution. What happens when such a house is no longer needed functionally for agricultural occupancy, as happens quite frequently, and the legitimate inhabitants, 'those engaged in or last engaged in agriculture', and their families have moved or died? The choice, simply, when an application is made for removal of the condition, is to refuse it in the belief, expectation or hope either that it will soon be found that the house is really needed for agricultural occupation after all or that, having served its turn in performing the particular function for which it was permitted, it should be allowed to wither and die. This would be ruthless, but I think quite often justified, because there is no point in imposing conditions in order to make what would otherwise be unacceptable acceptable, and then give in as soon as there is a squawk. On the other hand, ruthlessness should only be used if it is really justified, and with agricultural conditions it is by no means always justified. Figures 17.16 and 17.17 are cases where removal of the condition was refused, but clearly unjustifiably, and the consequent appeals were successful. In the first case, if the site was not within the village envelope it was so close to it that the distance could

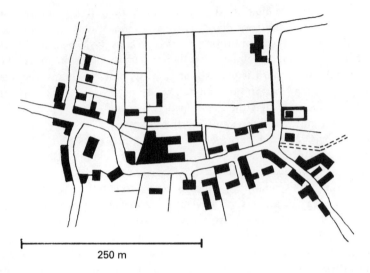

250 m

Fig. 17.16 Removal of an 'agricultural condition'. It is hard to see why permission should not be given for an ordinary house here and therefore even harder to think that demolition would be justified if it ceased to be occupied by an agricultural worker.

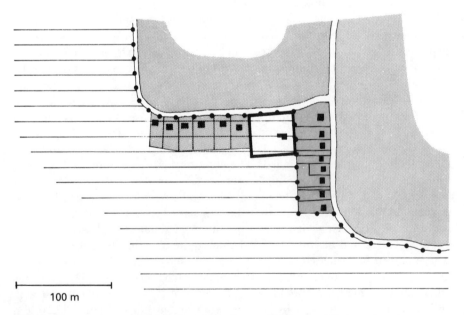

100 m

Fig. 17.17 Another 'agricultural condition' case. The green belt boundary is inappropriately drawn and, unusually for a house which has such a condition attached, it is, on any estimate, within a large urban area.

almost be measured in millimetres, and in the second case, the site quite obviously fell within what could quite reasonably be regarded as an urban area!

An opposite situation arises when agricultural development is refused on the grounds that it would be damaging to residential amenity. While one would not say that a refusal on such grounds is always inadmissible, it is nevertheless necessary to remember that the *raison d'être* of most villages is to serve agriculture. Figure 17.18 shows a quite extraordinary case. It brings in several issues.

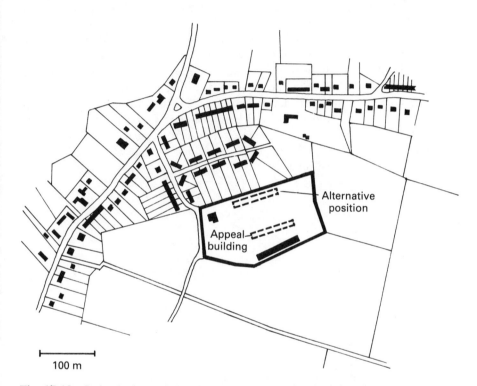

Fig. 17.18 Refusal of permission for an agricultural building. Because of a curious technicality in the General Development Order the appellant needed planning permission for the agricultural building in the position shown. If he had put it in the alternative position, more than ninety metres from the existing building, erected within the previous two years, he would not have needed permission, but the new building would have been *much* closer to the neighbours who complained vociferously!

There was a poultry farm using intensive methods (batteries). Much though one may deplore such activities, they are legal, and as already argued in several parts of this book, it is not the function of town planning to engage in moral argument. The farmer needed an additional battery house and applied for planning permission because it was so sited as to be just outside the tolerances given to agricultural buildings by the General Development Order. He was refused permission on the grounds that the amenities of nearby residents would be injured and that the view from a nearby public footpath would be injured. At the appeal it was duly pointed out that the nearby houses were just about as adventitious as any village houses could be, they and their occupiers having nothing whatever to do with the agricultural industry and that, subject to normal constraints regarding privacy and loss of light, there was no reason whatever for their interests to receive special consideration. It was further pointed out that a similar building could, taking account of the peculiarities of General Development Order exemptions, have been erected in a position which would have been much more harmful to neighbours without planning permission being sought at all. As to the footpath, very much as in the case of the riding school appeal mentioned on pp. 192–5, the building would only be visible from it for a total distance of about fifty metres. Almost incredibly, the appeal was dismissed on wishy-washy and evasive grounds, the inspector clearly wanting to please what he regarded as public opinion rather than think the whole thing through to a just determination. To finish a rather shameful affair, before the appellant could get on and build a building in a position which did not need planning permission, the council managed to push through an Article 4 direction which removed agricultural buildings in that area from General Development Order exemption.

18 _____

The urban fringe

As was mentioned in the last chapter, there is an overlap between the material dealt with there and that to be dealt with in this chapter. Some of the kinds of development dealt with in this chapter might in some circumstances be considered acceptable in open country as well as in the urban fringe, but we concentrate here on problems which typically and frequently arise in the urban fringe.

The expression perhaps needs explanation. The urban fringe is the area beyond the continuously built-up area of a town, but so close to it that it attracts uses which draw their living mostly from the adjacent urban area, uses which do not wish to or cannot afford to locate within the urban area because they need so much land, and look for sites just outside it. Some of these uses are harmless, suitable and useful; others very much otherwise. Nearly all urban areas tend to attract a sort of scurf around their edges which is liable to push genuine open country further away from urban dwellers. That is always undesirable, likely to be unsightly, and some uses are liable to attract much greater quantities of traffic than the local road system is designed for or can comfortably take. For all that, some urban fringe uses simply have to be accepted. It would not be economically feasible (or desirable, because of the need to maintain compact town texture) for large garden centres, for example, to locate themselves in the hearts of urban areas.

Consideration of the urban fringe can be divided into where the edge of the urban area ought to be, which uses ought to be allowed only within that edge and which can reasonably go outside.

The general principles of planning almost any town should be to allot enough land for all purposes that can be foreseen, allowing for full, but not excessively dense development of land, but, consistently with that, to keep the town as compact as possible and to provide a road system adequate to deal with the total amount and local intensities of traffic which will be produced by the allocation of uses in the town plan. It follows that any urban use which goes outside the urban perimeter is likely to have some disadvantages:

1. It may attract excessive traffic from the planned urban road network to the rural network, which is not designed to take much traffic.
2. It will increase noise, movement and disturbance in what should be the quiet of the rural area and may prove detrimental to the local ecology.
3. It may appreciably and undesirably increase the quantum of journeys to work by having to draw employees from a considerable distance.
4. It may visually blur the distinction between town and country.

A general planning principle, much more generally subscribed to than most and already referred to in relation to villages, is that there should be as sharp a line as possible drawn between town and country, that, almost literally, one ought to be able to stand with one foot in the town and the other in the country. Obviously, the more uses that are allowed in the urban fringe, the more this desirable distinction becomes blurred.

Ideally, it would be better for most activities associated with urban fringes to be placed within the urban area but in the less central and less accessible parts of it (see Fig. 18.1). There, specific allowance has been made for such uses in areas which would interfere least with the urban accessibility pattern, though within the urban perimeter. The hard truth is that at present we simply do not plan fully or decisively enough for this to be a generally feasible policy. In view of present aspirations regarding prices expected to be realised from urban land, it would be very difficult indeed for a council to succeed on appeal with such

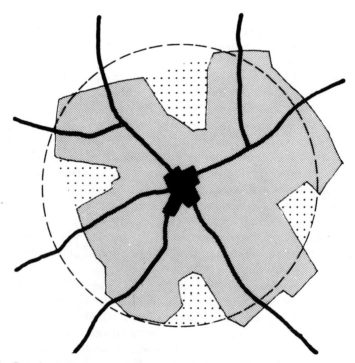

Fig. 18.1 Low intensity uses can appropriately be sited in areas such as those shown dotted, comparatively far from lines of communication.

a policy. Moreover, there is an inherent, severe difficulty in it: the difficulty of quantifying demand and need for uses of the kind under discussion is very great. Demand waxes and wanes; virtually new uses spring into prominence quite quickly. Who, fifteen years ago, could have foreseen and made provision in town plans for the amount of land now demanded for garden centres?

Two special cases cause difficulties, but also provide help:

1. Some very fine buildings outside the urban perimeter, previously distinguished dwellings, have to be found new uses if they are to be kept in existence as they should be. But any new use must not be of a kind which will attract too much traffic for local roads to carry.
2. Some recently erected buildings outside the urban perimeter, perhaps unwisely permitted, and erected for a particular purpose, have been deserted by the concerns that built them, and the economic loss of refusing to allow a new use, a loss ultimately directly and indirectly borne by all of us, is too great to justify leaving them to decay. This argument should not be taken too far. Generally speaking, it is a good thing for errors to be allowed to decay. How else would town planning ever ultimately succeed? But evidently there are limits to tolerable economic loss, though where those limits lie is a matter for judgement and argument. The issues involved are too complex to be dealt with by even the most refined cost-benefit analysis.

Some of the uses to be discussed could quite rationally be placed in urban industrial areas if these were made extensive enough. However, this would hardly be practicable for others, because for security reasons or the need for attendance throughout the night, a house needs to be provided on the site, and who would willingly live in it in the midst of an industrial area? Many claims for such needs are, nevertheless, exaggerated or bogus; a night time 'pad' might often be all that was really needed. But some of the activities under consideration, though going well beyond 'hobbies' and more than ancillary to the occupation of a house, are, none the less, pleasant, low-intensity activities which require living on the spot in order to carry them on, and which people would hardly want to carry on unless they could live in reasonably pleasant surroundings. Some, such as garden centres, to mention these once more, may also be activities which produce, in part at least, a pleasant appearance for the site. Others, such as used car dumps from which spare parts are sold, are inherently unsightly and need to be hidden as thoroughly as possible.

Obviously, greater tolerance can and should be shown to uses which can utilise existing buildings than to those which require new buildings to be erected; the greater the merit of a building to be so used and the narrower the range of uses for which it is suitable the greater should be the tolerance. But tolerance can never be absolute, and should not be given if appreciable disadvantages are likely to follow. There must be some sliding scale, ranging from: 'Even if it meant putting up a new building, this site would be acceptable for this purpose' to 'Even if this were the most beautiful building in the world and it could be put to no other use, putting it to this use would not be justifiable; too much planning harm would result.'

191

Here is an interesting borderline case from the north-west of England. Very extensive buildings, totalling several acres of floor-space, were erected only about a decade ago, some 2 km outside the edge of a town on farmland on a rather prominent site. The buildings have no visual merit and were erected for rather sinister research purposes. After some years, the owners and occupiers simply abandoned them. They must have been very well-to-do owners, for the buildings must have cost some millions of pounds. It is surprising that planning permission was given. The council concerned now look at the buildings rather differently and are reluctant to give permission for any other purpose. Are they right? On the one hand the buildings are unattractive. If they were used for a purpose which involved them being filled to capacity with workers the local road system might well be swamped. On the other hand, if they are left unoccupied they may take many years to fall down and will look increasingly unpleasant meanwhile. It also seems a shocking waste for the huge sums of money spent on them to be lost. Some use probably ought to be permitted, subject to a limit on the number of people employed, and perhaps subject to some of the less substantial and uglier buildings being removed. At the time of writing the issue has not been resolved.

Apart from public institutional uses, the kinds of uses which are likely to try to locate in urban fringes and which might reasonably be contemplated there, are:

- Garden centres (for which good road access is essential)
- Boarding kennels and breeding establishments for cats and dogs
- Riding schools
- Small private zoos
- Car dumps (needing to be thoroughly hidden)
- Nursing homes
- Private institutions of all kinds, including schools
- Hotels
- Filling stations
- Animal and vehicle race tracks

It needs to be borne in mind that while a proper site has to be found somewhere for any necessary use, there may not be a site in or adjacent to *every* town suitable for every such use. The location of things such as household refuse dumps, sewage disposal works and so on is not discussed, since these are 'one off' special, publicly promoted developments which do not fall within the ordinary development control and appeal system. The following examples illustrate the kinds of problems typically and commonly encountered in appeals relating to urban fringe problems.

Figure 18.2 illustrates an appeal more remarkable for the extraordinary course that the appeal took than for the inherent difficulty of the planning problem raised; but, taking these two aspects together, it deserves to be related fairly fully. The site lay within a green belt; this helped to confuse matters, because between the site and genuine countryside were a ridge fully developed for housing, and another ridge on which was massive development, of town size,

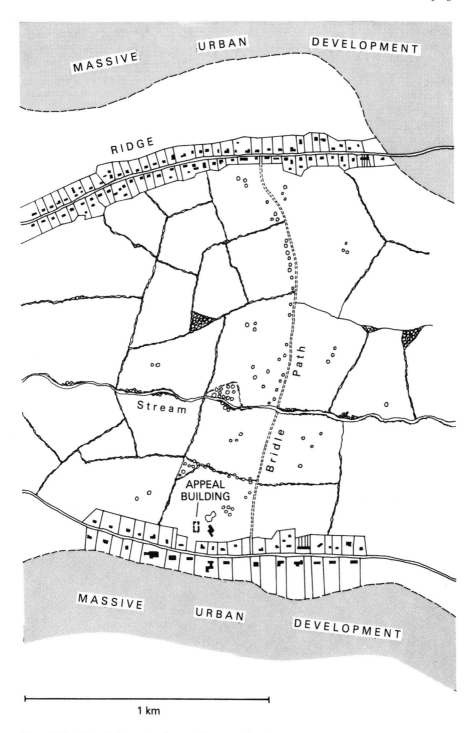

Fig. 18.2 The riding school case discussed in the text

which formed part of a conurbation. The actual open area of this particular piece of green belt was only of the order of 5 km². On a farm, the farmhouse of which actually lay within urban development, a horse riding school was operated. The associated farmland was genuine farmland but was not what one would regard as being very seriously farmed. It was intersected by bridle paths. The riding school was a very serious enterprise and it was found that in the English climate it suffered severely from all the teaching activities having to be carried on outdoors. A makeshift building, was erected to serve for indoor riding instruction. This was done without planning permission having been obtained and set the council's teeth on edge, and, after a great deal of *brouhaha*, it was removed. An architect was engaged and an application for planning permission was made for the erection of a purpose-built indoor riding school. The building was well designed and skilfully sited, being tucked away in a fold in the ground so as to be inconspicuous. Planning permission was refused on numerous and lengthily expressed grounds, the two principal ones being that the use of the proposed building was inconsistent with its location in the green belt and that in any case it would be visually offensive and injurious to the amenity of numerous nearby residents. It should be noted that the most vociferous of nearby residents in subsequent proceedings lived about 2 km away, along the first of the ridges previously mentioned.

The whole of the proceedings was marked by ill will and ill manners to an unusual extent. Before the inquiry took place, a conference was arranged between representatives of the appellants and of the council. It broke up in disorder after about twenty minutes because of the astonishingly rude and dictatorial manner of the Town Clerk who, uninvited, chaired it. The council briefed an able and exceedingly tough barrister to represent them, but it was noticed at the inquiry that his toughness was hardly matched by the strength of the evidence that he called. Residents allegedly affected, amenity groups and so on, were represented by exceedingly offensive solicitors.

The issues were simple. The recreational use was wholly compatible with the recreational purposes of the green belt; the proposed building, simply supplementary to the outdoor riding school activities, would make them much more effective. There was no question of a traffic problem. As has been said, the building, a pleasant-looking one, would hardly be visible from anywhere. Evidence was given for the appellants that out of a total length of about 2 km of public bridle path, the building would be visible over a total length of about 50 metres. Efforts to discredit this were made on behalf of the council, but at a subsequent site inspection it was seen to be perfectly true. Even if physically just capable of being viewed from the houses on the ridge, distance and the frequent mistiness of the English climate, together with much pleasant vegetation in the form of trees and hedges would render the building an object far from prominent in the landscape, even leaving out of account that it was the houses that were intrusions into the green belt, not the riding school. The appellant's barrister, rather appropriately in the atmosphere in which the inquiry was carried out, was better known for his advocacy in murder cases than in planning appeals, but acquitted himself very well. There was, metaphorically, a lot of blood on the floor, but practically all of it flowed from the council and the objectors.

The site inspection was very funny indeed. Almost at once the inspector detected something that the opposition had failed to, namely that the outline of the proposed building drawn on photographs produced by the council was vastly bigger than it would actually be (always be very careful about super-imposing proposed buildings on photographs; the opportunities for error are endless). One third-party objector alleged that the building would be visible from a number of places and was sent off to find them. He lost himself for a while and rejoined the inspecting party much later, tired and bedraggled and having to admit failure. Led by the inspector, the party entered the back garden of a house on the ridge, to be met by the surprised owner. The inspector explained the party's presence, whereupon the owner disclaimed all knowledge of having objected to the proposed development, although he had been legally represented at the inquiry as an objector. The appellants' representatives enjoyed a large and hilarious lunch.

The appeal was of course allowed, though this was the case, mentioned in Chapter 11, where the unfortunate inspector wrote 'dismissed' in his rec-ommendations where he meant to write 'allowed'. Thousands of pounds of public and private money were spent on this affair quite needlessly; the council had no case. They would not have had any case even if the housing on the ridge had not existed and the site had been on the edge of open country. It was as good and legitimate an urban fringe development as you could hope to find.

The next case is quite different. And here the appellant would probably have done better if the site had been more separated from urban development than it was. It is shown in Fig. 18.3. The site was on the edge of an urban area and was already used for breeding dogs. The proposal was to add to this a 'cat hotel'. There was no access or parking problem, and little objection from neigh-bours. The essence of the matter was that, nevertheless, the site was immedi-ately adjoined by houses with good-sized, but not enormous gardens. It seemed on common-sense grounds very probable that there would be from time to time often enough to cause serious disturbance to neighbours, not only an extra total quantity of noise issuing from the site because of the meows added to the existing woofs, but also (rather more seriously) disagreement between the dogs and cats however carefully they were kept, which would lead to noisy demonstrations.

It did not seem to either council or inspector that this was a risk which could reasonably be taken. This is an interesting case, because if only the adjoining houses had been twice as far away, the site would have been ideal for the purpose, and also because if much weight had been given to the comparative absence of third-party objection, council or inspector might well have concluded that permission should be given. They rightly acted to protect adjoining resi-dents against the likelihood of disturbance which they appeared not to have appreciated

Next, a fairly common type of case. A large, genuinely fine old house set in a small park, kept up in some style and with art treasures. It is occasionally

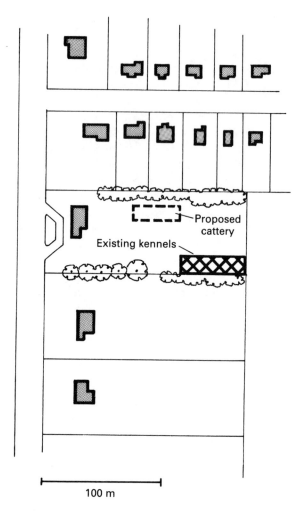

Fig. 18.3 Dogs and cats. This is a site just acceptable for a kennels. Add a cattery and trouble would be likely.

open to the public. There are various outbuildings, which include staff quarters. The application is to build two new dwellings for staff. The site is not even close to the outskirts of a town; it is a mile or more outside. An eminently reasonable proposal, except that there are thousands of houses for which similar reasons could be given for permitting ancillary staff houses. By permitting such applications, all the bad consequences set out on page 181 inevitably follow.

Places of worship are difficult to site suitably nowadays. They mostly now cannot find or afford the town centre sites or neighbourhood centre sites which might be thought appropriate for them. From the town planning point of view they tend to make noise and attract traffic. Though one must feel hesitant about the suitability of such central-area-oriented uses for urban fringe sites, these are

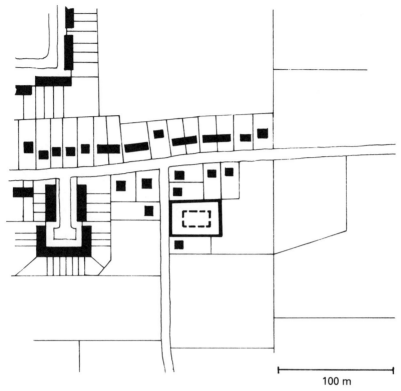

Fig. 18.4 A proposed church. The need for a sizeable urban site naturally made this attractive to the developers, but it is simply too close to houses to be acceptable.

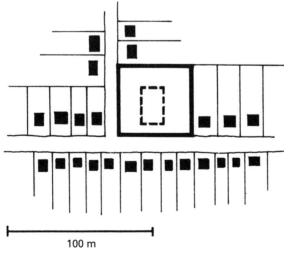

Fig. 18.5 Another proposed church. Objections arise similar to those in Fig. 18.4, but here there is also the disadvantage of substantial traffic having to manoeuvre and park very close to a road junction.

197

about the only practicable and harmless locations for many of them. Clearly, good access and a reasonable distance away from nearby houses are the essential minimum conditions. Figures 18.4 and 18.5 are examples of where they will not quite do.

19

Miscellaneous uses

The very varied topics dealt with in this chapter have two things in common: consideration of many of them involves the use of highly technical expertise of a specialist kind which is unlikely to be possessed by most chartered town planners, and they all, wholly or in large part, relate to the appearance of the appeal site and its surroundings.

About the first of these two factors, it would not be appropriate in this short book to offer more than a few general comments, but these are necessary because some of these specialised matters may be incidentally or peripherally involved in planning appeals where the main subject-matter of the appeal relates to ordinary town planning matters.

As regards the second factor, appearance, special difficulties are involved, because not only does it have to be debated how the control of appearance should be exercised, but also why and even whether it should be exercised. *Town Planning Made Plain*, (Ch. 6, pp. 120–34) discusses these issues, particularly the very difficult issue of whether these controls should be exercised from the viewpoint of pure aesthetics or that of 'the man on the Clapham omnibus' or somewhere in between.

To take the question of specialist knowledge a little further, it is foolish to purport to give expert evidence about something regarding which one is not in fact expert. For all that, where the main argument is about general town planning matters and the specialist aspects so subsidiary that calling in a specialist expert cannot be justified, it may be possible for a chartered town planner witness-advocate to score usefully in respect of the specialist aspects, not by way of giving evidence on them but in the course of cross-examining his opponents. To do so he may have to 'fish' a little and will of course do so the more effectively if he has at least armed himself with some sound information. For example, if the siting of a building is the main issue, but there is also involved the appropriateness or otherwise of its architectural design, one does not have to be an architect to be able to suggest that, say, a thin building with strong

199

vertical emphasis is likely to be a curious companion for adjoining wide buildings with strong horizontal emphasis. Nor does it take an architect to know that a keeper's house at a rural zoo (in effect a 'key worker's cottage') will be less conspicuous in the rural setting if it is a one-storey building rather than a two-storey building. One does not need to be an architect to be able to say with confidence that, on the other hand, an assertion that a building is out of character with its surroundings is not a good reason for refusal if the prevailing character of the surroundings is awful.

We now turn to brief consideration of some of the more important of these very varied matters.

Minerals

Building operations always cause some disturbance around them while they are going on, perhaps for months or even a year or so. This is inevitable and a normal part of the processes of change in the built environment. It can seldom, if ever, be a good reason for refusing an application. The situation is quite different with mineral workings, which may well, on a particular site, continue for very many years and be accompanied all the time by disturbances similar to those caused by building operations and also many more: very large and noisy machinery, explosions, dust, greatly increased traffic on nearby roads, a deposit of mud on these roads, and a changing, but always unpleasant effect on the landscape.

Different kinds of minerals are won in many different ways; the depths of the overburden and of the mineral seams and varying richness of yield produce widely varying amounts of spoil. There is an intermixture of matters which can be sensibly thought about and dealt with in the light of ordinary town planning knowledge and of those which can only be sensibly assessed in the light of specialist knowledge about minerals. Other individual items combine general and specialist aspects, both of which have to be taken into account for their proper determination. Here there is need to avoid being overborne by the specialist aspects, which may easily happen if a confident and loquacious specialist witness is employed in situations where the general or common-sense aspect is at least as, or more, important.

The sort of thing that often arises is the question of how good a mineral yield from a particular site has to be in order for working to be 'economic'. What does 'economic' mean? The word is often, sometimes ignorantly, sometimes deliberately, confused with 'economical'. 'Economic' means 'worth carrying on from the point of view of profitability'. 'Economical' means 'relatively cheap to carry on'. Something can therefore easily be economic without being very economical. Something could be relatively economical compared with something else, yet still not be economic.

There is often, in mineral working appeals, the predominant issue of necessity, linked with that of economy. This causes much confusion, because it is often difficult to disentangle whose needs and whose economics are being talked about and, if those of one party conflict with those of another, whose should prevail. Moreover, conflicts of interest in this area are frequently of a kind which preclude direct comparison of advantage and disadvantage being made. The distance of alternative mineral working sites from markets is often raised as an important issue, but, important though it may be, it ought not necessarily to be decisive. In relation to, say, roadstone, even if Rockshire is virtually made of roadstone, this may not be very helpful for Mudshire a hundred miles away, because of transport costs. Nevertheless, it might justly be urged that Mudshire should be required to make do with supplies of roadstone from Rockshire, despite the increased cost, if the only alternative is to use the limited roadstone resources of Mudshire in such a way that inevitably much of the very special and lovely landscape of Mudshire will be wrecked.

The role of the chartered town planner in matters of this kind may have to be limited to exposing the real issues; he may not be able to work out the best solution. The act of disentanglement may, however, be very valuable in enabling the best solution to be arrived at.

As a matter of design, the chartered town planner may be able to do a good deal to reconcile the use of an area for mineral working with concurrent and later land uses in the vicinity and to suggest general landscaping policies as part of after treatment. Even here, his role must be limited; he cannot be mineralogist, geologist, economist, landscape architect, ecologist and botanist rolled into one. This is where teamwork in the proper sense of the word should come in.

Tipping

If mineral working is essentially making holes, tipping is essentially filling in holes. Many of the problems are similar, especially those of traffic and appearance, but in addition many kinds of pollution, including those of underground water supply, may be involved, about which of course specialist expert evidence is necessary. One specialist item which does occur with mineral workings, but occurs much more crucially with tips, is the question of what can be grown on tips after they have been completed, and what measures are needed to ensure that successful planting will eventually be possible.

Caravans

Many aspects of this intractable problem are dealt with in other legislation, namely the Caravan Sites and Control of Development Act 1960. With caravans the planning aspects and public health aspects are both so important and so intertwined that, wisely I think on the whole, in order to avoid confusion between the two, separate control legislation has been introduced. However, general questions of location remain in relation to town planning.

It is necessary to distinguish sharply between holiday caravans and caravans as permanent residential accommodation. The siting of holiday caravans is evidently in many parts of the country predominantly a town planning problem, a question of countryside conservation and the avoidance of overwhelming approach roads. Permanent residential caravans, though quantitatively a smaller problem, pose quite different issues. As permanent homes, their location, density and layout should not, in my view, be regarded differently from houses. Privacy, traffic, accessibility to schools, shops and open spaces are or ought to be considerations to be dealt with similarly to those arising from any other housing project. As regards appearance, it is fairly clear that caravans do not sit very well if interspersed with ordinary houses, or if so sited as to form a prominent part of the urban scene. Concentration of residential caravans into a comparatively small number of sites is therefore desirable, and some tactful screening, purely on visual grounds, from nearby ordinary housing is also sensible. One cannot help thinking that just as allotments are a makeshift substitute for individual gardens, the need for which should be made to wither away as the result of the application of proper residential density policy, so more vigorous and enlightened housing policy should cause the need and demand for residential caravans to wither away.

Outdoor advertising

It is in a sense merely accidental that control of outdoor advertising should have been incorporated in the British legal planning code. Apart from its effect upon appearance, it has nothing to do with the subject of town planning: nothing to do with the allocation of appropriate quantities of land for various purposes in appropriate places. To draw a curious comparison, just as green belt policy, though intellectually indefensible, has been remarkably effective, so control of outdoor advertising has obvious intellectual weaknesses but has achieved remarkable success. *Planning Control of Signs and Posters* (HMSO, 1965) is an insufficiently known Ministry publication; it gives a large number of illustrated examples of appeal decisions about outdoor advertising. I find it impossible from this otherwise excellent publication to draw any conclusions about the principles, if any, upon which these decisions have been based.

The Advertisement Regulations, which are a kind of equivalent to the General Development Order and the Use Classes Order for outdoor advertisements, are complex and, I think, in some ways irrational, but they can be learned without very much difficulty. One would not want to tamper too much with a system which has been so successful, but the establishment of rational principles in relation to it would avoid the waste of a good deal of public and private time and money. Someone ought to write a short book on the subject.

Building and Tree Preservation orders

It is easy to understand the need to preserve superb architecture in the form of individual buildings and groups of buildings, though in the latter case the matter is complicated because some of the individual buildings included in the group may have no special merit themselves. It is equally easy to understand the need to preserve individual trees especially beautiful in themselves or in relation to their surroundings, groups of trees and, for rather different reasons, large areas of trees which form an important part of a landscape of merit.

It is also easy, though not quite so easy, to understand the desirability of preserving buildings or sites of exceptional historical interest. Whether or not one believes that some kind of magic quality is inherent in such places, at the very least, contemplation of them stimulates the imagination and creates or at least strengthens understanding of the past. But I think it is necessary to try to distinguish sensibly between the visual qualities of buildings and sites and their historical interest. The two, of course, are very often combined, but not always. As regards historical interest, the advance of technology makes it easier and easier to preserve detailed and vivid records of what a building or site looked like in relation to its historical interest without actual physical preservation. I therefore believe that there should be caution in insistence upon preservation for purely historical reasons. I do not think that Dickens having stayed in a house for a month is a reason for preservation of that house, while, without perhaps being able to justify the view in detail, I do think that a year's residence by a world-shaker such as Buddha, Jesus or Charles Darwin would.

Trees are even more difficult. However hard one tries, trees do not live for ever. Thought about tree preservation is in a state of some confusion. It is necessary in formulating tree preservation policy to accept that the preservation of a tree or trees on account of inherent botanical beauty is not permanent and that requirements to replant if a tree dies or becomes dangerous ought to be dependent upon whether it was the intrinsic botanical beauty of the original tree which was the reason for its preservation or if it was that in that particular location there ought permanently to be a tree or trees, independent of the inherent beauty of the trees.

I am the proud owner of an area of perhaps 200 m² of land, full of trees; because the land is in a village conservation area, regulations (SI 1975 No 148) prescribe that all those with a diameter of more than 75 mm at 1.75 m above ground level, are automatically subject to preservation. Some of the trees are dead or dying, none is a beautiful tree in itself, few if any (and in any case only the tops of them) are visible from any point to which the public has access. There must be thousands of sites like this. Can present blanket methods of preservation be thought to make any sense? Could they possibly be enforced to a worthwhile extent? Is not the impossibility of effective enforcement apt to bring the law into contempt?

A further confusion is for planning authorities to assume that tree preservation and building development on the same site are necessarily incompatible. Figure 19.1 illustrates an interesting appeal case. Here, a tree preservation order, quite legitimately applied, had as its purpose the maintenance of the appearance of a generally wooded skyline as viewed from a mile or more away. The proposal was to intersperse housing at fairly low density among the trees, the site being unquestionably within an urban area suitable for housing development. The

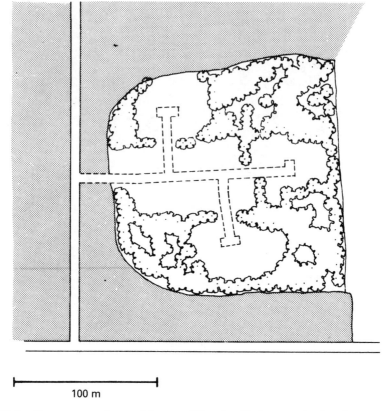

100 m

Fig. 19.1 Tree preservation and houses. Why should there not be housing among these trees? The location is suitable for houses and few, if any, good trees need be lost. Their only importance is that they form part of a silhouette seen from afar. The houses will not affect this.

appeal was lost despite incontrovertible evidence that the desired development could take place without the general effect of a wooded silhouette being damaged. Argument in that case was confused by the unpardonable failure of planning legislation to define, except in the case of automatic tree preservation orders in conservation areas, what a tree is. Is a beech seedling 5 cm high a tree? It might be said to be so, but if it is the position is absurd: in almost any tree preservation area one would be liable to destroy dozens of 'trees' merely by walking through the area!

To make the point once more, chartered town planners can have much that is useful and sensible to say in planning appeals involving tree preservation, but they cannot be expected to be botanists or foresters, to whose opinions they should defer in all matters about which the latter are expert.

20

Planning standards

It is, as has been suggested at various points throughout this book, desirable to steer a careful course with standards, neither, on the one hand, slavishly adhering to over-detailed, rigid and perhaps ill-based standards, nor, if possible, reverting to reliance upon a sort of intuitive or inspirational 'feeling' as to whether something is or is not satisfactory. Intuitive judgements based upon experience may often be sound enough from the point of view of the person who makes them, but very difficult to put in a form which will be acceptable or comprehensible to those to whom they are made, particularly to those disadvantaged by them.

The history of standards in British planning has been an odd one, proceeding from the traditional '1932 Act' array of minutely detailed, interlocking standards relating to density and space about buildings, often based upon nothing more than intuition or, at best, upon examples of good contemporary development. We moved to more scientifically based standards, such as the Daylight Code and the Floor Space Index. But because these were never sufficiently developed and refined, and in their comparatively crude state gave rise to numerous anomalies, there has been a movement away from these towards the purely intuitive.

That there is a need for properly based standards can hardly be denied; nor can it be denied that they would be very difficult to devise, based, as many would have to be, upon translation into specific dimensions of ethological concepts such as personal space, defensible territory and so forth. What has just been said does not of course fully apply to standards designed simply to bring parking space and traffic into rough accord with each other; these are, in principle, not difficult to devise and verify.

The more general a standard is, the surer we can be that it is roughly correct. General standards such as residential densities and amounts of public open space fall into this category. It is difficult if not impossible to define optima of this kind with precision, but not at all difficult to get them about right.

However, the establishment and maintenance of standards of that kind depend also, apart from new towns and similar development, upon the imposition of appropriate *detailed* standards in a multitude of individual development control cases. These are much more difficult because it is much less certain that the standards applied will be correct. The establishment of an appropriate general standard of space for public playing fields can readily be based upon a study of demands and trends, the results of which can produce standards which, though they may be capable of being challenged in detail, can hardly be challenged to an extent which would justify gross alteration in the standard. But an assertion (which I make myself) that there should be a distance of 'about a chain' between facing windows of habitable rooms and between rear elevations and rear garden boundaries is necessarily vague because no one has yet found a way of establishing its validity with precision. Worse, alterations to and relaxations of such a standard produce considerable differences in the amounts of land needed to accommodate a given number of people and the amounts and locations of neighbourhood facilities and services needed.

In the present state of knowledge, some simple space standards, especially for residential development, are certainly better than none, and probably the simpler they are the better, though the simpler they are the more exceptions to them will have to be accepted.

Leaving out of account, as irrelevant to most appeals, general standards such as overall amounts of urban land to be devoted to various uses, the standards needed are divisible into: (1) space about buildings; (2) traffic and parking; and (3) appearance.

Space about buildings

Space about buildings can be further divided into standards relating to privacy, (sub-divisible into privacy against sight, sound and smell) and standards to ensure sufficient access of daylight and sunlight to buildings and sites.

The 'sight' aspect of privacy

This is at once the most important and the easiest to deal with. It really only applies in relation to dwellings. In work-places, the need for visual privacy is very slight compared with that needed for the normal intimacies of domestic life. Little more needs to be said about it, since it has been discussed at intervals throughout this book, particularly in Chapter 14.

Privacy against sound

The main safeguard against house to house sound is adequate party walls, but garden to garden and garden to house sounds are different. Little mitigation is achieved by screen walls and fences; the effectiveness of spatial separation is unequalled.

Smells

The same applies to domestic smells, especially, of course, cooking smells. As regards industrial smells, I do not think that they (as distinct from atmospheric pollution by smoke, dust, etc.) have ever been quantified or are capable of quantification. However harmless to physical health they may be, they can be quite unpleasant, and spatial separation of the source may well be the only practicable remedy.

Daylight and sunlight

These are, by contrast, readily and precisely measurable items. In respect of them, excellent practical codes have been worked out. (See *Sunlight and Daylight*, HMSO, 1971.) Some practical difficulties arise because such codes, dependent as they are upon measurements of heights and angles, cannot take into account the very different amounts of light reflected by nearby buildings according to their colours and textures nor the reduction of light caused by nearby vegetation, especially trees (which may well be preserved trees!); nor, it has been found, are they of much use in ascertaining the probable effects of minor house extensions. Unfortunately, there really does not seem to be in this matter a practicable alternative to common sense and the application of experience, though as in so much else with planning appeals, a simple set of measurements based upon valid assumptions, whether made by contestants or inspector, may be worth more than pages of words.

Traffic and parking

These produce problems more difficult of solution than would at first sight appear likely. To illustrate this, let us pose a few questions.

In considering how much, if any, parking space should be provided in connection with a proposed development, to what extent should parking along adjacent roads be taken into account? To what extent should nearby public parking space be taken into account? To what extent should acknowledged and remediable deficiencies in nearby public parking provision be taken into account? To what extent should the physical impracticability of providing on-site parking be taken into account? To what extent should willingness to provide multi-storey parking either above or below ground be taken into account in assessing permissible intensity of development? There are no very easy answers to any of these questions.

To illustrate some of the difficulties, I mention a case from some time ago in which the foolish behaviour of a council and an inspector has burnt itself into my memory. There was, in a Midland town, a small and inconvenient pub, which its brewer owners wished to redevelop. Being a public-minded company, they were willing and indeed anxious to incorporate in the new building a theatre club on an upper floor. They were refused planning permission because

207

they did not, and indeed could not, provide the number of on-site parking spaces required by the council's parking standard policy. The site was very small, within the central area of an impoverished town. There was a lot of public parking space within two or three hundred metres. If necessary, more could readily have been provided by the council on derelict sites within a hundred metres. There was little traffic or parking in the streets and it was hardly conceivable that any additional parking produced by the proposed development could not have been readily accommodated by kerbside parking without detriment to traffic flow or inconvenience to occupiers of premises. There were no central area redevelopment proposals which might have been in conflict with the proposed development. The council really did seem to be trying to cut its nose off to spite its face. The appeal was feebly contested by the council, but the inspector found for them on the grounds that the proposed development did not comply with the council's parking standards. The town lost its free theatre club. The moral is: planning standards are necessary and desirable in order to ensure the sound and consistent application of development control, but if ill-conceived or badly applied they do even more harm than an absence of standards.

Residential parking standards also present grave difficulties, as discussed in Chapter 14. A very commonly imposed standard is to require new residential development to have two parking spaces off the road for each dwelling; in simple terms, two cars for each household or one car and a visitor's car. Does this make sense? It all depends. It certainly is not a bad idea in relation to a new housing estate. It ensures that the local roads will not get blocked. But what are local roads for? They are made in order to provide access to houses. Access to houses implies that calling vehicles will park on the road. The milkman is not going to pull off the road and park 'on-site' at every house at which he calls.

An elementary common-sense principle for residential roads is that they should at least be wide enough for two wide vehicles to pass each other or for a vehicle in motion to be able to pass a parked vehicle; with widths for house plots of ten metres or more numerous vehicles can park on both sides of the road, yet allow slowly and prudently driven vehicles to thread their way through. Put very simply, therefore, normal rules for road widths in ordinary housing areas (widths which could not sensibly be further relaxed even if there were no parking), in fact allow for normal parking traffic to be accommodated without danger or congestion. Requirements for two off-street parking places per house are therefore no more than a useful bonus, a bonus which can quite legitimately be imposed without loss or detriment to anyone in 'estate' housing development, and necessary if the plots are narrower than about ten metres but they do not make sense when sought to be imposed in relation to a single house nudged into a gap between existing houses. In such situations they ought to be deemed to be inapplicable. Few applications for the erection of a house which is, on locational grounds, desirable, ought to be refused merely because it cannot meet off-street parking standards. Of course, if it can be shown that such a house is likely to create a traffic hazard because it would be located on a sharp bend and/or adjacent to a carriageway of inadequate width, that is quite a different matter. As I have said earlier it is very interesting that in many cases in which the land use issues are finely balanced, inadequate and dangerous access may well be the determining factor against the proposal. My conclusion is that a standard of two parking spaces per house off the road is a sensible and reasonable one for estate development, but not at all a reasonable one for individual houses nudged in between existing development.

As regards general traffic considerations it seems to me that too much reliance is placed by councils upon existing traffic conditions compared with the traffic conditions which would or could obtain if the council had carried out thoroughly, conscientiously and efficiently its planning duties in relation to improvement of the highway system. A single example may serve to illustrate this; it is typical of many.

In East Anglia, the council opposed the conversion of a house to offices solely on the ground that the conversion would be likely to cast more traffic on a nearby main road which was already overloaded with traffic. The main road in question was one of the principal roads leading from the surrounding region to the heart of quite a large town. The land use suitability, *per se*, of the site in question was not in doubt. The council had done nothing whatever to prepare or implement plans for the improvement of the main road in order to make it a safe and efficient primary radial road. In the particular case, therefore, (no doubt there were many others in the vicinity) they were seeking to inhibit sensible and desirable development simply because they had failed in their town planning duty to provide for a proper main road framework for the town.

The 'standard', I think, which ought to be applied in such cases is whether the proposal would fit in with proposals which the council ought to have produced and implemented rather than the effects likely to be produced in terms of their inefficiency and inaction.

In relation to more general effects upon traffic, it seems to me that, as constantly emphasised, especially in Chapter 14, and failing some subtler method of testing, *Roads in Urban Areas* provides an admirable standard. If, on traffic grounds, a proposed development will not be likely to violate the figures given in Fig. 10.1 thereof, then, if on land use planning grounds it is acceptable, it ought to be allowed, and in assessing this there ought to be taken into account, and discounted, any sensible improvements to the existing road framework which the council have failed to carry out.

Appearance

It is at the very least doubtful whether standards, in the sense in which we have been using the term in this chapter, can sensibly be applied to matters of appearance. To do so is liable to reduce the subtle to the ludicrous. The inappropriateness and ineffectiveness of definitions of items such as 'infilling' and 'rounding off' have already been shown in Chapter 14. This applies, I think, even to general and essentially sensible statements about using local materials and the use of gabled rather than hipped roofs or vice versa. Here, I believe, we are in territory not amenable to codification or standardisation. To attempt either is likely to produce worse results than those produced by the outcome of argument based on educated aesthetic judgement.

However great the abuses to which the term has been put, 'functionalism' has a good deal to recommend it in relation to development control. If a proposal is made for something which can be shown to be suitable for its purpose on a suitable site, then it is likely that it is or can readily be made aesthetically suitable. As regards aesthetics, 'neighbour reaction' is likely to be even more wildly astray and unreliable than in other matters. I once saw this dramatically demonstrated. In reading papers before inspecting an appeal site, I saw that several third-party objections referred to the generally high visual

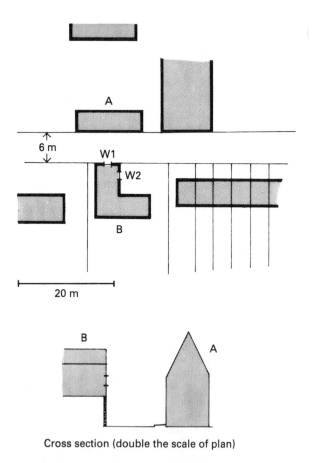

Cross section (double the scale of plan)

Fig. 20.1 Daylight. Any rule of thumb application of standards would prevent good redevelopment here. Building A is an old agricultural building, now used as an outbuilding to the adjoining house. Building B is a bungalow. But together they form a very suitable, closed termination to a village street which ought to remain even if the buildings are eventually replaced. Despite the differences in level of the two sides of the narrow street compliance with daylight standards applied in the ordinary way is hardly possible, but in fact all is well because W2 lights the same room as W1.

quality of the area in question, marred, they said, only by 'one recent aberration'. I suspected that this might in fact be the only decent house in the area; indeed it was; it was a very good design; all the other houses around it were quite without merit.

In a very unsophisticated planning situation it is just possible that a few broad pronouncements about aesthetic acceptability might be useful. In Queensland, which is unquestionably unsophisticated in planning, I once suggested that there should be a general requirement that not more than four houses (detached houses in the Queensland context) should be allowed to be sited in a straight line along a road. After that, subsequent houses should be required to be set either back or forward by the normal depth of a house, i.e. about eight metres. This may sound so crude as to be laughable, but if it had been applied in Queensland from 1970 onwards, Queensland housing would be better to look at and live in than it is.

To illustrate the difficulties in applying standards in such a way as to ensure good performance without imposing counter-productive rigidity, I close this chapter with two examples.

Figure 20.1 shows the existing situation in a street. The reader is invited to consider to what extent the imposition of planning standards would assist in or handicap good development control.

Second, consider Fig. 20.2. To what extent would reliance upon minimum standards suffice to promote sensible and equitable development, or is something special needed in such circumstances?

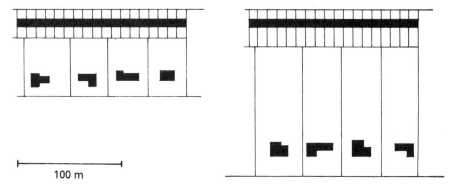

100 m

Fig. 20.2 Boundary between high and low density housing areas. (*Right*) There can be no legitimate grumble by the low density dwellers at the bottom if the houses shown above, with normal depth back gardens, are built. They still have reasonable privacy, even at the far ends of their back gardens. (*Left*) Occupants of the more modest low density development at the bottom *might* legitimately grumble about the building of very high density housing above. But perhaps not; they are still very privileged; it is a moot point.

211

21

Summary

I end as I began by saying that we have in this country a good, probably uniquely good, system for the settlement of development control disputes. If in the course of discussion that opinion has from time to time been overlaid by emphasis on defects, that is natural. Nothing is so good that it cannot be made better, and there is always a danger that if it is not made better it will become worse. The following, all already discussed in previous chapters, appear to me to be the main ways in which improvement is needed and the means which might be used to effect improvements. I like to think that a Secretary of State for the Environment might pin some such list above his desk and consider quarterly to what extent he had contributed towards their implementation in the preceding quarter.

Better appeal decisions

Try as one may to think otherwise, it is virtually certain that an undue proportion of appeal decisions are wrong decisions. That is to say, decisions which are likely to produce a worsening, however small, in the physical environment, rather than an improvement. To improve that situation, I think that the employment of better inspectors is the key. Better inspectors means, among other things, that all inspectors except for a tiny minority of specialists should be chartered town planners and should, despite the evident difficulties in the way of this (discussed in Ch. 11), be encouraged to be more independent in their decisions, more imaginative, more venturesome, relying less on conventional wisdom and more on technical expertise. Obviously, too, the better the information and evidence presented to an inspector from all sides, the better the chance of his being fully and accurately informed about the issues and of coming to a right decision. For this to happen as a matter of course, I am personally convinced that the resolution of every appeal should include a discussion between the inspector and the parties face to face, not confined to written representations (see Ch. 4).

Quicker decisions

Whatever minor speeding-up successes may be achieved by administrative re-arrangement and ingenuity, radical improvement must come from willingness by the DoE to take more risks and cut down the amount and meticulousness of their checking (see Ch. 4).

Pressure on councils to make decisions quickly and to respond quickly to requests for Statements of Case would also help. As regards the latter, progress-ively stronger pressure by the DoE is perhaps already producing results. As regards the former, however, I am convinced that levying substantial fines on councils which did not make and issue decisions on applications for planning permission within the allowed time would be likely to be effective. It is, indeed, probably the only effective means of speeding them up. Representatives of appellants also delay matters by failing to submit representations or supply information promptly. Quantitively, however, this must surely be a small item compared with the dilatoriness of councils.

Delays produced by the intervention and dilatoriness of third parties (not only private third parties, but County Engineers, Water Boards, etc.) have some effect. The relevance or otherwise of third-party contributions has been discussed in Chapter 5. One feels sure that less rather than more third-party participation would speed up the determination of appeals without reducing the quality of decisions.

Fewer appeals

It would be good if there were fewer appeals. One would not want to see a situ-ation in which any genuine disputes failed to be brought to appeal, but rather, more care being taken to ensure that a dispute genuinely existed before an appeal was set in train or determined. Applicants need to take much more care than many of them do to ensure that the applications they make are clear, accurate and unambiguous. Councils need to do the same for their decisions, but in addition to make sure that they are not refusing permission for something that does not need permission, and that they are using their planning powers for planning purposes, not illegitimately for some other purpose. As suggested in Chapter 11, I believe it would be a good thing if inspectors were permitted and encouraged to criticise in their decision letters exceptionally bad decisions by councils and exceptionally unreasonable applications. This might well have some deterrent effect; so would a somewhat tougher policy with regard to the award of costs. The last thing one would want would be for applicants to be deterred from making reasonable appeals or councils to be deterred from reasonable refusals, but both appellants and councils get away unpenalised with outrageous behaviour. In this regard it would be some help if award of costs in appeals dealt with by means of written representations was not entirely barred.

The three desiderata described above would all be assisted to fulfilment if more solid, technical, professional expertise were brought to bear throughout the planning process. This includes, very importantly, a recurrent theme throughout this book, namely the need for competent and appropriately detailed development plans to cover all developed and developing parts of the country. This in turn implies the use of more and even better trained chartered town planners. This would produce more solid evidence based on performance standards established by careful research as valid, applied against a background of properly established planning theory. The whole town planning field is still controlled to far too great an extent by those who know far too little about the subject.

Further reading ──────────────

As frequently indicated throughout the book Sweet and Maxwell's *Encyclopedia of Planning Law and Practice* is the principal, essential aid for anyone seriously involved with planning appeals. It is bound in four, large, loose-leaf volumes and costs (1984) £145. Revisions are frequently printed of parts which need updating and are supplied, with directions for places of insertion and old pages to be discarded, for an annual payment (1984) of £70. The savings in time, effort and peace of mind secured by its possession rapidly repay the cost many times over. It is not, initially, a very easy publication to use; indeed a short course of instruction in how to use it would be useful; but after a little practice almost any item of information one needs about the law of planning (and clues to related items) can quickly be found. What it does not include, and hardly could include, is graphic material of the kind included in, for example, the DoE's *Settlement in the Countryside* (Planning Bulletin No. 8. 1967). Very broadly, in fact, no strictly technical material is included in the Encyclopedia unless it is closely connected with legal points. Part 1, 'A General Statement of the Law relating to Town and Country Planning' is a quite admirable summary of the development and present state of the English planning system, while 'Planning Law and Practice from the Decisions' (Part VI, in vol. 4) by Harold J. J. Brown is an equally valuable summary of legal and ministerial decisions.

For a brief, accurate, readable book on planning law there is nothing to beat Sir Desmond Heap's *An Outline of Planning Law* (Sweet and Maxwell (8th edn) 1982). It excellently describes the wood without classifying the bark on the trees as the Encyclopedia so fully does. *The Journal of Planning and Property Law*, from the same house, published monthly, keeps information right up to date.

Professor P. McAuslan's *Land, Law and Planning* (Weidenfeld and Nicholson 1975) and *The Ideologies of Planning* (Pergamon Press 1980) are admirable discussions of the political philosophy of planning law, but will not and are not intended to help you win planning appeals. They would certainly help you to draft good planning legislation if it fell to you to have to do that.

So much for legal reading. When it comes to technical matters it is less easy to make suggestions. It is to be noted that the *Encyclopedia of Planning Law and Practice* deals with legal and administrative practice, not at all with technical practice. Here there is a surprising lack of publications and I can only, however unbecomingly, refer to my own *Town Planning Made Plain* (Construction Press 1983). Even this deals mainly with the 'why' and 'what' of planning and little with the 'how'. For details of the 'how' nothing has yet replaced my *Principles and Practice of Town and Country Planning* (Estates Gazette (4th edn) 1969). It is out of print.

Delegated legislation and Department of the Environment (HMSO) publications likely to be useful in connection with planning appeals include orders, circulars, memoranda, notes and handbooks. As suggested in Chapter 11, many are able, sensible and helpful in setting out the conventional wisdom at a particular time, but are so studded with 'normally' and 'in many, but not all cases', etc., that they provide only a watery diet; a diet, what is more, of ambiguous flavour. It is not at all uncommon for opposed parties at an appeal both to cite the same paragraph of the same DoE publication in support of their cases. The following is a list of the most useful as containing material which may be directly useful in fighting planning appeals, though others, too numerous to list, contain valuable items for that purpose.

The Town and Country Planning General Development Order (SI 1977 No. 289) and amendments to it (SI 1980 No. 1946 and SI 1981 No. 245), together with *The Town and Country Planning (Use Classes) Order* (SI 1972 No. 1385) are indispensable, complex material, great familiarity with which is necessary in many cases in order to decide with any confidence whether something needs planning permission. All have been extensively referred to in this book. To them must be added *The Town and Country Planning (National Parks, Areas of Outstanding Natural Beauty and Conservation Areas) Special Development Order* (SI 1981 No. 246). This, essentially, cuts down, in such areas, the amount of permitted development which is available elsewhere for house extensions, development within the curtilage of a dwelling-house and for certain industrial operations.

Ministry of Housing and Local Government Circular 5 of 1968, *The Use of Conditions in Planning Permissions* is very good and sensible. Most importantly it suggests tests for deciding whether to impose a condition: is it (a) necessary, (b) relevant to planning, (c) relevant to the development to be permitted, (d) enforceable, (e) precise and (f) reasonable?

DoE Circular No. 75 of 1976, *Development Involving Agricultural Land.* This contains material useful for embarrassing slipshod councils.

DoE Circular No. 36 of 1978, *Trees and Forestry* tells most of us more than we want to know.

DoE Circular No. 22 of 1980, *Development Control – Policy and Practice.* The great Tory 'planning liberalisation' document, but it does not really open the floodgates; councils find it as useful to resist appeals as developers do to promote them.

DoE Circular No. 9 of 1981 contains information and advice about, *inter alia*, SI 1981 No. 245 and SI 1981 No. 246 (see above).

Roads in Urban Areas, HMSO 1966, is an admirable technical treatise about urban road design.

Development Control Policy Notes. The conventional wisdom of the DoE in 1969 issued under numerous headings, ranging from *General Principles* to *Amusement Centres*; plenty of good if timidly expressed sense.

Settlement in the Countryside (Planning Bulletin No. 8 1967). Not recommended. Listed here simply because it has been mentioned in Chapter 17.

Sunlight and Daylight. Planning criteria and design of buildings. 1971 (2 volumes; second volume consists of transparent indicators). As explained in Chapter 14, the elegant technique described is not appropriate for use with minor development such as house extensions. For larger projects it is very useful, though insufficiently understood and used. If you master it and point it at your opponent it may well disquiet him, but be careful not to confuse the inspector.

Planning Appeals: a guide (HMSO 1983). Referred to in the Introduction to this book, this is an admirably clear and concise procedural guide.

Note added in proof

DoE Circular 1 of 1985, *The use of conditions in planning permissions*, was published just after the book was printed. It is a full and able reaffirmation and expansion of the principles, previously set out in Circular 5 of 1968, which should govern the imposition and wording of planning conditions.

Index _____

limited growth, 52
Local Government, Planning and Land Act 1980, 13
local plans, 26–7, 49, 57, 64, 83–7, 103, 104, 124, 152

Macmillan pledge, 175
magistrates, 23–4
maisonette defined, 133–4
mandarins, characteristics of, 89
maps, uses of, 66, 83–5
material change of use, 6, 16, 18, 19, 113, 114
methods of investigating appeals, 30 *et seq.*
minerals, 200, 201
Ministers, 23–5
minor development, 10
miscellaneous uses, Ch. 19 199–204
mixed areas, 77–8
mixed uses, 163–5
moorings, 108–21 *passim*
morals, 158
motherhood statements, 26, 84, 86
multiple restrictions in countryside, 84, 166, 168

'necessary' and 'essential', 76
need, 75–6
need for permission, 13–16
neighbours, 4, 43, 210
new development plan system, 89, 90
'nice' and 'nasty' areas, 77, 78
noise, 7, 152, 160, 161
Northern Ireland, 26
noxious industry *see* industry
nursing homes, 170, 192

oaths, 32
offices, 150, 153, 156, 159, 209
office use, 10, 11
officialese, avoidance of, 67
ombudsman, 69
open country, development in, Ch. 17 166–87
'operations', 6, 9
opinion, 22
opinion the determining factor, 15, 16, 113
opponent, trouserless, visualisation of, 69
ordnance maps, 83–5
outdoor advertising, viii

outline applications, 13, 21, 51
outline plan, 52
overbearing effect, 147
ownership, irrelevance of, 116, 120

Parker, Lord, 19, 113
Parker-Morris standards, 137
parking, 140, 141, 152, 165, 207–9
pedestrian precincts, 151–2
perimeter of nuisance, 151–9
permissions
    applications for, 4
    fees, 13, 14
    need for, 4–6, 13–16
    personal, 76–7
    temporary, 14, 76–7
permitted development, 116, 161, 187–8
Perry Mason, don't try to be, 68
personal permissions, 76–7
photographs, 67, 195
'place' contrasted with 'row', 179
Planning Advisory Group, 84, 89, 90
planning aid, 45–6
Planning Appeals: A Guide, viii
Planning Bulletin, *Settlement in the Countryside*, 181
'*Planning, Law and Practice from the Decisions*', 8
planning permission, obligation to apply for, vii, 4–6, 8, 13–16
planning policies, established, 24
planning schemes, 166
planning systems, 1974 Act, 167
planning unit, 111, 112, 117
plot ratio, 90
poles, 55, 113
post offices, 150
pottery, 17, 18
poultry farm, 187–8
precedents, 104, 115
prematurity, 76, 103
preparation for appeals, Ch. 7 49–71 *passim*
presentation of case at appeals, 66 *et seq.*
principal roads, 59
Principles and Practice of Town and Country Planning, 83
privacy, 143–7, 152, 164–5, 206, 207
privacy distances, 145–7
procedures, Ch. 5 36–43 *passim*
    at public inquiries, 36–9
    suggested alternative, 40–3
professional integrity, 46
programme maps, 64

221

programming, 64, 167
public inquiries, 31–2, 36–8
  procedures at, 36–8
public open space, 205, 206
pubs, 150–2, 157–9

Queensland, 23–4; 211
questions by inspector, 37–8

race tracks, 192
reasons for refusal and conditions, 7, Ch. 8 72–9
  illegitimate, 72 *et seq.*
  legitimate, 72 *et seq.*
recommendations of inspectors, 92–3, 119, 120, 169, 171, 195
re-examination, 37, 69, 70
  statement by way of, 58
refusal notice, 53
refusal of planning permission, 3, 109 *et seq.*
  legitimate and illegitimate reasons for, 72 *et seq.*
refuse, 9, 201
regional planning, 83, 87, 169
regulations for structure and local plans, 83
representation at appeals, Ch. 6 44–8
reserved matters in outline permissions, 21
reserves, holding back, 68
responsibilities of parties, vii, viii
restaurants, 150
reviews of plans, 85–6, 99
revised applications, 14
riding schools, 192–5
roads, 208, 209
  principal, 59
  widths, 137
Roads in Urban Areas, 91, 138
rounding off, 141–2, 148, 175–6, 209, 210
routes to appeal, 3–7
'row' contrasted with 'place', 179
Royal Town Planning Institute, 45–8, 65, 94, 100
  constraints on advocacy in Charter of, 47–8, 65

safety, 7
schools, suitability of sites for, 124, 126
Scott Report, 174

Secretary of State for the Environment, (SoS), functions of, vii, 65
Secton 53 application, 4, 6, 14, 16
services, lack of, 166
Settlement in the Countryside, 181
sewage disposal, 128–30
sewage works, 122, 192
sewers, repair of, 9
shopping centres, 151–2
  hypermarket, 152
  out of town, 152
shops, 10, 11
  betting, 157–8
  defined, 150
  for sale of motor vehicles, 151
  isolated, 152, 157
  special, 10, 151–9, 161
site visits, 3, 39, 42, 71, 195
Siting and Design Review Committee, Canberra, 40–2
smell, 7, 122, 158, 160–1, 207
smoke, 160, 161
solicitors, 44–5
sound, 206
Southbank, Ms, 50–71 *passim*
space about buildings, 206
speaking, hints about, 68–9
Speakwell Mr, 50–71 *passim*
Special Development Orders, 11, 12
special industry *see* industry
spoken content in appeals, 31
sporadic development, 182
staging, 167
Standards, 143–5, Ch. 20 205–12
  Parker-Morris, 137
  parking, 140–1
statements, 36–8, 42–3, 53–6, 68, 84–5, 111–18, 213
  final, 71
Stop Notices, 8, 12
structure plans, 26, 49, 62, 63, 65, 83–7, 124, 152, 156
subject plans, 85
sunlight, 146, 207
Sunlight and Daylight, 207
supplementary town maps, 64, 152
surveys, 51
  existing use, 51, 67

tactics at appeals, 66 *et seq.*
tandem development, 142
technical assessors, 24
temporary permissions, 14
tests for conditions, 73